How to Become
A
Critical Thinker

BY

Dr. Hesham Mohamed Elsherif

ABOUT THE AUTHOR

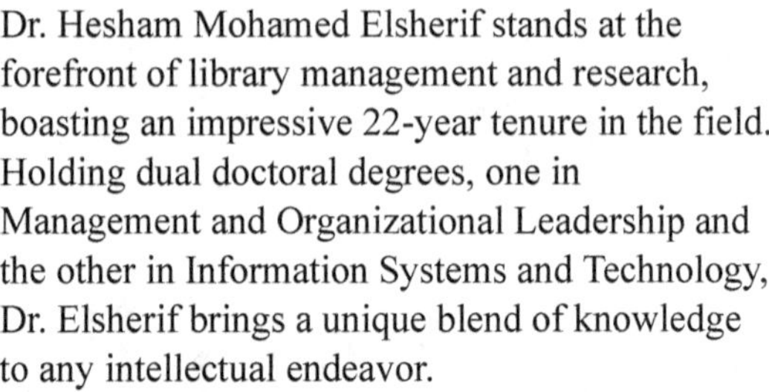

Dr. Hesham Mohamed Elsherif stands at the forefront of library management and research, boasting an impressive 22-year tenure in the field. Holding dual doctoral degrees, one in Management and Organizational Leadership and the other in Information Systems and Technology, Dr. Elsherif brings a unique blend of knowledge to any intellectual endeavor.

An expert in Empirical research methodology, Dr. Elsherif specializes particularly in the Qualitative approach and Action research. This specialization has not only strengthened his research endeavors but has also allowed him to contribute invaluable insights and advancements in these areas.

Over the years, Dr. Elsherif has made significant contributions to the academic world not only as a professional researcher but also as an Adjunct Professor. This multifaceted role in the educational landscape has further solidified his reputation as a thought leader and pioneer.

Furthermore, Dr. Elsherif's expertise isn't confined to one region. He has served as a consultant to numerous educational institutions on an international scale, sharing best practices, innovative strategies, and his deep insights into the ever-evolving realms of management and technology.

Combining a passion for education with an unparalleled depth of knowledge, Dr. Elsherif continues to inspire, educate, and lead in both the library and academic communities.

PREFACE

Welcome to "How to Become a Critical Thinker," a book dedicated to exploring the art and science of critical thinking. This journey into the world of reasoned analysis and thoughtful consideration is more than an academic pursuit—it's a fundamental skill that can transform the way you engage with the world around you.

My Journey and Motivation

As the author of this book, my journey into the field of critical thinking began in the early days of my academic career. With a background in management, leadership, philosophy, cognitive science, and education, I have always been intrigued by the ways in which we process information, make decisions, and form beliefs. Over the years, teaching and researching in various academic institutions, I have come to realize the immense value of critical thinking skills in all areas of life—from personal decisions to professional practices.

The motivation behind this book is a simple yet profound realization: in our rapidly changing, information-saturated world, the ability to think critically is not just valuable; it is essential. Whether it's navigating the complexities of everyday decisions, understanding the barrage of information (and misinformation) online, or engaging in constructive social and political discourse, critical thinking empowers us to approach these challenges with clarity and confidence.

Target Audience

This book is designed for a diverse audience. Whether you are a student eager to sharpen your analytical skills, a professional seeking to make more informed decisions, or simply a curious individual interested in understanding the world more deeply, this book is for you. It assumes no prior expertise in philosophy or logic, making it accessible to readers from all backgrounds.

How to Use This Book

"How to Become a Critical Thinker" is structured to guide you through the fundamental aspects of critical thinking in a progressive manner. Each chapter builds upon the previous one, though they are also designed to stand alone, allowing you to dive into topics of particular interest.

The chapters include real-life examples, exercises, and case studies to help you apply the concepts discussed. At the end of each chapter, you will find a summary and a set of questions or activities intended to reinforce your understanding and stimulate further reflection.

I encourage you to approach this book not just as a reader, but as an active participant. Engage with the exercises, challenge the ideas presented, and perhaps most importantly, apply these concepts to your everyday life.

Final Thoughts

As you embark on this journey of becoming a critical thinker, remember that this is a skill, much like any other, that improves with practice. It's my hope that this book will not only teach you about critical thinking but also inspire you to continually apply and refine these skills throughout your life.

Thank you for choosing to embark on this journey with me. Let's begin.

Dr. Hesham Mohamed Elsherif

WHO SHOULD READ THIS BOOK?

"How to Become a Critical Thinker" is designed with a wide audience in mind, encompassing individuals from various walks of life who share a common goal: to sharpen their critical thinking skills. Whether you are just embarking on your intellectual journey or are a seasoned thinker seeking to refine your skills, this book offers valuable insights and practical tools. Below are some of the key groups that will find this book particularly beneficial:

1. **Students and Educators**: Whether you're a high school student, an undergraduate, or a postgraduate scholar, this book provides the tools to enhance your analytical skills, which are essential for academic success. Educators across disciplines will find resources to help inculcate critical thinking skills in their students, making learning a more engaging and effective process.

2. **Professionals and Business Leaders**: In the fast-paced and complex world of business, the ability to think critically is invaluable. This book offers strategies to improve decision-making, problem-solving, and strategic planning. Business leaders will find these skills crucial for navigating challenges, driving innovation, and maintaining a competitive edge.

3. **Policy Makers and Public Servants**: For those involved in policy development and public administration, critical thinking is key to understanding complex social issues and making informed decisions. This book provides frameworks for analyzing data, evaluating impacts, and considering diverse perspectives in policy formulation.

4. **Healthcare Professionals**: In fields where evidence-based practice is paramount, such as medicine, nursing, and public health, critical thinking is essential. This book can help healthcare professionals assess clinical evidence, make better diagnostic decisions, and provide more effective patient care.

5. **Scientists and Researchers**: Critical thinking is the cornerstone of scientific inquiry. This book offers techniques for formulating hypotheses, interpreting data, and evaluating the validity of research findings, which are invaluable skills for anyone involved in scientific research.

6. **Anyone with a Curious Mind**: If you are someone who is naturally inquisitive and always seeking to understand the world better, this book is

for you. It will help you refine your ability to question, analyze, and evaluate the information that you encounter in everyday life.

7. **Lifelong Learners and Hobbyists**: For those who are committed to lifelong learning, whether for professional development or personal fulfillment, this book offers a structured approach to enhance cognitive abilities and approach learning with a critical eye.

8. **Activists and Social Advocates**: In an era where social and political activism is more important than ever, the ability to critically evaluate information, arguments, and strategies is crucial. This book equips activists with the skills to make stronger arguments and develop more effective strategies for change.

9. **Media Professionals and Journalists**: In the world of media and journalism, where the rapid assessment and reporting of information are vital, critical thinking skills can enhance the accuracy and depth of reporting and analysis.

10. **Parents and Guardians**: For those responsible for nurturing the next generation, this book provides insights into teaching critical thinking to children and teenagers, helping them to become thoughtful and informed adults.

In short, "How to Become a Critical Thinker" is a valuable resource for anyone interested in improving their reasoning skills, making better decisions, and fostering a deeper understanding of the world around them.

Dr. Hesham Mohamed Elsherif

WHY THIS BOOK IS ESSENTIAL READING?

In a world inundated with information and increasingly complex challenges, "How to Become a Critical Thinker" is not just beneficial reading—it's essential. This book stands out as a vital resource for several key reasons:

1. **Navigating the Information Age**: We live in an era where information is abundant and constantly at our fingertips. This book equips you with the skills to discern fact from fiction, critically evaluate sources, and navigate the often-overwhelming landscape of digital and traditional media.

2. **Enhancing Decision-Making Abilities**: Whether in personal life, academia, or the professional world, the ability to make well-informed decisions is invaluable. This book offers tools and techniques to analyze situations, consider various perspectives, and make decisions that are both informed and reasoned.

3. **Developing Analytical and Reasoning Skills**: At its core, critical thinking is about improving how we think. This book helps refine your analytical and reasoning abilities, enabling you to break down complex problems, identify underlying assumptions, and understand the implications of your thoughts and actions.

4. **Improving Communication and Persuasion Skills**: Critical thinking is not just about analyzing; it's also about effectively communicating your ideas. This book teaches you how to construct clear, logical, and persuasive arguments, enhancing both personal and professional interactions.

5. **Fostering Intellectual Independence**: In cultivating critical thinking, this book empowers you to form your own opinions and challenge prevailing narratives. This intellectual independence is crucial for personal growth, academic success, and active citizenship.

6. **Adapting to a Changing World**: The world is constantly evolving, presenting new challenges and opportunities. Critical thinkers can adapt more easily to change, as they possess the skills to understand and evaluate new information quickly and efficiently.

7. **Promoting Social and Ethical Responsibility**: Critical thinking involves considering the ethical implications of our beliefs and actions. This book encourages a deeper understanding of social responsibility and the impact of our decisions on others and the environment.

8. **Building a Foundation for Lifelong Learning**: Critical thinking is a foundational skill that supports lifelong learning. By mastering these skills, you set yourself up for continuous growth and development, regardless of your field or interests.

9. **Preparing for the Future of Work**: In an ever-changing job market, critical thinking skills are increasingly in demand. This book prepares you to meet the challenges of the modern workplace, where problem-solving, creativity, and analytical thinking are key competencies.

10. **Creating a More Informed Society**: By developing critical thinkers, this book contributes to a more informed, rational, and discerning society. Critical thinkers are better equipped to engage in constructive public discourse and contribute meaningfully to societal progress.

In essence, "How to Become a Critical Thinker" is more than a guide—it's an essential companion for anyone looking to thrive in a complex world. By honing your critical thinking skills, you prepare yourself not just to succeed, but to lead a more informed, reasoned, and fulfilling life.

Happy Reading!

Dr. Hesham Mohamed Elsherif

Table of Contents

Introduction..11

Definition of Critical Thinking:.. 12

Importance in the Modern World:.. 13

Overview of the Book's Structure: 14

Chapter 1: Foundations of Critical Thinking................................. 17

The History of Critical Thinking:.. 18

Key Philosophers and Theories:.. 19

The Brain and Critical Thinking:... 29

Chapter 2: The Characteristics of a Critical Thinker 31

Curiosity and Skepticism: 40

Open-mindedness:.. 42

The Ability to Analyze and Evaluate:.. 43

Chapter 3: Logic and Reasoning 45

Introduction to Logic:.. 46

Types of Reasoning: Deductive vs. Inductive: 58

Common Logical Fallacies:.. 59

Chapter 4: The Role of Argumentation 62

Constructing a Sound Argument: 77

Analyzing Arguments:.. 78

The Art of Persuasion and Rhetoric:.. 79

Chapter 5: Emotional Intelligence and Critical Thinking............... 81

Understanding Emotions in Reasoning: 91

Bias and Heuristics:.. 92

The Balance of Emotion and Logic:... 93

Chapter 6: Critical Thinking in the Digital Age............................. 95

Information Overload:... 104

Evaluating Sources and Fake News: 106

Digital Literacy and Critical Thinking: 107

Chapter 7: Strategies for Effective Critical Thinking 109

Questioning Techniques: 120

Creative and Lateral Thinking 132

Problem-solving Strategies: 134

Chapter 8: Critical Thinking in Everyday Life 136

Personal Decision Making: 146

In the Workplace 156

Social and Ethical Implications 157

Chapter 9: Critical Thinking in Academia 160

Critical Reading and Writing: 172

Research Methodologies: 173

Debate and Discussion in the Classroom: 175

Chapter 10: Continuing Your Journey 178

Lifelong Learning: 189

Resources and Further Reading: 197

Developing a Personal Critical Thinking Plan: 199

Appendix 201

Exercises and Case Studies: 201

Glossary of Key Terms: 203

References 206

Introduction

Critical thinking, a multifaceted and essential skill, is pivotal in a wide range of contexts, from personal decision-making to academic research and professional practices. It involves disciplined thinking that is clear, rational, open-minded, and informed by evidence (Paul & Elder, 2006). This introductory section lays the foundation for understanding the essence, importance, and practical applications of critical thinking.

Essence of Critical Thinking

Critical thinking is often defined as the ability to engage in reflective and independent thinking. It involves being skeptical of arguments and assertions until evidence and reason are used to support them (Dewey, 1933). Critical thinkers question assumptions, evaluate evidence, and use logic and reason to come to conclusions (Glaser, 1941).

Components of Critical Thinking

Critical thinking comprises various components such as interpretation, analysis, evaluation, inference, explanation, and self-regulation (Facione, 1990). Interpretation involves understanding and expressing the meaning or significance of a wide variety of experiences, situations, data, events, judgments, conventions, beliefs, rules, procedures, or criteria. Analysis, evaluation, and inference are the core processes involved in critical thinking, enabling the thinker to break down complex material, assess its value, and draw reasoned conclusions.

Importance of Critical Thinking

In a rapidly changing world, critical thinking is more important than ever. It enables individuals to process information effectively, make reasoned judgments, and solve problems efficiently (Halpern, 2014). In the professional realm, critical thinking is crucial for decision-making and innovation (Brookfield, 1987). In academia, it underpins effective research and scholarly discourse (Kuhn, 1999).

Critical Thinking in Education

Education systems around the world have recognized the importance of critical thinking as a fundamental goal of education (Paul, 1992). Educational strategies that encourage questioning, problem-solving, and analytical thinking contribute to the development of critical thinking skills (Abrami et al., 2008).

Challenges to Critical Thinking

Despite its importance, critical thinking faces several challenges. These include cognitive biases, emotional influences, cultural norms, and societal pressures, which can impede objective reasoning (Stanovich & West, 2007). Educators and thinkers are tasked with recognizing and overcoming these challenges to foster a more critical and reflective society.

Definition of Critical Thinking:

Understanding what constitutes critical thinking is the first step in developing this crucial skill set. Critical thinking is a multifaceted and dynamic cognitive process that involves the objective analysis and evaluation of information to form a judgment (Paul & Elder, 2006). It is characterized by the ability to engage in reflective and independent thinking, where one is aware of the influence of context and personal biases on their reasoning (Halpern, 2014).

The Nature of Critical Thinking

Critical thinking involves several key components: analysis, evaluation, inference, explanation, and self-regulation (Facione, 1990). Analysis refers to the ability to break down complex information into smaller, more manageable parts. Evaluation involves assessing the credibility and relevance of information (Ennis, 1987). Inference is the ability to draw reasoned conclusions from available data, while explanation encompasses the ability to clearly and coherently articulate one's reasoning process. Self-regulation implies a conscious effort to monitor and correct one's thinking processes (Ku & Ho, 2010).

Skills and Dispositions

Critical thinking is not just about possessing certain skills but also about having a specific mindset or disposition towards thinking. Critical thinkers are typically curious, open-minded, skeptical, and committed to rational inquiry (Perkins, Jay, & Tishman, 1993). They are also willing to consider alternative perspectives and are aware of the limitations of their own knowledge (Bailin, Case, Coombs, & Daniels, 1999).

Critical Thinking in Context

The application of critical thinking varies across different contexts. In the scientific domain, it involves empirical reasoning and the application of scientific methods (Kuhn, 1999). In ethical reasoning, it encompasses the consideration of moral principles and the impact of decisions on others (Noddings, 2010). In everyday life, it relates to making reasoned judgments in situations that range from personal decisions to understanding societal issues (Lipman, 2003).

Critical Thinking and Education

Education plays a pivotal role in fostering critical thinking. Educational approaches that emphasize active learning, problem-solving, and inquiry-based learning are effective in developing critical thinking skills (Abrami et al., 2008). The role of educators is crucial in modeling and nurturing these skills through effective pedagogy (Brookfield, 1987).

Importance in the Modern World:

In today's rapidly changing and complex world, critical thinking has become more than a valuable skill—it is a necessity for navigating life's challenges both professionally and personally. The ability to think critically is crucial in a world characterized by information overload, technological advancements, and increasingly complex social and political issues (Halpern, 2014).

Adapting to Information Overload

With the advent of the internet and social media, we are bombarded with a deluge of information daily. Critical thinking helps in discerning reliable information from misinformation, thus fostering informed decision-making (Wineburg & McGrew, 2016). It enables individuals to evaluate sources critically, identify biases, and understand the context of the information they consume (Bråten, Strømsø, & Salmerón, 2011).

Technological Advancements and Innovation

The rapid pace of technological innovation demands a workforce that can think critically, solve complex problems, and adapt to new scenarios (Binkley et al., 2012). In fields ranging from artificial intelligence to healthcare, critical thinking aids in the ethical and practical implications of new technologies, ensuring responsible innovation (Moor & Bynum, 2002).

Navigating Social and Political Complexities

Critical thinking is vital for understanding and engaging with social and political issues. It fosters the ability to analyze arguments, recognize persuasive techniques, and understand the broader context of societal debates (Nussbaum, 2010). This skill is particularly important in a democratic society, where informed citizenry is key to the functioning of democratic institutions (Dewey, 1916).

Critical Thinking in the Workplace

In the professional world, critical thinking is essential for effective leadership and management. It enables professionals to solve problems creatively, make informed decisions, and manage resources efficiently (Paul & Elder, 2006). Employers value critical thinkers for their ability to analyze situations and come up with innovative solutions (Cottrell, 2005).

Educational Implications

The importance of critical thinking in education cannot be overstated. Educators are increasingly focusing on developing these skills in students to prepare them for the complexities of the modern world (Abrami et al., 2008). Critical thinking in education promotes deeper learning, encourages active participation, and prepares students for lifelong learning (Bailin et al., 1999).

Overview of the Book's Structure:

"How to Become a Critical Thinker" is structured to provide a comprehensive guide on developing and applying critical thinking skills in various aspects of life. The book is divided into distinct but interconnected chapters, each addressing a specific dimension of critical thinking. This structure is designed to facilitate a thorough understanding of the concept, its importance, and its practical application in various contexts.

1. **Chapter 1: Foundations of Critical Thinking**

    - This chapter explores the historical and philosophical roots of critical thinking. It delves into the evolution of critical thought from ancient times to the present day, emphasizing contributions from key thinkers such as Socrates, Descartes, and Dewey (Paul & Elder, 2006).

2. **Chapter 2: The Characteristics of a Critical Thinker**

   - Here, the focus is on the traits and habits that define a critical thinker. It discusses characteristics such as skepticism, open-mindedness, and the ability to reason logically, drawing on insights from psychology and education research (Facione, 1990).

3. **Chapter 3: Logic and Reasoning**

   - This chapter introduces the principles of logical reasoning and argument analysis. It covers types of reasoning, common fallacies, and the structure of arguments (Toulmin, 1958).

4. **Chapter 4: The Role of Argumentation**

   - The art of argumentation and its role in critical thinking is the focus here. The chapter explores how to construct and deconstruct arguments, including understanding rhetorical strategies (van Eemeren & Grootendorst, 2004).

5. **Chapter 5: Emotional Intelligence and Critical Thinking**

   - This chapter examines the relationship between emotional intelligence and critical thinking, discussing how emotions can both hinder and enhance critical thinking (Salovey & Mayer, 1990).

6. **Chapter 6: Critical Thinking in the Digital Age**

   - Addressing the challenges and opportunities presented by the digital era, this chapter focuses on digital literacy, information evaluation, and the impact of social media on critical thinking (Wineburg & McGrew, 2016).

7. **Chapter 7: Strategies for Effective Critical Thinking**

   - Practical strategies and techniques for enhancing critical thinking skills are presented in this chapter. It includes questioning techniques, problem-solving methods, and creative thinking approaches (Paul & Elder, 2006).

8. **Chapter 8: Critical Thinking in Everyday Life**

   • The application of critical thinking in daily life, including personal decision-making and social interaction, is explored in this chapter (Halpern, 2014).

9. **Chapter 9: Critical Thinking in Academia**

   • This chapter discusses the role of critical thinking in academic contexts, focusing on critical reading, writing, and research methodologies (Abrami et al., 2008).

10. **Chapter 10: Continuing Your Journey**

   • The final chapter provides guidance on continuing to develop critical thinking skills beyond the book. It includes resources for further reading and strategies for lifelong learning (Brookfield, 1987).

Each chapter in this book is carefully crafted to build upon the knowledge established in previous sections, providing a holistic understanding of critical thinking. The chapters are supplemented with case studies, practical exercises, and real-world examples to enhance learning and application.

Chapter 1: Foundations of Critical Thinking

The concept of critical thinking, though seemingly modern, has roots extending back to ancient philosophy. Understanding these foundations is crucial for appreciating the depth and breadth of critical thinking as a discipline. This section delves into the historical evolution, key philosophical underpinnings, and the cognitive aspects of critical thinking.

Historical Evolution of Critical Thinking

Critical thinking, as a formal concept, has its genesis in the Socratic method of ancient Greece, where questioning and dialogue were used to stimulate critical analysis (Paul & Elder, 2006). This tradition was further developed by philosophers like Plato and Aristotle, who laid the groundwork for logical reasoning and empirical inquiry (McPeck, 1981).

During the Enlightenment, thinkers like Descartes and Kant emphasized the importance of skepticism and the questioning of established doctrines, further shaping the modern concept of critical thinking (Durant, 1926). In the 20th century, educational theorists like Dewey advocated for the role of critical thinking in education, emphasizing its importance for an informed and democratic society (Dewey, 1933).

Key Philosophical Theories

Several key philosophical theories have contributed to the understanding of critical thinking. Rationalism, championed by Descartes, posits that reason is the primary source of knowledge, highlighting the role of logical analysis (Kemerling, 2001). Empiricism, on the other hand, emphasizes experience and sensory perception as sources of knowledge, as seen in the works of Hume and Locke (Markie, 2004).

Pragmatism, a philosophy developed by Peirce and later expanded by James and Dewey, argues that thought must be tied to action and practical outcomes, a perspective that has significantly influenced contemporary critical thinking (Thayer-Bacon, 2000).

The Brain and Critical Thinking

The cognitive science perspective provides insights into how the brain engages in critical thinking. Neuroscientific research suggests that critical thinking involves a complex interplay of various cognitive processes, including memory, attention, and executive functions (D'Esposito, Postle, & Rypma, 2000). The prefrontal cortex, in particular, plays a crucial role in higher-order thinking and decision-making (Miller & Cohen, 2001).

The History of Critical Thinking:

Critical thinking, as a distinct and valued form of reasoned inquiry, has a rich historical background spanning several millennia. Understanding its history helps in appreciating its development, evolution, and importance in various spheres of human endeavor.

Ancient Beginnings

The earliest recorded thoughts on critical thinking are found in the works of ancient philosophers. In ancient Greece, Socrates developed the Socratic method, a form of cooperative argumentative dialogue to stimulate critical thinking and to draw out ideas and underlying presuppositions (Vlastos, 1991). Plato, Socrates' student, further developed these ideas, emphasizing the role of reasoning in the pursuit of truth (Cooper, 1997).

The Influence of Aristotle

Aristotle, a student of Plato, made significant contributions to the field of logic, particularly with his work on syllogisms which provided a foundation for deductive reasoning (Smith, 1989). His emphasis on empirical observation and systematic inquiry laid the groundwork for scientific methodology, which is inherently linked to critical thinking (Barnes, 1995).

Medieval and Renaissance Developments

During the Middle Ages, critical thinking was influenced by religious and theological studies. However, the Renaissance rekindled interest in scientific inquiry and skeptical thinking, with figures like Leonardo da Vinci and Galileo challenging established norms and promoting empirical observation (Shapin, 1996).

The Enlightenment Era

The Enlightenment was a pivotal period in the development of critical thinking. Philosophers like René Descartes, John Locke, and Immanuel Kant emphasized individual reason and skepticism over tradition and dogma (Kenny, 2008). Descartes' famous dictum, "Cogito, ergo sum" (I think, therefore I am), underscored the importance of doubt and questioning as a path to true knowledge (Williams, 2005).

18

Modern and Contemporary Perspectives

In the 20th century, thinkers like John Dewey brought critical thinking into the realm of education, advocating for reflective thinking as a core educational goal (Dewey, 1933). The later part of the century saw the development of formal critical thinking frameworks and models, notably by scholars like Richard Paul, who emphasized the need for critical thinking to be an explicit part of instruction (Paul, 1992).

Key Philosophers and Theories:

The development of critical thinking has been influenced by numerous philosophers and their theories over centuries. This section highlights some key figures and their contributions, which have laid the groundwork for our understanding and practice of critical thinking.

Socrates and the Socratic Method

Socrates, often regarded as the father of Western philosophy, introduced the Socratic Method—a form of cooperative argumentative dialogue that stimulates critical thinking. This method involves asking and answering questions to stimulate critical thinking and to illuminate ideas (Vlastos, 1991).

One of the most significant contributions to the field of critical thinking comes from the ancient Greek philosopher Socrates and his development of the Socratic Method. This method remains a foundational tool for cultivating critical thinking and is widely used in various educational and professional disciplines.

Socrates: The Father of Critical Thinking

Socrates (469-399 BCE), often hailed as the father of Western philosophy, emphasized the importance of seeking knowledge and understanding through persistent questioning and dialogue. His approach was not to convey knowledge but to create a process by which knowledge could be discovered (Vlastos, 1991).

The Socratic Method

The Socratic Method involves asking a series of questions to challenge assumptions and illuminate ideas. This method is a form of cooperative argumentative dialogue that encourages participants to think critically and logically analyze their beliefs and ideas (Brickhouse & Smith, 1994).

Key Aspects of the Socratic Method

1. **Elenchus (Refutation)**: Socrates used refutation as a way to disprove or refute the beliefs held by others, thereby encouraging them to seek a deeper understanding of the subject matter (Vlastos, 1991).

2. **Inductive Reasoning**: Socrates often employed inductive reasoning, drawing general conclusions from specific instances. This form of reasoning is essential in forming logical conclusions and is a key aspect of critical thinking (Hughes, 2011).

3. **Intellectual Humility**: A hallmark of the Socratic method is the recognition of one's own ignorance. Socrates famously claimed to know nothing, which underscored the importance of intellectual humility in the pursuit of knowledge (Kahn, 1996).

Impact on Education and Critical Thinking

The Socratic Method has had a profound impact on education, particularly in developing critical thinking skills. By engaging students in dialogue and encouraging them to question, it fosters an active learning environment conducive to critical analysis and reasoning (McKeachie, 2013).

Contemporary Applications

Today, the Socratic Method is applied in various fields, from law to medicine, as a means of exploring complex ideas, uncovering underlying assumptions, and developing critical thinking skills (Mills, 1996).

Plato and the Theory of Forms

Plato, a student of Socrates, contributed significantly to the concept of critical thinking through his Theory of Forms. He argued that the material world as it appears to us is not the real world, but only a shadow or imitation of the real world (Cooper, 1997). His emphasis on abstract thinking and questioning the nature of reality has influenced the philosophical approach to critical thinking.

Plato, a pivotal figure in the history of Western philosophy and a student of Socrates, made significant contributions to critical thinking, notably through his Theory of Forms. This theory has profound implications for understanding reality and the process of reasoning.

Plato's Philosophy

Plato (c. 428–348 BCE) was a foundational figure in Western thought. His work laid the groundwork for many areas of philosophy, including epistemology, metaphysics, and ethics (Cooper, 1997). Plato's philosophy is characterized by a search for the true form of justice, beauty, equality, and other ideals.

The Theory of Forms

At the heart of Plato's philosophy is his Theory of Forms (or Ideas). This theory posits that the material world, as perceived through the senses, is not the real world but merely a shadow of the real world. The Forms are abstract, perfect, unchanging concepts or ideals that transcend time and space (Fine, 1993).

Key Aspects of the Theory of Forms

1. **Abstract Reality**: The Forms represent the most accurate reality. For instance, a circle in the physical world is just an imperfect manifestation of the 'perfect' circle that exists in the world of Forms (Fine, 1993).

2. **Knowledge and Remembrance**: According to Plato, knowledge is a matter of recollecting the Forms, which the soul knew before it was incarnated in the body (Cooper, 1997).

3. **Critical Thinking and the Forms**: Plato's theory challenges individuals to think beyond their sensory experiences. It encourages a form of critical thinking that seeks to understand the essence of things, rather than just their physical manifestations (Sedley, 2007).

Impact on Critical Thinking

Plato's Theory of Forms has significantly influenced the field of critical thinking by promoting an abstract approach to understanding concepts and ideas. It encourages critical thinkers to question the reality of their sensory experiences and seek deeper, more universal truths (Grube, 1993).

Plato's Influence on Education

Plato's emphasis on the importance of seeking knowledge and truth has had a lasting impact on educational philosophy. His work supports the idea that education is not just about imparting information but about guiding students toward a deeper understanding of fundamental truths (Cooper, 1997).

Aristotle's Logic and Empiricism

Aristotle, Plato's student, is known for his contributions to logic, particularly his development of the syllogism as a tool for deductive reasoning. His work in empiricism—basing conclusions on observable evidence—has been fundamental in shaping the scientific approach to critical thinking (Barnes, 1995).

Aristotle, a student of Plato, made significant contributions to critical thinking, particularly through his development of formal logic and his approach to empiricism. His work laid foundational principles that continue to influence modern critical thinking and scientific methodology.

Aristotle's Contributions to Logic

Aristotle (384–322 BCE) is often referred to as the "Father of Logic." He was the first to develop a formalized system for reasoning, an achievement that has had a lasting impact on the field of critical thinking (Smith, 1989).

1. **Organon**: Aristotle's collection of works known as the "Organon" lays out the basic principles of logical reasoning. It includes discussions on syllogisms, propositions, and the structure of logical arguments (Barnes, 1995).

2. **Syllogistic Logic**: Aristotle's syllogistic logic was a breakthrough in thinking about reasoning. It is a form of deductive reasoning that involves drawing conclusions from two premises, a method still central to logical argumentation today (Smith, 1989).

Aristotle's Empiricism

In contrast to Plato's emphasis on abstract Forms, Aristotle argued for the primacy of empirical observation and experience in acquiring knowledge.

1. **Empirical Observation**: Aristotle believed that all knowledge starts with sensory experiences. He emphasized the importance of observing the natural world and gathering data as the basis for understanding (Lloyd, 1996).

2. **Inductive Reasoning**: Building from empirical data, Aristotle advocated for inductive reasoning. This method involves drawing

general conclusions from specific observations, a fundamental process in scientific investigation (Lloyd, 1996).

Aristotle's Impact on Critical Thinking

Aristotle's approach to logic and empiricism significantly shaped the development of critical thinking. His emphasis on structured reasoning, empirical evidence, and inductive processes laid the groundwork for scientific inquiry and rational analysis (Barnes, 1995).

Aristotle's Influence in Various Fields

The principles of Aristotelian logic and empiricism have influenced a range of fields, from science and mathematics to philosophy and education. His ideas about logical consistency, empirical evidence, and ethical reasoning continue to form the basis of many contemporary critical thinking models (Hughes, 2011).

Descartes and Rationalism

René Descartes, a key figure in the development of modern philosophy, advocated for methodological skepticism and rationalism. His famous statement, "Cogito, ergo sum" (I think, therefore I am), underscores the importance of doubting as a path to knowledge (Williams, 2005).

René Descartes, a 17th-century French philosopher, mathematician, and scientist, profoundly impacted critical thinking with his approach to rationalism. His philosophy marked a significant shift towards a new method of inquiry based on reason and skepticism.

Descartes' Rationalism

Descartes' approach to knowledge, known as rationalism, posits that reason is the primary source of knowledge, distinct from and superior to sensory experience (Cottingham, 1992). He argued that through the application of reason alone, individuals can arrive at fundamental truths.

"Cogito, ergo sum"

One of Descartes' most famous contributions is the statement "Cogito, ergo sum" ("I think, therefore I am"). This phrase encapsulates his view that the act of thinking itself serves as indisputable proof of one's existence and became a fundamental element in Western philosophy (Williams, 2005).

Methodological Skepticism

Descartes is renowned for his methodological skepticism. He advocated for the systematic doubt of all beliefs that could be subject to even the slightest uncertainty. This approach was intended to strip away all unreliable beliefs, leaving only those that could be known with absolute certainty (Broughton, 2002).

Descartes' Deductive Method

Building upon his rationalist philosophy, Descartes developed a deductive method for acquiring knowledge. This method begins with basic, indubitable principles and proceeds through logical steps to more complex conclusions, a process that heavily influenced subsequent scientific and philosophical methods (Cottingham, 1992).

Impact on Critical Thinking

Descartes' emphasis on doubt and reason has had a lasting impact on critical thinking. His approach encourages individuals to question commonly accepted knowledge and to base their beliefs on clear, rational thought processes (Hatfield, 2003).

Influence Across Disciplines

Descartes' rationalist ideas have influenced numerous disciplines beyond philosophy, including mathematics, science, and psychology. His approach laid the groundwork for the Enlightenment and significantly shaped modern Western thought (Clarke, 2006).

Kant and the Critique of Pure Reason

Immanuel Kant's work, particularly the "Critique of Pure Reason," delved into the relationship between experience and reason. His exploration of the limits of reason and the role of experience in forming knowledge has significantly influenced critical thinking in the context of epistemology (Guyer, 2006).

Immanuel Kant, a central figure in modern philosophy, made groundbreaking contributions to critical thinking through his work "Critique of Pure Reason." Kant's philosophy represents a pivotal shift in epistemology, challenging the basic assumptions of knowledge, perception, and reasoning.

Kant's Epistemological Revolution

Kant's work marked an epistemological revolution by synthesizing the rationalist and empiricist traditions that preceded him. He proposed that while our knowledge begins with experience, it does not necessarily arise from experience (Guyer, 2006). This approach sought to bridge the gap between rationalism, which prioritized innate ideas and deduction, and empiricism, which emphasized sensory experience and induction.

The Critique of Pure Reason

In "Critique of Pure Reason" (1781), Kant examines the foundations of human knowledge and understanding. He argues that the human mind plays an active role in constructing the experience of the external world, rather than merely receiving passive sensory data (Kant, 1781/1998).

Key Concepts in Kant's Philosophy

1. **Synthetic a priori Knowledge**: Kant introduced the concept of synthetic a priori knowledge, which refers to knowledge that is both informative and necessary, derived independent of experience. This concept challenges the traditional dichotomy between empirical knowledge and pure reasoning (Kant, 1781/1998).

2. **Phenomena and Noumena**: Kant distinguishes between phenomena (things as they appear) and noumena (things in themselves). He argued that while we can know phenomena through our sensory experience, noumena remain ultimately unknowable, a notion that has profound implications for the limits and capabilities of human understanding (Guyer, 2006).

3. **Categorical Imperative**: Although more ethical than epistemological, Kant's concept of the Categorical Imperative, which asserts that one should act only according to that maxim by which you can at the same time will that it should become a universal law, has influenced critical thinking in moral and ethical reasoning (Wood, 1999).

Impact on Critical Thinking

Kant's work has significantly influenced critical thinking by highlighting the active role of the mind in shaping experience and knowledge. His ideas challenge thinkers to consider the ways in which their perceptions and reasoning are framed by the inherent structures of the human mind (Allison, 2004).

Kant's Enduring Influence

Kant's critical philosophy, particularly his analysis of the limits of human reason and understanding, continues to influence a wide range of fields, from philosophy and science to ethics and politics. His work remains a cornerstone in the study of epistemology and critical thinking (Guyer, 2006).

John Dewey and Reflective Thinking

John Dewey, an American philosopher and educator, emphasized the role of education in developing critical thinking skills. He advocated for reflective thinking—a careful consideration of a belief or supposed form of knowledge in light of the grounds that support it (Dewey, 1933).

John Dewey, an American philosopher, psychologist, and educational reformer, significantly influenced the concept of critical thinking, particularly through his advocacy for reflective thinking in education. His progressive approach to education emphasized the development of critical thinking skills as essential for full participation in democratic society.

John Dewey's Educational Philosophy

Dewey's philosophy of education is centered on the idea that learning occurs through experience and interaction with the world. He criticized traditional education for its focus on rote memorization and passive learning, advocating instead for active and experiential learning processes (Dewey, 1938).

Reflective Thinking

1. **Definition**: Dewey defined reflective thinking as the active, persistent, and careful consideration of a belief or supposed form of knowledge in light of the grounds that support it and the further conclusions to which it tends (Dewey, 1933).

2. **Characteristics**: According to Dewey, reflective thinking involves a willingness to engage in a thoughtful process of evaluating evidence, analyzing assumptions, and synthesizing information to arrive at reasoned conclusions (Dewey, 1933).

Impact on Education

Dewey's emphasis on reflective thinking had a transformative effect on education. He argued that fostering critical thinking skills should be a primary goal of education, as it develops students' ability to think independently, solve problems, and understand the world around them (Dewey, 1910).

Dewey's Method of Inquiry

Dewey developed a method of inquiry based on the scientific method, which involves identifying problems, formulating hypotheses, gathering data, and reaching conclusions. This method emphasizes the importance of questioning, evidence evaluation, and reasoned argumentation in the learning process (Dewey, 1938).

Relevance in Contemporary Education

Dewey's ideas about reflective thinking and experiential learning remain highly relevant in contemporary education. His work has influenced modern pedagogical approaches that prioritize critical thinking, problem-solving skills, and the active engagement of students in their own learning (Hickman, 2009).

Richard Paul's Model of Critical Thinking

In the contemporary context, Richard Paul has been influential in developing a model of critical thinking that emphasizes its importance in education. His model focuses on the skills and dispositions required for critical thinking, and how these can be taught and learned (Paul, 1992).

Richard Paul, an influential figure in the field of critical thinking, contributed significantly to its conceptualization and teaching methodology. His model of critical thinking is one of the most recognized and widely used frameworks in educational settings.

Richard Paul's Contributions to Critical Thinking

Paul's work in critical thinking is distinguished by its focus on practical application in educational contexts. He emphasized the importance of critical thinking as a fundamental skill for effective reasoning, problem-solving, and decision-making (Paul & Elder, 2006).

Key Elements of Paul's Model

1. **Elements of Thought**: Paul identified several core components of thinking, including purpose, question at issue, information, interpretation, concepts, assumptions, implications, and point of view. These elements serve as a guide to dissect and analyze thinking (Paul, 1990).

2. **Intellectual Standards**: Paul proposed intellectual standards for assessing critical thinking, such as clarity, accuracy, precision, relevance, depth, breadth, logic, significance, and fairness. These standards are used to evaluate the quality of reasoning and argumentation (Paul & Elder, 2006).

3. **Socratic Questioning**: Building on the Socratic tradition, Paul emphasized the role of deep questioning in developing critical thinking. He advocated for questions that probe reasoning, evidence, perspectives, and implications (Paul & Elder, 1990).

Paul's Influence on Education

Paul's model has had a substantial impact on teaching and learning practices. His framework provides educators with tools to foster critical thinking skills in students, encouraging them to become more thoughtful, reflective, and independent thinkers (Paul & Elder, 2008).

Critical Thinking and Lifelong Learning

Paul argued that critical thinking is not only essential for academic success but also for lifelong learning and personal development. He believed that developing critical thinking skills enables individuals to better navigate complex life situations and societal issues (Paul, 1992).

Challenges and Critiques

While Paul's model has been widely adopted, it has also faced critiques. Some educators argue that the model can be overly prescriptive and may not account for the role of emotion and cultural context in thinking processes (Ennis, 2011).

The Brain and Critical Thinking:

Understanding how the brain engages in critical thinking is a burgeoning area of research, combining insights from psychology, neuroscience, and cognitive science. This interdisciplinary approach provides a deeper understanding of the biological and cognitive processes underpinning critical thinking.

Cognitive Processes in Critical Thinking

Critical thinking involves a variety of cognitive processes including reasoning, decision-making, problem-solving, and the ability to process and organize information. These functions are associated with specific areas of the brain, particularly within the frontal lobes, which are responsible for higher-order cognitive skills (D'Esposito, Postle, & Rypma, 2000).

Neurological Basis of Reasoning and Judgment

1. **Frontal Lobes**: The prefrontal cortex, a part of the frontal lobes, plays a crucial role in critical thinking. It is involved in planning complex cognitive behaviors, personality expression, decision-making, and moderating social behavior (Miller & Cohen, 2001).

2. **Neural Networks**: Critical thinking tasks activate a network of brain regions, including the lateral prefrontal cortex, anterior cingulate cortex, and parietal lobes. These areas work together to process information, evaluate evidence, and make reasoned judgments (Goel, 2007).

The Role of Memory and Knowledge

Critical thinking also involves the retrieval and application of knowledge, a process that engages the brain's memory systems. The hippocampus and associated structures in the medial temporal lobe are integral to memory formation and recall, essential for applying past knowledge to new situations (Eichenbaum, 2017).

Emotional Intelligence and Critical Thinking

Recent research indicates that emotional intelligence, which involves the ability to recognize and regulate emotions, plays a role in critical thinking. The limbic system, particularly the amygdala, is key in processing emotional responses, which can influence decision-making and reasoning (Salovey & Mayer, 1990).

Neuroplasticity and Learning Critical Thinking Skills

The brain's ability to change and adapt (neuroplasticity) is fundamental to learning and developing new skills, including critical thinking. Engaging in challenging cognitive tasks can strengthen neural connections and even lead to the development of new neurons, enhancing critical thinking abilities over time (Draganski et al., 2006).

Chapter 2: The Characteristics of a Critical Thinker

Understanding the characteristics of a critical thinker is essential in recognizing and developing these skills in oneself and others. Critical thinkers possess a set of cognitive abilities, habits of mind, and attitudes that enable them to approach problems effectively and rationally.

Key Characteristics of a Critical Thinker

I.   **Analytical Skills:**

A critical thinker has the ability to analyze information and arguments, dissecting them into their constituent parts to understand their structure and basis (Facione, 1990).

Analytical skills are a cornerstone in the repertoire of a critical thinker. These skills enable individuals to break down complex information into manageable parts, assess data, and understand underlying connections, which are essential for effective problem-solving and decision-making.

Understanding Analytical Skills

Analytical skills involve the ability to deconstruct information into smaller components to understand the structure, function, and relationships within it. This process is crucial for evaluating arguments, identifying assumptions, and drawing reasoned conclusions (Facione, 1990).

Components of Analytical Skills

1. **Identification**: Recognizing various elements of information, such as arguments, ideas, and facts, and understanding how they relate to each other (Halpern, 2014).

2. **Comparison**: Analyzing similarities and differences between pieces of information, which is vital for categorizing and understanding relationships (Bloom et al., 1956).

3. **Evaluation**: Assessing the credibility and relevance of information, including the identification of biases, fallacies, and logical inconsistencies (Ennis, 1987).

4. **Synthesis**: Integrating various pieces of information to form a cohesive and comprehensive understanding (Anderson et al., 2001).

Developing Analytical Skills

Analytical skills can be enhanced through specific educational strategies and practices. These include engaging in activities that require sorting, categorizing, prioritizing, and evaluating information (Abrami et al., 2008).

Application in Problem-Solving

In problem-solving, analytical skills are used to dissect a problem, understand its components, and develop a systematic approach to finding a solution. This process often involves considering multiple perspectives and solutions (Mayer, 1990).

Analytical Skills in Everyday Life

Beyond academic and professional settings, analytical skills are invaluable in everyday decision-making. They enable individuals to navigate complex life situations, understand current events, and make informed choices (Facione, 1990).

II.   **Open-mindedness**:

Critical thinkers are open to new ideas and perspectives and are willing to reconsider their beliefs in light of new information or compelling arguments (Halpern, 2014).

Open-mindedness is a pivotal characteristic of a critical thinker. It involves a willingness to consider new ideas, perspectives, and evidence, even when they contradict one's preconceptions or beliefs. This trait is essential for unbiased and effective reasoning.

Defining Open-mindedness

Open-mindedness in critical thinking refers to the ability to approach problems, situations, and viewpoints with a genuine willingness to consider all relevant information and perspectives (Baron, 1993). It is the antithesis of dogmatism and involves a readiness to change one's mind in light of new evidence or arguments.

Aspects of Open-mindedness

1. **Receptiveness to New Ideas**: Being open to new and different ideas, even if they challenge established beliefs (Stanovich & West, 2007).

2. **Tolerance for Ambiguity**: Comfort with uncertainty and the ability to process complex, conflicting, or ambiguous information without rushing to judgment (Facione, 2000).

3. **Fair-mindedness**: The ability to consider opposing viewpoints objectively and to weigh evidence impartially (Paul & Elder, 2006).

Cultivating Open-mindedness

Open-mindedness can be cultivated through practices that encourage critical reflection, exposure to diverse viewpoints, and engagement in open and respectful discourse. Educational approaches that emphasize inquiry-based learning and critical discussion can foster this trait in students (Abrami et al., 2008).

Challenges to Open-mindedness

Maintaining open-mindedness can be challenging, especially in the face of strongly held beliefs or societal pressures. Cognitive biases, such as confirmation bias and the Dunning-Kruger effect, can impede open-mindedness (Kahneman, 2011).

Open-mindedness in Decision-Making

Open-mindedness enhances decision-making by allowing for the consideration of a wide range of options and alternatives. It enables critical thinkers to make more informed and balanced decisions, free from the constraints of prejudice or undue influence (Halpern, 2014).

III.   **Skepticism**:

While being open-minded, critical thinkers are also appropriately skeptical. They question claims and seek evidence rather than accepting things at face value (Paul & Elder, 2006).

Skepticism is a fundamental characteristic of critical thinking, involving a questioning attitude towards knowledge, facts, or opinions stated as facts. It is not about cynicism or disbelief but rather a thoughtful and rational approach to questioning and verifying information.

Understanding Skepticism in Critical Thinking

Skepticism in critical thinking is the practice of not taking things at face value without sufficient evidence. It involves questioning the validity of claims, seeking clarity, and demanding adequate justification before accepting any statement as true (Paul & Elder, 2006).

Components of Skepticism

1. **Questioning Attitude**: Being skeptical means having a habit of questioning and not accepting information, assertions, or arguments without questioning and analyzing them (Ennis, 1987).

2. **Demand for Evidence**: Skeptical thinkers require evidence and sound reasoning to support claims. They are wary of basing decisions or conclusions on assumptions, rumors, or unverified information (Facione, 1990).

3. **Recognizing Bias and Fallacies**: Skepticism involves identifying biases, both in others' arguments and one's own thinking, and recognizing logical fallacies that can undermine the validity of arguments (Bowell & Kemp, 2005).

Cultivating Skepticism

Developing a healthy level of skepticism involves education and practice. It requires the development of analytical skills, understanding of logical fallacies, and awareness of cognitive biases. Educators can foster skepticism by encouraging students to question and critically analyze what they read, hear, and observe (Abrami et al., 2008).

Balancing Skepticism and Open-mindedness

While skepticism is crucial, it needs to be balanced with open-mindedness. A critical thinker should be open to considering new ideas and perspectives while maintaining a cautious and scrutinizing attitude towards them (Baron, 1993).

Skepticism in the Digital Age

In the digital age, where information is abundant and not always reliable, skepticism is increasingly important. Critical thinkers must navigate through a vast array of sources, discerning credible information from misinformation and understanding the context and purpose behind the information presented (Wineburg & McGrew, 2016).

IV.   **Reasoning Skills**:

Good critical thinkers can follow the logic of arguments, identify faulty reasoning, and construct well-reasoned arguments of their own (Ennis, 1987).

Reasoning skills are at the heart of critical thinking, enabling individuals to make sense of information, draw logical conclusions, and make well-reasoned decisions. These skills involve the ability to think in a structured, logical manner and are fundamental for problem-solving and analysis.

Understanding Reasoning Skills

Reasoning skills in critical thinking refer to the capacity to process information in a logical way, to form sound judgments, and to make decisions based on evidence and logical analysis rather than emotion or intuition (Facione, 1990).

Types of Reasoning

1. **Deductive Reasoning**: This involves drawing specific conclusions from general principles or premises. It is a process of top-down reasoning where the conclusion necessarily follows from the premises if they are true (Copi, Cohen, & McMahon, 2016).

2. **Inductive Reasoning**: Inductive reasoning involves making generalizations based on specific observations or instances. It is bottom-up reasoning, where the conclusions are probable and may need further verification (Salmon, 2013).

3. **Abductive Reasoning**: Abductive reasoning involves starting with an incomplete set of observations and proceeding to the likeliest possible explanation for the group of observations (Walton, 2004).

Developing Reasoning Skills

Reasoning skills can be developed through practice and education. Engaging in activities that require logical analysis, such as problem-solving exercises, puzzles, and debates, can enhance these skills. Education that emphasizes critical thinking and analysis also plays a key role in developing reasoning abilities (Abrami et al., 2008).

Application in Problem-Solving

In problem-solving, reasoning skills are used to assess situations, identify problems, generate solutions, and decide on the most appropriate course of action. Good reasoning ensures that decisions are well-founded and justifiable (Halpern, 2014).

Reasoning Skills in Everyday Life

Beyond academic and professional contexts, reasoning skills are essential in everyday life. They enable individuals to navigate complex situations, understand and evaluate arguments, and make informed decisions (Ennis, 1987).

V.   **Creativity**:

They often approach problems and issues in innovative ways, thinking outside of conventional frameworks (Cropley, 2006).

Creativity, often seen as the ability to generate new and original ideas, is a key aspect of critical thinking. It involves thinking outside of conventional boundaries and developing innovative solutions to problems. Creativity in critical thinking goes beyond artistic expression, encompassing the ability to see new connections, generate multiple solutions, and approach problems from different perspectives.

Creativity in Critical Thinking

Creativity in critical thinking is characterized by the ability to conceive of alternative possibilities, to generate novel ideas, and to view situations from multiple viewpoints. It is essential for problem-solving, particularly in complex situations where traditional approaches may not be effective (Cropley, 2006).

Aspects of Creativity in Critical Thinking

1. **Divergent Thinking**: This involves thinking in a non-linear fashion, generating many different ideas or solutions to a problem (Guilford, 1967).

2. **Innovative Problem Solving**: Creative critical thinkers are able to approach problems in innovative ways, often leading to more effective and efficient solutions (Runco, 2004).

3. **Integration of Knowledge and Skills**: Creativity in critical thinking often involves integrating various types of knowledge and skills to create something new or to approach a problem in a novel way (Sternberg & Lubart, 1999).

Developing Creative Thinking

Creative thinking skills can be developed through practices that encourage exploration, experimentation, and the questioning of assumptions. Activities that stimulate imagination, such as brainstorming, role-playing, and engaging with diverse forms of knowledge, can enhance creativity (Starko, 2013).

The Role of Creativity in Decision Making

In decision-making, creativity enables individuals to consider a wider range of options, to think beyond conventional solutions, and to anticipate possible future scenarios. This broadened perspective can lead to more effective and forward-thinking decisions (Paul & Elder, 2006).

Creativity in Collaboration

Creative critical thinking is often enhanced through collaboration, as interacting with others can bring new perspectives and ideas, fostering a more dynamic and innovative approach to problem-solving (Sawyer, 2007).

VI. **Reflectiveness**:

Reflectiveness involves thinking about one's own thinking, being aware of one's own biases and assumptions, and being willing to change one's mind (Dewey, 1933).

Reflectiveness is a crucial characteristic of a critical thinker. It involves the ability to think about one's own thinking, to evaluate and improve one's cognitive processes, and to be aware of one's biases and assumptions. This introspective aspect of critical thinking is essential for continuous learning and self-improvement.

Understanding Reflectiveness

Reflectiveness in critical thinking refers to a person's ability to engage in a thoughtful and conscious examination of their own beliefs, arguments, and decision-making processes. It is about being aware of one's cognitive biases, evaluating the validity of one's reasoning, and being open to revising one's viewpoints (Dewey, 1933).

Components of Reflectiveness

1. **Self-awareness**: Being aware of one's own thinking patterns, biases, and preferences. This self-awareness is crucial for recognizing when and why one might be inclined to biased thinking or logical fallacies (Metcalfe & Shimamura, 1994).

2. **Self-regulation**: The ability to regulate one's thinking processes and strategies. It includes monitoring one's own cognitive activities and adjusting strategies as needed (Zimmerman, 2002).

3. **Metacognition**: Metacognition, or thinking about thinking, involves reflecting on how one processes and organizes information, solves problems, and makes decisions (Flavell, 1979).

Developing Reflectiveness

Reflectiveness can be developed through practices that encourage self-examination and feedback. Keeping journals, engaging in discussion and debate, and seeking constructive criticism are ways to enhance reflectiveness (Kitchener & King, 1990).

Importance in Learning and Problem-Solving

Reflectiveness is important in learning and problem-solving as it allows individuals to evaluate their thought processes and approaches, leading to more effective learning strategies and problem-solving techniques (Schön, 1983).

Challenges in Cultivating Reflectiveness

One of the challenges in cultivating reflectiveness is overcoming inherent biases and the discomfort that may come with questioning one's own beliefs and assumptions. Developing reflectiveness requires an open-minded and humble approach to learning and personal growth (Paul & Elder, 2006).

VII.   **Independence:**

Critical thinkers are independent thinkers. They do not rely solely on authority or the opinions of others but use their own judgment to make decisions (Bailin et al., 1999).

Independence in critical thinking refers to the ability to think autonomously, making judgments and decisions based on one's own reasoning and analysis rather than relying solely on external authority or the opinions of others. This self-directed aspect of critical thinking is crucial for intellectual growth and informed decision-making.

Understanding Independence in Critical Thinking

Independence in critical thinking involves forming one's own opinions and conclusions through careful evaluation and analysis of information. It requires the courage to question popular opinion, challenge norms, and stand by one's reasoning even in the face of opposition or criticism (Bailin et al., 1999).

Aspects of Independence

1. **Autonomous Judgment**: Making decisions based on one's analysis and reasoning, free from undue influence or external pressure (Paul & Elder, 2006).

2. **Critical Self-reliance**: Relying on one's cognitive abilities to evaluate information and arguments, rather than depending on others to provide answers or solutions (Ennis, 1987).

3. **Challenging Authority and Norms**: Willingness to question authoritative sources and societal norms, understanding that authority does not automatically equate to correctness (Brookfield, 1987).

Developing Independence in Thinking

Developing independence in thinking can be fostered through practices that encourage self-exploration, questioning, and the pursuit of knowledge. Engaging in activities that require individual analysis, such as research projects or reflective writing, can enhance independent thinking skills (Abrami et al., 2008).

Importance in Personal and Professional Life

Independence in thinking is essential in both personal and professional contexts. It enables individuals to navigate life's complexities with self-assurance and to contribute original ideas and solutions in professional settings (Facione, 1990).

Balancing Independence and Collaboration

While independence is important, it needs to be balanced with the ability to collaborate and consider other viewpoints. The most effective critical thinkers are those who can think independently while also valuing and integrating the perspectives of others (Paul & Elder, 2006).

Challenges in Cultivating Independence

One of the challenges in cultivating independence is overcoming societal pressures and cognitive biases that can lead to conformity. Encouraging a culture that values individual thought and critical inquiry can help in developing independent thinking (Brookfield, 1987).

Developing Critical Thinking Skills

Critical thinking skills are not innate; they can be developed through education and practice. Teaching methods that encourage active participation, questioning, debate, and problem-solving can foster these skills (Abrami et al., 2008).

Emotional Intelligence in Critical Thinking

Emotional intelligence, the ability to understand and manage emotions, plays a crucial role in critical thinking. Emotions can influence the way we perceive and reason about information, and being aware of this influence is a key aspect of critical thinking (Salovey & Mayer, 1990).

Cultural and Contextual Influences

Critical thinking does not occur in a vacuum. Cultural, social, and personal factors influence how individuals think critically. Understanding these influences is important for a well-rounded approach to critical thinking (Bailin et al., 1999).

Curiosity and Skepticism:

Curiosity and skepticism are two intertwined and essential characteristics of a critical thinker. Curiosity drives the desire to learn and explore, while skepticism provides a cautious and questioning approach to the information encountered. Together, these traits foster a mindset that is both inquisitive and discerning.

Curiosity in Critical Thinking

Curiosity in critical thinking is the eagerness to acquire knowledge and understanding. It involves a deep interest in exploring ideas, investigating problems, and understanding the world (Kashdan & Fincham, 2004).

Aspects of Curiosity

1. **Inquisitiveness**: A desire to learn more about various subjects and to delve deeper into topics of interest.

2. **Openness to Experience**: Being open to new experiences and ideas, and willing to explore unfamiliar concepts (McCrae & Costa, 1987).

3. **Continuous Learning**: A lifelong commitment to learning and self-improvement.

Skepticism in Critical Thinking

Skepticism in critical thinking is the practice of questioning the validity and authenticity of information. It involves a cautious approach to accepting claims, requiring evidence and logical reasoning before forming a belief (Shermer, 2002).

Aspects of Skepticism

1. **Questioning Attitude**: Not accepting information at face value and seeking to understand the evidence and reasoning behind claims.

2. **Critical Evaluation**: Assessing the credibility of sources, the quality of evidence, and the soundness of arguments.

3. **Awareness of Bias and Fallacies**: Recognizing potential biases in information and being aware of common logical fallacies that can mislead reasoning.

Developing Curiosity and Skepticism

Fostering curiosity and skepticism involves creating environments that encourage questioning and exploration. This can be achieved through educational methods that emphasize inquiry-based learning, critical discussion, and problem-solving activities (Paul & Elder, 2006).

The Balance Between Curiosity and Skepticism

Balancing curiosity and skepticism is crucial in critical thinking. While curiosity drives the pursuit of knowledge, skepticism ensures a careful and thorough evaluation of the information. Together, they prevent gullibility while encouraging a rich and active intellectual life (Ennis, 1987).

Open-mindedness:

Open-mindedness is a vital characteristic of a critical thinker, encompassing the willingness to consider different viewpoints and entertain new ideas, even when they conflict with one's preconceived notions or beliefs. This trait is fundamental in allowing for unbiased and effective analysis and reasoning.

Understanding Open-mindedness in Critical Thinking

Open-mindedness in critical thinking refers to the readiness to evaluate and possibly accept ideas and viewpoints different from one's own. It involves a fair and impartial consideration of evidence, arguments, and perspectives, regardless of one's own biases or preferences (Baron, 1993).

Key Aspects of Open-mindedness

1. **Willingness to Consider Alternative Views**: Being open to ideas and arguments that contradict one's own beliefs and being prepared to revise one's viewpoints in light of new evidence (Halpern, 2014).

2. **Resistance to Premature Closure**: Avoiding the tendency to hastily form conclusions without adequate evidence and reasoning (Dweck, 2006).

3. **Appreciation of Diverse Perspectives**: Valuing the diversity of thought and recognizing the potential benefits of considering a wide range of viewpoints (Stanovich & West, 2007).

Cultivating Open-mindedness

Open-mindedness can be cultivated by exposing oneself to a variety of perspectives, actively seeking out information that challenges one's beliefs, and engaging in dialogue with individuals who have differing viewpoints (Paul & Elder, 2006).

Challenges to Open-mindedness

Maintaining open-mindedness can be challenging due to innate cognitive biases, such as confirmation bias, which can lead individuals to favor information that confirms their existing beliefs (Nickerson, 1998).

Open-mindedness in Problem-Solving and Decision-Making

In problem-solving and decision-making, open-mindedness enables a more comprehensive analysis of the situation, consideration of alternative solutions, and a greater likelihood of reaching effective and innovative outcomes (Facione, 1990).

The Ability to Analyze and Evaluate:

A defining characteristic of a critical thinker is the ability to analyze and evaluate information effectively. This skill set involves breaking down complex material into its constituent parts, understanding its structure, and assessing its value in a reasoned, systematic manner.

Understanding Analysis and Evaluation

1. **Analysis**: Analysis in critical thinking involves examining information in detail to understand its structure, components, and relationships. It includes identifying arguments, discerning underlying assumptions, and recognizing patterns and inconsistencies (Bloom, 1956).

2. **Evaluation**: Evaluation is the process of judging the credibility and validity of information, arguments, and findings. It involves assessing the logical coherence of arguments, the reliability of sources, and the relevance and sufficiency of evidence (Facione, 1990).

Developing Analytical and Evaluative Skills

1. **Critical Reading and Listening**: Developing analytical and evaluative skills involves engaging critically with texts and arguments, questioning the information presented, and actively seeking to understand the underlying reasoning (Paul & Elder, 2006).

2. **Practicing Logical Reasoning**: Regularly engaging in activities that require logical reasoning, such as solving puzzles, debating, and discussing complex issues, can enhance these skills (Halpern, 2014).

3. **Reflective Thinking**: Reflective thinking, or thinking about one's own thinking process, is key to developing analytical and evaluative skills.

It involves self-assessment of one's reasoning and the ability to revise one's thinking based on this reflection (Dewey, 1933).

The Role of Analysis and Evaluation in Problem-Solving

In problem-solving, the ability to analyze and evaluate is crucial for identifying the core of the problem, understanding its context, and developing effective solutions. It allows critical thinkers to distinguish between more and less plausible solutions and to make decisions based on sound judgments (Ennis, 1987).

Challenges in Developing Analytical and Evaluative Skills

One of the challenges in developing these skills is overcoming cognitive biases and emotional influences that can affect objective analysis and evaluation. Education and training that emphasize critical thinking and reasoning can help mitigate these challenges (Nickerson, 1998).

Chapter 3: Logic and Reasoning

Logic and reasoning are foundational elements in the skill set of a critical thinker. These cognitive processes enable individuals to make sense of information, draw logical conclusions, and formulate sound arguments. They involve the application of systematic and rational thinking to assess validity and solve problems.

Understanding Logic and Reasoning in Critical Thinking

1. **Logic**: Logic in critical thinking refers to the framework or set of rules used to structure reasoning. It ensures that arguments are coherent and conclusions follow logically from premises (Copi, Cohen, & McMahon, 2016).

2. **Reasoning**: Reasoning involves the mental process of deriving conclusions from premises or evidence. It is the application of logical principles to specific problems or arguments (Salmon, 2013).

Types of Reasoning in Critical Thinking

1. **Deductive Reasoning**: This is a top-down approach where general principles are applied to specific cases. If the premises are true and the argument is valid, the conclusion must be true (Copi, Cohen, & McMahon, 2016).

2. **Inductive Reasoning**: Inductive reasoning is a bottom-up approach that involves making generalizations based on specific observations or instances. The conclusions are probable but not guaranteed (Salmon, 2013).

3. **Abductive Reasoning**: Abductive reasoning involves starting with incomplete observations and proposing the most likely explanation. It is often used in diagnostic processes and hypothesis formation (Walton, 2004).

Developing Logic and Reasoning Skills

Developing logic and reasoning skills can be achieved through critical thinking exercises, engaging in debates and discussions, and practicing problem-solving scenarios. Education that emphasizes these skills can significantly enhance one's ability to think logically and reason effectively (Paul & Elder, 2006).

The Role of Logic and Reasoning in Problem-Solving

In problem-solving, logic and reasoning are used to identify the root of the problem, generate potential solutions, and evaluate the feasibility and effectiveness of these solutions. These skills are essential for making well-reasoned decisions and for effective argumentation (Halpern, 2014).

Challenges in Applying Logic and Reasoning

Applying logic and reasoning can be challenging due to cognitive biases, emotional influences, and lack of knowledge or information. Recognizing and addressing these challenges is a critical part of effective critical thinking (Nickerson, 1998).

Introduction to Logic:

Logic is a fundamental aspect of critical thinking, providing a framework for analyzing arguments and reasoning. An understanding of logic helps critical thinkers evaluate the validity and soundness of arguments and develop their reasoning skills.

Fundamentals of Logic in Critical Thinking

I.   **Definition**:

Logic is the study of reasoning, particularly the evaluation of arguments according to well-defined principles. It involves understanding how to construct valid arguments and how to identify fallacious reasoning (Copi, Cohen, & McMahon, 2016).

Logic is a crucial component in the arsenal of a critical thinker. It forms the basis of rational thought, allowing for the systematic evaluation and construction of arguments. Understanding the fundamentals of logic is essential for effective critical thinking.

Definition of Logic in Critical Thinking

1. **Logic as the Study of Reasoning**: At its core, logic is the study of correct reasoning. It involves the analysis of arguments and the principles that govern sound reasoning processes (Copi, Cohen, & McMahon, 2016).

2. **Formal Logic**: Formal logic, also known as symbolic logic, involves the use of symbols and formal methods to represent and evaluate

arguments. It focuses on the form rather than the content of arguments (Hurley, 2015).

3. **Informal Logic**: Informal logic pertains to the evaluation of arguments as they occur in natural language. It deals with aspects of reasoning that are not captured by formal systems, such as the use of context and the evaluation of evidence (Walton, 2004).

The Role of Logic in Critical Thinking

Logic plays a vital role in critical thinking by providing a framework for distinguishing good reasoning from bad. It enables critical thinkers to assess whether conclusions follow logically from premises and to identify flaws in arguments (Facione, 1990).

Importance of Understanding Logical Principles

1. **Valid vs. Invalid Arguments**: Understanding logic helps in distinguishing valid arguments (where the conclusion necessarily follows from the premises) from invalid ones (Hurley, 2015).

2. **Sound vs. Unsound Arguments**: Beyond validity, logic helps in assessing the soundness of arguments, considering both the structure of the argument and the truthfulness of its premises (Copi, Cohen, & McMahon, 2016).

Application of Logic in Everyday Thinking

Logic is not confined to academic disciplines; it is a practical tool that applies to everyday thinking. Whether evaluating a news article, formulating a business strategy, or making personal decisions, logic provides a critical framework for analysis and decision-making (Paul & Elder, 2006).

Developing Logical Thinking Skills

Developing skills in logic involves studying the principles of logical reasoning, practicing the analysis of arguments, and engaging in exercises that challenge one's reasoning abilities, such as puzzles and logical problems (Ennis, 1987).

II.   **Components of Logical Arguments**:

A logical argument consists of premises (statements or propositions) and a conclusion. The validity of an argument depends on the relationship between the premises and the conclusion (Hurley, 2015).]

A fundamental aspect of logic in critical thinking involves understanding the components that constitute a logical argument. These components are the building blocks of rational discourse and are crucial for analyzing and constructing coherent arguments.

Components of a Logical Argument

1.   **Premises**: Premises are statements or propositions that provide the basis or evidence for a conclusion. They are the foundational assertions that an argument is built upon (Copi, Cohen, & McMahon, 2016).

2.   **Conclusion**: The conclusion is the statement or proposition that the premises are intended to support or prove. It is the outcome or result of the argument, logically derived from the premises (Hurley, 2015).

3.   **Logical Connectives**: Logical connectives are the terms that join premises and conclusions, such as "and," "or," "if...then," and "not." They help in structuring the argument and clarifying the relationships between different parts of the argument (Tarski & Corcoran, 1983).

Structuring Logical Arguments

Understanding how to structure a logical argument is key in critical thinking. A well-structured argument will clearly present its premises, use logical connectives appropriately, and lead to a conclusion that is supported by the premises.

Evaluating the Strength of Arguments

1.   **Validity**: An argument is valid if its conclusion logically follows from its premises. Validity concerns the form of the argument and whether the conclusion is a necessary outcome of the premises (Copi, Cohen, & McMahon, 2016).

2.   **Soundness**: An argument is sound if it is both valid and its premises are true. Soundness is a stronger condition than validity as it pertains to both the form and content of the argument (Hurley, 2015).

The Role of Logic in Critical Analysis

Logic plays a critical role in analyzing arguments, whether in academic discourse, media, or everyday conversations. By understanding the components of logical arguments, critical thinkers can assess the credibility and persuasiveness of arguments presented to them.

Developing Skills in Logical Argumentation

Developing skills in logical argumentation involves practice in identifying, constructing, and evaluating arguments. Engaging in debates, analyzing case studies, and studying examples of logical arguments can enhance these skills (Ennis, 1987).

Types of Logic

I.   **Deductive Logic**:

Deductive logic involves arguments where the truth of the premises guarantees the truth of the conclusion. It is characterized by reasoning from general principles to specific instances (Copi, Cohen, & McMahon, 2016).

Deductive logic is a fundamental type of reasoning in critical thinking, characterized by deriving specific conclusions from general principles or premises. It is a process of top-down reasoning that plays a crucial role in formulating sound arguments and rational decision-making.

Understanding Deductive Logic

1. **Definition**: Deductive logic involves drawing specific conclusions from general statements or premises. If the premises are true and the logic is correctly applied, the conclusion must also be true (Copi, Cohen, & McMahon, 2016).

2. **Structure of Deductive Arguments**: A deductive argument typically starts with a general statement or hypothesis (major premise), relates it to a specific instance (minor premise), and deduces a conclusion that applies to that instance (Hurley, 2015).

Characteristics of Deductive Reasoning

1. **Validity**: A deductive argument is valid if its conclusion logically follows from its premises. Validity refers to the form of the argument rather than the truth of its premises (Copi, Cohen, & McMahon, 2016).

2. **Predictability and Certainty**: Deductive reasoning provides a high degree of certainty. If the premises are true and the argument is valid, the conclusion cannot be false (Hurley, 2015).

Examples of Deductive Logic

- Syllogisms: Classical forms of deductive reasoning that follow a three-part structure: a major premise, a minor premise, and a conclusion (Copi, Cohen, & McMahon, 2016).

- Mathematical Proofs: Deductive reasoning is fundamental in mathematics, where conclusions (theorems) are derived from axioms and previously established theorems (Tarski & Corcoran, 1983).

Application in Critical Thinking

Deductive reasoning is widely used in various fields, including science, mathematics, and philosophy. It is essential for constructing logical arguments, testing hypotheses, and developing theories based on established principles (Ennis, 1987).

Developing Deductive Reasoning Skills

Improving deductive reasoning skills involves practicing the construction and analysis of deductive arguments, familiarizing oneself with common logical forms, and engaging in exercises that challenge deductive reasoning abilities (Paul & Elder, 2006).

Challenges in Deductive Reasoning

While deductive reasoning can provide certainty, its efficacy is contingent on the truth of the premises. Critical thinkers must ensure that their premises are accurate and relevant to ensure sound conclusions (Hurley, 2015).

II. **Inductive Logic:**

Inductive logic involves reasoning from specific observations to broader generalizations. While inductive arguments can provide strong evidence, they do not guarantee the conclusion's truth (Salmon, 2013).

Inductive logic is a key type of reasoning in critical thinking, involving the formulation of generalizations based on specific observations or instances. Unlike deductive logic, where conclusions are certain if premises are true, inductive logic deals with probabilities and likelihoods.

Understanding Inductive Logic

1. **Definition**: Inductive logic involves reasoning from specific cases to general principles. It starts with observations and moves towards broader generalizations and theories (Salmon, 2013).

2. **Characteristics of Inductive Reasoning**: Inductive arguments do not guarantee the truth of the conclusion but suggest that the conclusion is probable, given the evidence. The strength of an inductive argument depends on the quality and quantity of the evidence (Copi, Cohen, & McMahon, 2016).

Types of Inductive Reasoning

1. **Generalization**: Drawing a general conclusion from a set of specific observations. For example, observing that many instances of a phenomenon share a characteristic and concluding that all instances of the phenomenon likely share that characteristic.

2. **Statistical Induction**: Using statistical data to infer a general conclusion. This involves reasoning from a sample to a population (Hurley, 2015).

3. **Causal Inference**: Establishing a cause-and-effect relationship based on observed patterns or correlations (Salmon, 2013).

Applications of Inductive Logic

Inductive reasoning is widely used in scientific research, where hypotheses are often developed based on observed data. It is also used in everyday decision-making, where people make predictions about future events based on past experiences (Ennis, 1987).

Developing Inductive Reasoning Skills

Improving inductive reasoning involves practicing the interpretation of data, understanding statistical reasoning, and learning to identify patterns and correlations. Engaging in scientific research methods and data analysis can enhance these skills (Paul & Elder, 2006).

Challenges in Inductive Reasoning

One challenge of Inductive reasoning is the risk of overgeneralization or drawing conclusions based on insufficient or biased data. Critical thinkers must be vigilant about the quality and representativeness of the data they use (Nickerson, 1998).

Principles of Logical Reasoning

I.   **Validity and Soundness**:

Validity refers to an argument where if the premises are true, the conclusion must be true. Soundness is when an argument is both valid and its premises are actually true (Hurley, 2015).

In the realm of logical reasoning, two fundamental concepts are crucial for critical thinkers to understand: validity and soundness. These principles are integral in evaluating the strength and reliability of arguments.

Validity in Logical Reasoning

1.   **Definition**: Validity refers to the formal correctness of an argument. An argument is valid if, assuming the premises are true, the conclusion must also be true. Validity is about the logical structure of an argument, not the actual truth of the premises or conclusion (Copi, Cohen, & McMahon, 2016).

2.   **Determining Validity**: To assess an argument's validity, one must examine the logical form of the argument. Even if an argument has false premises, it can still be valid if the conclusion logically follows from those premises (Hurley, 2015).

Soundness in Logical Reasoning

1.   **Definition**: Soundness is a stronger criterion than validity. An argument is sound if it is both valid and its premises are actually true. Thus, a sound argument guarantees the truth of the conclusion (Copi, Cohen, & McMahon, 2016).

2.   **Assessing Soundness**: Evaluating soundness involves two steps: determining the validity of the argument and then assessing the truth of all its premises. If both criteria are met, the argument is sound (Hurley, 2015).

Importance of Validity and Soundness in Critical Thinking

1. **Building Strong Arguments**: Understanding validity and soundness allows critical thinkers to construct arguments that are not only logically consistent but also factually accurate.

2. **Evaluating Arguments**: These principles are tools for evaluating the strength and credibility of arguments encountered, whether in academic discourse, media, or everyday conversations (Ennis, 1987).

Challenges in Applying Validity and Soundness

1. **Identifying Logical Form**: It can be challenging to discern the underlying logical structure of real-world arguments, as they may not be presented in a clear, formal manner.

2. **Verifying Truth of Premises**: Assessing the truth of premises often requires external verification and fact-checking, which can be complex and multifaceted (Paul & Elder, 2006).

Developing Skills in Logical Assessment

1. **Education and Practice**: Developing skills in assessing validity and soundness can be achieved through studying logic, practicing with various forms of arguments, and engaging in critical discussions.

2. **Critical Analysis Exercises**: Exercises that involve dissecting arguments, identifying their logical form, and evaluating their validity and soundness are beneficial for honing these skills (Tarski & Corcoran, 1983).

II. **Recognizing Logical Fallacies**:

Logical fallacies are errors in reasoning that undermine the logic of an argument. Understanding common fallacies, such as ad hominem attacks or false dichotomies, is crucial in evaluating arguments (Walton, 2004).

Logical fallacies are flaws or errors in reasoning that can undermine the validity of an argument. For critical thinkers, recognizing and understanding these fallacies is crucial to evaluate arguments correctly and to avoid faulty reasoning in their thought processes.

Understanding Logical Fallacies

1. **Definition**: A logical fallacy is a mistake in reasoning. These errors occur when an argument is based on unsound premises or incorrect reasoning, leading to invalid or deceptive conclusions (Walton, 1995).

2. **Categories of Fallacies**: Logical fallacies are often categorized into formal and informal fallacies. Formal fallacies are errors in the structure of the argument, while informal fallacies relate to errors in content or context (Copi, Cohen, & McMahon, 2016).

Common Types of Logical Fallacies

1. **Ad Hominem**: Attacking the person making the argument rather than the argument itself.

2. **Straw Man**: Misrepresenting an opponent's argument to make it easier to attack.

3. **Appeal to Ignorance**: Arguing that a claim is true because it has not been proven false, or vice versa.

4. **False Dilemma**: Presenting two opposing options as the only possibilities when others exist.

5. **Slippery Slope**: Arguing that a relatively small first step leads to a chain of related events culminating in some significant effect (Damer, 2009).

Importance of Recognizing Logical Fallacies

1. **Evaluating Arguments**: Understanding logical fallacies is essential for critically assessing the strength and validity of arguments presented in discourse, media, and everyday conversations.

2. **Avoiding Misleading Reasoning**: Awareness of common fallacies helps individuals avoid reliance on faulty reasoning in their thought processes, leading to more rational and sound conclusions (Schick & Vaughn, 2014).

Developing Skills to Identify Fallacies

1. **Education and Awareness**: Learning about different types of logical fallacies through study and practice is essential for developing the ability to recognize them.

2. **Critical Analysis**: Regular practice in analyzing arguments, identifying potential fallacies, and questioning the underlying reasoning is key to honing this skill (Paul & Elder, 2006).

Challenges in Identifying Fallacies

1. **Complex Arguments**: Some arguments may contain subtle fallacies that are not immediately apparent, requiring careful analysis to uncover.

2. **Biases and Prejudices**: Personal biases can sometimes hinder the ability to recognize fallacies, especially in arguments that align with one's beliefs (Nickerson, 1998).

Developing Logical Skills

Developing logical skills involves both the study of formal logic and practical exercises in reasoning. Engaging in activities that require constructing and evaluating arguments, such as debates or analytical writing, can enhance these skills (Paul & Elder, 2006).

Developing logical skills is a vital aspect of becoming an effective critical thinker. This process involves enhancing one's ability to reason accurately, to analyze arguments rigorously, and to construct coherent, valid arguments.

Strategies for Developing Logical Skills

1. **Formal Study of Logic**: Engaging in formal study through courses or textbooks on logic can provide a foundational understanding of logical principles and argument structures (Hurley, 2015).

2. **Practicing with Logical Puzzles and Games**: Engaging in activities that challenge logical thinking, such as puzzles, brain teasers, and strategic games, can enhance one's ability to reason systematically (Paul & Elder, 2006).

3. **Analyzing and Constructing Arguments**: Regularly practicing the analysis of arguments in texts, debates, or media, and attempting to construct one's own arguments, can improve the ability to identify logical flaws and to argue coherently (Copi, Cohen, & McMahon, 2016).

4. **Critical Discussion and Debate**: Participating in discussions and debates on various topics encourages the application of logical skills in

real-world scenarios and exposes one to different viewpoints and argumentation styles (Damer, 2009).

Importance of Logical Skills in Critical Thinking

1. **Evaluating Information and Arguments**: Logical skills are essential for effectively evaluating the vast amount of information and arguments we encounter in our daily lives.

2. **Problem-Solving and Decision-Making**: Logical reasoning is crucial in problem-solving and decision-making processes, allowing one to navigate complex situations and arrive at well-reasoned conclusions (Ennis, 1987).

Challenges in Developing Logical Skills

1. **Overcoming Cognitive Biases**: Recognizing and overcoming innate cognitive biases and emotional influences that can affect logical reasoning is a challenge in developing logical skills (Nickerson, 1998).

2. **Complexity of Real-World Arguments**: Applying logic to real-world arguments can be challenging, as such arguments may not always be presented in a clear, structured manner (Walton, 1995).

Tools and Resources

1. **Educational Resources**: Utilizing educational resources such as online courses, workshops, and logic textbooks can provide structured guidance in developing logical skills.

2. **Mentorship and Peer Learning**: Engaging with mentors or peers who are skilled in logical reasoning can provide practical insights and feedback.

Importance of Logic in Everyday Life

Understanding logic is not just important in academic contexts; it is crucial for making sound decisions and understanding complex issues in everyday life. It enables individuals to reason through problems, identify misinformation, and make informed decisions (Facione, 1990).

Logic, often perceived as a formal and academic discipline, plays a significant role in everyday life. Understanding and applying logic is crucial for critical thinking, enabling individuals to make sound decisions, solve problems effectively, and navigate the complexities of daily life.

Application of Logic in Daily Decision-Making

1. **Evaluating Information**: In an age of information overload, logic is essential for evaluating the credibility and relevance of the information we encounter daily, from news sources to social media (Paul & Elder, 2006).

2. **Problem-Solving**: Logical thinking aids in breaking down complex problems into manageable parts, identifying cause-and-effect relationships, and developing effective solutions (Hurley, 2015).

Enhancing Communication and Persuasion

1. **Constructing Coherent Arguments**: Logic helps individuals to construct clear, coherent, and persuasive arguments, whether in personal discussions, professional presentations, or written communications (Tindale, 2007).

2. **Identifying and Countering Fallacies**: Understanding logical fallacies enables individuals to recognize flawed reasoning in arguments presented by others, and to respond or counter them effectively (Walton, 1995).

Improving Critical Analysis and Reflection

1. **Critical Analysis of Media and Politics**: Logic is instrumental in critically analyzing political rhetoric, advertising, and media content, allowing individuals to discern biases, agendas, and manipulative tactics (Nickerson, 1998).

2. **Self-Reflection and Personal Growth**: Logic also plays a role in personal reflection, helping individuals to assess their beliefs and decisions critically, and to consider different perspectives (Ennis, 1987).

Challenges in Applying Logic to Everyday Life

1. **Emotional Influence**: Emotional factors can sometimes override logical thinking, leading to biased or irrational decisions (Kahneman, 2011).

2. **Complexity of Real-Life Situations**: Applying logic to real-life situations can be challenging due to their complexity, ambiguity, and the interplay of various factors (Copi, Cohen, & McMahon, 2016).

Encouraging Logical Thinking in Everyday Contexts

1. **Education and Awareness**: Promoting education and awareness about the principles of logic and their practical applications can help individuals apply logical thinking more effectively in everyday life.

2. **Practice and Engagement**: Regularly engaging in activities that require logical thinking, such as discussions, debates, and analytical reading, can sharpen one's ability to apply logic in daily contexts (Paul & Elder, 2006).

Types of Reasoning: Deductive vs. Inductive:

Understanding the distinction between deductive and inductive reasoning is fundamental for critical thinkers. These two primary forms of reasoning provide the basis for logical analysis and are essential in various aspects of problem-solving, decision-making, and argument construction.

Deductive Reasoning

1. **Definition**: Deductive reasoning is a process of reasoning from one or more general statements (premises) to reach a logically certain conclusion. It is often referred to as a top-down approach (Copi, Cohen, & McMahon, 2016).

2. **Characteristics**: Deductive arguments are structured so that if the premises are true, the conclusion must also be true. The strength of a deductive argument lies in its validity and logical form (Hurley, 2015).

3. **Examples**: Mathematical proofs and syllogistic reasoning are classic examples of deductive reasoning.

Inductive Reasoning

1. **Definition**: Inductive reasoning involves making generalizations based on specific observations, experiences, or facts. It is known as a bottom-up approach and deals with probabilities rather than certainties (Salmon, 2013).

2. **Characteristics**: Inductive reasoning does not guarantee the truth of the conclusion; instead, it renders the conclusion probable, based on the strength of the evidence (Copi, Cohen, & McMahon, 2016).

3. **Examples**: Scientific hypothesis formation and statistical inference are typical instances of inductive reasoning.

Comparing Deductive and Inductive Reasoning

1. **Nature of Conclusions**: Deductive reasoning provides conclusions that are logically certain, while inductive reasoning offers probabilistic conclusions.

2. **Application**: Deductive reasoning is often used in situations where the premises are known to be true and one needs to deduce specific conclusions. Inductive reasoning is common in scientific inquiry, where observations lead to broader generalizations and theories (Ennis, 1987).

3. **Validity and Strength**: In deductive reasoning, validity is a key criterion, while in inductive reasoning, the strength of the argument depends on the quality and quantity of evidence.

Developing Deductive and Inductive Reasoning Skills

1. **Education and Practice**: Engaging in activities that require both deductive and inductive reasoning, such as logic puzzles, scientific experiments, and critical analysis of texts, can help develop these skills (Paul & Elder, 2006).

2. **Understanding Logical Structures**: Familiarity with the structures of logical arguments, including common forms and patterns, is essential for both types of reasoning (Hurley, 2015).

Challenges in Applying Deductive and Inductive Reasoning

1. **Ensuring Validity and Reliability**: For deductive reasoning, ensuring the validity of the logical structure is crucial. In inductive reasoning, the challenge lies in ensuring the reliability and representativeness of the observations or data used (Salmon, 2013).

Common Logical Fallacies:

Logical fallacies are errors in reasoning that undermine the logic of an argument. They are common pitfalls in reasoning that can easily mislead or deceive. Understanding these fallacies is crucial for critical thinkers to evaluate arguments accurately and to avoid such errors in their reasoning.

Overview of Common Logical Fallacies

1. **Ad Hominem (Attack on the Person)**: This fallacy occurs when the argument focuses on discrediting or attacking the person making the argument rather than addressing the argument itself (Walton, 1998).

2. **Straw Man**: Involves misrepresenting someone's argument to make it easier to attack or refute. It is an oversimplification or distortion of the original argument (Tindale, 2007).

3. **Appeal to Ignorance (Argumentum ad Ignorantiam)**: This fallacy occurs when it is argued that a proposition is true because it has not been proven false, or vice versa (Copi, Cohen, & McMahon, 2016).

4. **False Dilemma (Either/Or Fallacy)**: This involves presenting two opposing options as the only possibilities, when in fact more options exist (Damer, 2009).

5. **Slippery Slope**: A claim that a relatively small first step leads to a chain of related events culminating in some significant impact, often negative and dire (Schick & Vaughn, 2014).

6. **Circular Reasoning (Begging the Question)**: This fallacy occurs when the conclusion of an argument is assumed in the phrasing of the question or premises (Hurley, 2015).

7. **Hasty Generalization**: Making a generalization based on a small or unrepresentative sample (Paul & Elder, 2006).

8. **Post Hoc Ergo Propter Hoc (After This, Therefore Because of This)**: Assuming that because B follows A, B was caused by A (Copi, Cohen, & McMahon, 2016).

Importance of Recognizing Logical Fallacies

1. **Evaluating Arguments**: Identifying logical fallacies is crucial for critically assessing the validity of arguments encountered in everyday life, media, and academic discourse.

2. **Avoiding Flawed Reasoning**: Awareness of these fallacies helps individuals avoid relying on faulty reasoning in their own arguments and decisions.

Challenges in Identifying Fallacies

1. **Subtlety of Fallacies**: Some fallacies are not overtly obvious and require careful analysis to identify.

2. **Bias and Prejudice**: Personal biases can sometimes hinder the recognition of fallacies, especially in arguments that align with one's own beliefs.

Developing Skills to Identify Fallacies

1. **Education and Practice**: Learning about different types of fallacies and practicing their identification in various contexts can enhance this critical skill.

2. **Critical Thinking Exercises**: Engaging in exercises that involve analyzing arguments for logical soundness and identifying any fallacies present.

Chapter 4: The Role of Argumentation

Argumentation plays a pivotal role in critical thinking, as it involves constructing, analyzing, and evaluating arguments to reach reasoned conclusions. It is a fundamental skill in the pursuit of knowledge, problem-solving, and decision-making across various contexts.

Understanding the Role of Argumentation

Definition:

Argumentation is the process of developing and presenting arguments. It involves reasoning logically to persuade or explain a point of view (Toulmin, 2003).

1. **Argumentation as a Process**: Argumentation is defined as the process of reasoning systematically in support of an idea, action, or theory. It involves presenting a set of reasons or evidence in support of a conclusion (van Eemeren & Grootendorst, 2004).

2. **Components of an Argument**: A typical argument consists of premises (statements or propositions that provide the rationale or evidence) leading logically to a conclusion (Toulmin, 2003).

Characteristics of Argumentation

1. **Rational Persuasion**: At its core, argumentation is about persuading others using rational methods. It is not about coercion or manipulation but about convincing others through logical and reasoned discourse (Johnson & Blair, 2006).

2. **Constructive Dialogue**: Argumentation often takes place in the context of a dialogue or discussion, where different viewpoints are presented and critically examined (Walton, 1996).

The Role of Argumentation in Critical Thinking

1. **Facilitating Understanding and Insight**: Through argumentation, complex ideas can be broken down, examined, and communicated effectively, leading to greater understanding and insight (Paul & Elder, 2006).

2. **Promoting Sound Decision-Making**: By evaluating the strength of arguments, individuals can make more informed and sound decisions, whether in personal, professional, or public spheres (Facione, 1990).

Developing Argumentation Skills

1. **Educational Approach**: Formal education in logic and reasoning, as well as participation in debate and public speaking courses, can greatly enhance argumentation skills.

2. **Practical Application**: Engaging in discussions and debates, writing essays, and analyzing arguments in media and literature are practical ways to develop argumentation skills.

Challenges in Argumentation

1. **Avoiding Fallacies**: One of the challenges in argumentation is to construct arguments that are free from logical fallacies, which can undermine the argument's validity (Tindale, 2007).

2. **Maintaining Objectivity**: It is important to maintain objectivity and avoid letting personal biases cloud judgment during argumentation (Nickerson, 1998).

Components of Argumentation:

Effective argumentation includes the assertion of claims, the support of these claims with evidence and reasoning, and the anticipation and refutation of counterarguments (van Eemeren & Grootendorst, 2004).

1. **Claim**: The claim is the statement or proposition that the argument seeks to prove. It is the conclusion that the arguer wants others to accept (Toulmin, 2003).

2. **Evidence**: Evidence consists of the facts, data, or information used to support the claim. It provides the foundation upon which the argument is built (van Eemeren & Grootendorst, 2004).

3. **Warrant**: The warrant is the logical link connecting the evidence to the claim. It explains why the evidence supports the claim and often relies on underlying assumptions (Toulmin, 2003).

4. **Backing**: Backing refers to the additional support or justification provided for the warrant. It strengthens the connection between the evidence and the

claim, especially when the warrant itself is not self-evident (Toulmin, 2003).

5. **Qualifier**: Qualifiers are words or phrases that limit the claim's scope, indicating the degree of certainty or generality. They acknowledge that arguments may not be universally applicable (Toulmin, 2003).

6. **Rebuttal**: The rebuttal addresses potential counterarguments or exceptions to the claim. It demonstrates the arguer's awareness of alternative viewpoints and potential criticisms (Tindale, 2007).

Importance of Understanding Argumentation Components

1. **Effective Argument Construction**: Knowledge of these components enables individuals to construct clear, logical, and persuasive arguments. It helps in organizing thoughts and presenting ideas coherently (Johnson & Blair, 2006).

2. **Critical Evaluation of Arguments**: Understanding the components of argumentation aids in the critical evaluation of arguments presented by others. It allows for a systematic analysis of the argument's strength and validity (Walton, 1996).

Developing Skills in Argumentation

1. **Educational Training**: Formal education in logic, rhetoric, or debate can provide a structured understanding of argumentation components.

2. **Practical Application**: Engaging in discussions, writing essays, and analyzing arguments in various media helps in applying these components practically (Paul & Elder, 2006).

Challenges in Argumentation

1. **Identifying Implicit Components**: Some components, like warrants or backings, may be implicit, making them more challenging to identify and analyze (Walton, 1996).

2. **Balancing Components**: Effectively balancing all components to construct a coherent and persuasive argument can be challenging, especially in complex or contentious issues (Tindale, 2007).

Importance of Argumentation in Critical Thinking

Facilitating Reasoned Discourse:

Argumentation fosters the ability to engage in reasoned discourse, which is essential for collaborative problem-solving, scholarly discussions, and civic engagement (Johnson & Blair, 2006).

1. **Promoting Rational Dialogue**: Argumentation provides a structured approach to discussing ideas. It encourages participants to present their thoughts logically and coherently, leading to more productive and rational dialogue (van Eemeren & Grootendorst, 2004).

2. **Enhancing Understanding and Insight**: Through argumentation, complex issues are broken down and examined critically. This process helps all participants to gain a deeper understanding of the subject matter and to consider perspectives they may not have previously entertained (Johnson & Blair, 2006).

3. **Resolving Conflicts and Disagreements**: Argumentation is a constructive way to handle disagreements, allowing individuals to present their viewpoints and to understand and evaluate opposing views. This often leads to the resolution of conflicts or to a compromise (Tindale, 2007).

Role of Argumentation in Various Contexts

1. **Academic and Educational Settings**: In educational contexts, argumentation is used to explore theories, interpret texts, and engage students in critical thinking. It fosters a learning environment where ideas are scrutinized and knowledge is constructed collaboratively (Paul & Elder, 2006).

2. **Public and Political Arenas**: Argumentation is crucial in democratic societies, as it forms the basis of public discourse. It allows citizens to debate policies, laws, and societal issues, contributing to informed decision-making and governance (Walton, 1996).

3. **Professional and Organizational Contexts**: In professional settings, argumentation aids in decision-making processes, problem-solving, and innovation. It enables teams to evaluate different strategies and solutions critically (Toulmin, 2003).

Developing Skills for Facilitating Reasoned Discourse

1. **Active Listening and Open-mindedness**: Effective argumentation in discourse requires active listening skills and an open-minded approach to considering and understanding different viewpoints (Nickerson, 1998).

2. **Critical Thinking and Communication Skills**: Developing strong critical thinking and communication skills is essential for engaging in reasoned discourse. This includes the ability to analyze information, construct clear arguments, and articulate thoughts effectively (Facione, 1990).

Challenges in Facilitating Reasoned Discourse

1. **Overcoming Emotional Biases and Barriers**: Emotional biases and barriers can hinder effective argumentation and reasoned discourse. Participants may become entrenched in their views, impeding open and rational discussion (Kahneman, 2011).

2. **Navigating Complex and Diverse Perspectives**: In discussions involving complex issues or diverse perspectives, maintaining a structured and productive argumentation process can be challenging. It requires balancing differing opinions while ensuring that the discourse remains focused and constructive (Tindale, 2007).

Enhancing Decision-Making:

Well-structured arguments aid in making informed decisions by considering different perspectives and weighing evidence and reasoning (Facione, 1990).

1. **Informed Decision-Making**: Argumentation equips individuals with the skills to gather, assess, and interpret relevant information and evidence, enabling them to make more informed decisions (Facione, 1990).

2. **Critical Evaluation of Options**: Through argumentation, different options or solutions can be critically evaluated. This process involves weighing the pros and cons, assessing risks, and considering the implications of each option (Toulmin, 2003).

3. **Logical Reasoning and Justification**: Effective argumentation involves logical reasoning, which is essential in justifying decisions and persuading others of their validity. Logical and well-structured arguments lend credibility and strength to the decision-making process (Johnson & Blair, 2006).

Application in Various Contexts

1. **Professional and Business Decisions**: In business and professional contexts, argumentation skills are crucial for strategic planning, policy development, and problem-solving. Logical argumentation helps in presenting and defending business cases or proposals (van Eemeren & Grootendorst, 2004).

2. **Personal and Ethical Decisions**: Argumentation aids in making personal and ethical decisions by allowing individuals to consider different viewpoints, values, and ethical implications before reaching a conclusion (Tindale, 2007).

Developing Argumentation Skills for Decision-Making

1. **Training in Logic and Critical Thinking**: Formal training in logic, critical thinking, and argumentation can significantly enhance decision-making skills.

2. **Practical Exercises**: Engaging in debates, discussions, and case study analyses helps in applying argumentation skills to practical decision-making scenarios (Paul & Elder, 2006).

Challenges in Using Argumentation for Decision-Making

1. **Complexity of Real-World Decisions**: Real-world decision-making often involves complex and multifaceted issues, requiring the ability to navigate through ambiguity and uncertainty (Walton, 1996).

2. **Overcoming Cognitive Biases**: Biases and emotional influences can impede objective decision-making. Argumentation requires the awareness and management of these biases to ensure rational and impartial decisions (Nickerson, 1998).

3. **Balancing Diverse Perspectives**: In decision-making, especially in group settings, balancing and integrating diverse perspectives and interests can be challenging. Effective argumentation skills are necessary to reconcile these differences and to arrive at a consensus or optimal decision (Johnson & Blair, 2006).

Developing Argumentation Skills

Learning Argument Structure:

Understanding the structure of arguments, including premises, conclusions, and logical connections, is crucial for effective argumentation (Toulmin, 2003).

1. **Basic Elements of an Argument**: The basic structure of an argument typically includes a claim (the conclusion that the argument is trying to prove), supporting evidence or premises (the reasons given to support the claim), and a warrant (the logical connection between the claim and the evidence) (Toulmin, 2003).

2. **Types of Arguments**: Familiarity with different types of arguments, such as deductive, inductive, and abductive, is essential. Each type follows a distinct structure and logic (Copi, Cohen, & McMahon, 2016).

3. **Recognizing Implicit and Explicit Components**: Arguments often have both explicit components (clearly stated) and implicit components (assumed or not directly stated). Understanding how to identify and assess these is crucial in argument analysis (Walton, 1996).

Importance of Argument Structure in Critical Thinking

edge of argument structure is essential for constructing clear and coherent arguments. It logically consistent and persuasive manner (Johnson & Blair, 2006).

structure of arguments aids in the critical evaluation of the strength and validity of arguments demic discourse (van Eemeren & Grootendorst, 2004).

Developing Skills in Argument Structure

1. **Educational Courses and Resources**: Engaging in courses or utilizing resources focused on logic, critical thinking, and rhetoric can provide foundational knowledge in argument structure.

2. **Practice and Application**: Regular practice in constructing and dissecting arguments, such as through debate, essay writing, and critical discussion, enhances one's ability to understand and apply argument structures effectively (Paul & Elder, 2006).

Challenges in Learning Argument Structure

1. **Complexity of Real-World Arguments**: Real-world arguments can be complex and multifaceted, making it challenging to identify and analyze their structure.

2. **Overcoming Cognitive Biases**: Personal biases can affect the ability to objectively analyze and construct arguments. Awareness and management of these biases are important in dealing with argument structures (Nickerson, 1998).

Practicing Argumentation:

Engaging in debates, discussions, and writing exercises helps in honing the skills of constructing and analyzing arguments (Paul & Elder, 2006).

1. **Engaging in Debates and Discussions**: Participating in debates, whether in formal settings or informal discussions, sharpens one's ability to formulate arguments quickly, respond to counterarguments, and think on one's feet (van Eemeren & Grootendorst, 2004).

2. **Writing Argumentative Essays**: Writing essays that require defending a thesis or viewpoint helps in structuring arguments logically and coherently, and in developing the skill of presenting evidence effectively (Toulmin, 2003).

3. **Analyzing Arguments in Various Media**: Critically analyzing arguments presented in books, newspapers, blogs, and other media sources can enhance one's ability to discern the strength of arguments and to identify logical fallacies (Paul & Elder, 2006).

Importance of Practicing Argumentation

1. **Enhancing Critical Thinking**: Regular practice in argumentation strengthens critical thinking skills, as it involves analyzing information, identifying biases, and assessing the validity of evidence and logic (Johnson & Blair, 2006).

2. **Improving Communication Skills**: Argumentation practice enhances one's ability to communicate ideas clearly and persuasively, an essential skill in both personal and professional contexts (Nickerson, 1998).

Challenges in Practicing Argumentation

1. **Overcoming Emotional Responses**: One challenge in argumentation is managing emotional responses and maintaining objectivity, especially in contentious or personal topics (Kahneman, 2011).

2. **Balancing Persuasion with Open-mindedness**: While arguing persuasively, it's crucial to remain open to new evidence and alternative viewpoints, avoiding the trap of becoming dogmatically attached to one's position (Tindale, 2007).

Strategies for Effective Argumentation Practice

1. **Seeking Diverse Perspectives**: Engaging with a variety of viewpoints, especially those that challenge one's own, can broaden understanding and enhance argumentation skills.

2. **Feedback and Reflection**: Seeking feedback from peers or mentors and reflecting on one's argumentative strategies can provide insights into areas for improvement (Walton, 1996).

3. **Participation in Structured Formats**: Involvement in structured formats like debate clubs, moot courts, or public speaking events provides a controlled environment for honing argumentation skills (van Eemeren & Grootendorst, 2004).

Critical Evaluation of Arguments:

Regularly evaluating the strength of arguments, identifying logical fallacies, and considering counterarguments are essential practices in developing argumentation skills (Walton, 1996).

1. **Analyzing Argument Structure**: Understanding the structure of an argument is essential. This involves identifying its premises, conclusions, and the logical connections between them. Evaluating how well the premises support the conclusion is crucial (Toulmin, 2003).

2. **Identifying Logical Fallacies**: A key part of evaluating arguments is identifying logical fallacies – errors in reasoning that weaken arguments. Recognizing these fallacies helps in assessing the argument's validity (Walton, 1996).

3. **Assessing Evidence**: Evaluating the quality, relevance, and sufficiency of the evidence supporting an argument is vital. This includes considering the sources of evidence and whether they are credible and reliable (Johnson & Blair, 2006).

Importance of Evaluating Arguments

1. **Informed Decision Making**: The ability to critically evaluate arguments enables individuals to make well-informed decisions, especially in situations where they are presented with competing claims or perspectives (Facione, 1990).

2. **Effective Communication**: By critically evaluating arguments, individuals can strengthen their ability to communicate effectively, particularly in persuasive contexts or when presenting complex information (van Eemeren & Grootendorst, 2004).

Developing Skills for Critical Evaluation

1. **Educational Training**: Formal education in logic, rhetoric, and critical thinking can provide a solid foundation for the critical evaluation of arguments.

2. **Practice and Application**: Regular practice in analyzing and critiquing arguments, such as through class discussions, debate, or essay writing, is essential for honing these skills (Paul & Elder, 2006).

Challenges in Argument Evaluation

1. **Overcoming Cognitive Biases**: Biases can affect the objectivity of one's evaluation. Being aware of and managing personal biases is crucial for fair and accurate assessment (Nickerson, 1998).

2. **Dealing with Complex Arguments**: Some arguments, especially in real-world scenarios, can be complex and multifaceted, making them challenging to analyze and evaluate thoroughly (Tindale, 2007).

3. **Distinguishing between Emotional and Logical Appeals**: Arguments often contain emotional appeals. Distinguishing these from logical reasoning is important for an objective evaluation (Kahneman, 2011).

Strategies for Effective Argument Evaluation

1. **Active and Reflective Listening**: Active listening and reflection are essential when evaluating others' arguments. This involves not just hearing but understanding and considering the arguments presented.

2. **Seeking Diverse Perspectives**: Exposing oneself to a range of viewpoints can enhance one's ability to evaluate arguments from different perspectives.

3. **Continuous Learning and Adaptation**: The landscape of argumentation is ever-evolving, especially with the influx of information in the digital age. Continuous learning and adaptation are key to staying adept at evaluating arguments (Walton, 1996).

Challenges in Argumentation

Avoiding Logical Fallacies:

One of the challenges in argumentation is to avoid logical fallacies, which can undermine the strength of an argument.

Understanding Logical Fallacies

1. **Definition**: Logical fallacies are flawed patterns of reasoning that can appear persuasive but lack logical validity. They often arise from misunderstandings, misinterpretations, or manipulations of reasoning (Walton, 1996).

2. **Types of Fallacies**: Common logical fallacies include ad hominem attacks, straw man arguments, false dilemmas, hasty generalizations, slippery slope arguments, and circular reasoning (Tindale, 2007).

Challenges in Avoiding Logical Fallacies

1. **Recognition and Identification**: One of the main challenges is the ability to recognize fallacies, especially when they are subtly embedded in persuasive language or complex arguments (Johnson & Blair, 2006).

2. **Cognitive Biases**: Cognitive biases like confirmation bias can lead individuals to unintentionally commit logical fallacies, particularly in arguments that align with their preexisting beliefs (Nickerson, 1998).

Strategies for Avoiding Logical Fallacies

1. **Education and Awareness**: Familiarity with different types of logical fallacies through education is crucial. Learning about these fallacies enables individuals to identify and avoid them in their reasoning (Toulmin, 2003).

2. **Critical Analysis**: Actively analyzing arguments for logical consistency and questioning the underlying premises can help in spotting potential fallacies (Paul & Elder, 2006).

3. **Seeking Feedback**: Engaging in discussions and seeking feedback from others can provide diverse perspectives that help in identifying overlooked fallacies.

Applying Strategies in Different Contexts

1. **Academic and Professional Settings**: In these settings, avoiding logical fallacies is essential for the integrity and credibility of arguments, research, and decision-making.

2. **Everyday Arguments**: In everyday life, being vigilant against logical fallacies is important for rational decision-making and productive discussions.

Overcoming Cognitive Biases:

Recognizing and overcoming personal biases is essential for objective and fair argumentation (Nickerson, 1998).

Understanding Cognitive Biases

1. **Definition**: Cognitive biases are psychological tendencies that cause the human brain to draw incorrect conclusions. They are often a result of the brain's attempt to simplify information processing (Kahneman, 2011).

2. **Common Biases in Argumentation**: These include confirmation bias (favoring information that confirms existing beliefs), anchoring bias (relying too heavily on the first piece of information encountered), and availability heuristic (overestimating the importance of information that is readily available) (Nickerson, 1998).

Challenges Posed by Cognitive Biases

1. **Impairment of Objective Reasoning**: Cognitive biases can impair the ability to reason objectively, as they can lead to skewed interpretations and judgments.

2. **Difficulty in Identifying Biases**: Often, individuals are not aware of their biases, making them difficult to identify and address (Tindale, 2007).

Strategies for Overcoming Cognitive Biases

1. **Awareness and Education**: Being aware of common cognitive biases and understanding their influence is the first step in mitigating their effects.

Education about these biases can be an eye-opener and a tool for self-reflection (Facione, 1990).

2. **Critical Self-Reflection**: Regularly questioning one's own beliefs and reasoning processes helps in recognizing potential biases. This involves actively seeking information that challenges one's preconceptions (Paul & Elder, 2006).

3. **Diverse Perspectives and Dialogue**: Engaging with a variety of viewpoints can provide alternative perspectives and mitigate the tunnel vision caused by personal biases. This encourages more balanced and comprehensive argumentation (Johnson & Blair, 2006).

4. **Structured Decision-Making Processes**: Implementing structured decision-making processes that involve step-by-step analysis and consideration of multiple factors can reduce the impact of biases on conclusions (Toulmin, 2003).

Application in Different Contexts

1. **Academic and Professional Environments**: In these settings, overcoming cognitive biases is crucial for sound research, ethical decision-making, and effective problem-solving.

2. **Personal Interactions and Daily Life**: Awareness of cognitive biases is also important in personal interactions and everyday decision-making, as it leads to more reasoned and less prejudiced judgments.

Argumentation in Different Contexts

Academic and Professional Contexts:

In academic research and professional settings, argumentation is crucial for proposing theories, discussing ideas, and justifying decisions.

Challenges in Academic Contexts

1. **Complexity of Subjects**: Academic arguments often involve complex and abstract subjects, requiring a deep understanding and the ability to communicate complex ideas clearly (Toulmin, 2003).

2. **Evidence and Research-Based Arguments**: Academic argumentation demands rigorous evidence and research. Finding, interpreting, and

presenting relevant data to support arguments can be challenging (Facione, 1990).

3. **Balancing Perspectives**: In academia, there's a need to acknowledge and critically evaluate multiple perspectives, which can be challenging, especially in areas with diverse views and theories (Paul & Elder, 2006).

Challenges in Professional Contexts

1. **Persuasion and Stakeholder Interests**: Professional arguments often involve persuading different stakeholders who have varying interests and priorities. Balancing these interests while making a compelling argument can be complex (Johnson & Blair, 2006).

2. **Practical Constraints**: In the professional world, arguments must often be made within the constraints of time, resources, and organizational structures, which can limit the depth and breadth of argumentation (Tindale, 2007).

3. **Ethical Considerations**: Professional argumentation can involve ethical considerations, where the arguer must

balance persuasive effectiveness with ethical responsibility, ensuring that arguments are not only compelling but also ethically sound and responsible (Walton, 1996).

Strategies for Overcoming Challenges in Academic and Professional Argumentation

1. **Thorough Research and Preparation**: In both academic and professional settings, thorough research and preparation are key. This involves not just understanding the subject matter but also being aware of the audience and their perspectives (Facione, 1990).

2. **Clear and Structured Communication**: Effective communication, including clarity of expression and logical structure, is crucial. Practicing structured argumentation can help in presenting complex ideas more clearly (Toulmin, 2003).

3. **Critical Thinking and Analysis**: Developing strong critical thinking and analytical skills is essential for evaluating evidence, identifying biases, and constructing balanced arguments (Paul & Elder, 2006).

4. **Collaboration and Feedback**: Collaborating with peers or colleagues and seeking feedback can provide new insights and help in refining arguments. It also aids in understanding various viewpoints and interests (Johnson & Blair, 2006).

5. **Ethical Considerations**: Being mindful of ethical standards and incorporating them into argumentation practices is vital, especially in professional contexts where decisions can have significant consequences (Tindale, 2007).

Everyday Life:

In everyday life, argumentation skills are used in personal decision-making, resolving conflicts, and persuading others.

1. **Emotional Involvement**: Arguments in personal or everyday contexts often involve emotional aspects, making it challenging to maintain objectivity and rationality. Emotional attachments can cloud judgment and lead to fallacious reasoning (Kahneman, 2011).

2. **Informal Settings and Unstructured Arguments**: Everyday arguments typically occur in informal settings and may lack a structured format. This can make it difficult to follow a clear line of reasoning and to distinguish between valid arguments and mere opinions (Tindale, 2007).

3. **Diverse Audiences**: In daily life, one encounters a wide range of individuals with varying levels of understanding and different perspectives. Tailoring arguments to effectively communicate with diverse audiences can be challenging (Johnson & Blair, 2006).

Strategies for Overcoming Challenges in Everyday Argumentation

1. **Practicing Active Listening**: Active listening is crucial in understanding the viewpoints of others and responding thoughtfully. It involves not just hearing but comprehending and considering the arguments of others (Paul & Elder, 2006).

2. **Managing Emotions**: Developing skills in emotional intelligence, such as recognizing one's own emotional responses and empathizing with others, can help in maintaining objectivity and respect during arguments (Goleman, 1995).

3. **Clear and Concise Communication**: Communicating in a clear, concise, and structured manner helps in making arguments more comprehensible and persuasive, especially in informal settings (Toulmin, 2003).

4. Adapting to the Audience: Tailoring the argument to the audience's level of understanding and interest is key. This involves using appropriate language, examples, and analogies that resonate with the audience (Walton, 1996).

5. **Seeking Common Ground**: Finding common ground or shared values can facilitate more productive and less confrontational arguments in everyday interactions (van Eemeren & Grootendorst, 2004).

Application in Diverse Everyday Contexts

1. **Family and Personal Relationships**: Effective argumentation skills can aid in resolving conflicts, making collective decisions, and discussing important matters with family members and friends.

2. **Consumer Decisions and Interactions**: In consumer scenarios, such as negotiating purchases or discussing services, argumentation skills are valuable for making informed choices and effectively presenting one's case.

Constructing a Sound Argument:

To become a proficient critical thinker, understanding the role of argumentation is essential. Argumentation is not just about winning debates; it's a fundamental process in reasoning, critical thinking, and problem-solving. This involves constructing sound arguments, which are logical, well-structured, and backed by evidence.

Constructing a Sound Argument

1. **Clear and Precise Language**: The use of clear, precise language is crucial (Toulmin, Rieke, & Janik, 1984). Ambiguity and vagueness can lead to misunderstandings and weak arguments.

2. **Logical Structure**: Every sound argument has a logical structure, with premises leading to a conclusion (Fisher, 2001). This logical progression is essential for the argument to be valid.

3. **Relevant and Strong Premises**: The strength of an argument depends on the relevance and solidity of its premises (Govier, 2010). Premises should be directly related to the conclusion and supported by evidence.

4. **Use of Evidence**: Sound arguments are supported by appropriate and credible evidence (Walton, Reed, & Macagno, 2008). This evidence must be accurately represented and relevant to the argument.

5. **Consideration of Counterarguments**: Acknowledging and addressing counterarguments strengthens an argument (van Eemeren & Grootendorst, 2004). This shows an understanding of the complexity of the issue and adds credibility.

6. **Avoiding Logical Fallacies**: Avoiding logical fallacies is crucial (Damer, 2009). Fallacies, such as ad hominem attacks or false dilemmas, weaken arguments and hinder critical thinking.

7. **Emotional Appeal and Ethical Consideration**: While primarily logical, effective arguments can also include an ethical dimension or emotional appeal, as long as these do not overshadow logical reasoning (Perelman & Olbrechts-Tyteca, 1969).

Becoming a critical thinker involves the skillful construction of sound arguments. This requires clear language, logical structure, strong and relevant premises, the use of credible evidence, consideration of counterarguments, avoidance of logical fallacies, and sometimes, ethical and emotional appeals. By mastering these elements, individuals enhance their critical thinking abilities, enabling them to analyze, evaluate, and create more effective arguments in various contexts.

Analyzing Arguments:

Becoming a critical thinker involves the skill of analyzing arguments effectively. This process requires understanding the structure of arguments, evaluating the evidence presented, and identifying logical fallacies or biases. In this context, argumentation plays a pivotal role.

Analyzing Arguments

1. **Understanding Argument Structure**: Recognize the components of an argument: premises, conclusions, and the inferential link between them (Fisher, 2001). This helps in discerning the argument's foundation and its purported outcome.

2. **Evaluating Evidence**: Critical thinkers assess the quality of evidence supporting an argument. This involves considering the source's credibility, the evidence's relevance, and its sufficiency (Walton, Reed, & Macagno, 2008).

78

3. **Identifying Assumptions**: Every argument has underlying assumptions. Critical analysis involves bringing these to light and assessing their validity (Toulmin, Rieke, & Janik, 1984).

4. **Recognizing Logical Fallacies**: Identifying logical fallacies, like ad hominem attacks or slippery slope arguments, is crucial (Damer, 2009). These fallacies can undermine an argument's validity.

5. **Distinguishing between Emotional and Logical Appeals**: While emotional appeals can be persuasive, they do not necessarily validate an argument (Perelman & Olbrechts-Tyteca, 1969). Distinguishing these from logical reasoning is key.

6. **Considering the Counterarguments**: Evaluating an argument also involves considering potential counterarguments (van Eemeren & Grootendorst, 2004). This broadens understanding and tests the argument's strength.

7. **Contextual Analysis**: Understanding the context in which an argument is made can provide insights into its validity and purpose (Govier, 2010).

In summary, analyzing arguments is a critical component of developing critical thinking skills. It involves understanding the structure of arguments, evaluating evidence, recognizing assumptions and logical fallacies, distinguishing between types of appeals, considering counterarguments, and understanding the context. Mastery of these skills enables individuals to engage more effectively in reasoning, decision-making, and problem-solving activities.

The Art of Persuasion and Rhetoric:

To become an adept critical thinker, one must understand the intricacies of persuasion and rhetoric within the realm of argumentation. The art of persuasion is not merely about convincing others but also about understanding and analyzing how arguments are constructed and presented to persuade. Rhetoric, the art of effective or persuasive speaking or writing, plays a pivotal role in this process.

The Art of Persuasion and Rhetoric in Argumentation

1. **Understanding Rhetorical Strategies**: Aristotle identified three primary forms of rhetoric: ethos (credibility), pathos (emotional appeal), and logos (logical reasoning) (Aristotle, 1991). A critical thinker needs to understand how these elements are used in arguments to persuade.

2. **Analyzing the Use of Ethos**: Ethos refers to the credibility or ethical appeal of the speaker or writer (Garver, 1994). Evaluating the authority, expertise, and reliability of the source is a key aspect of critical thinking.

3. **Evaluating Pathos**: Pathos involves appealing to the audience's emotions. Critical thinkers should discern when emotional appeals are used and whether they complement or overshadow logical arguments (Perelman & Olbrechts-Tyteca, 1969).

4. **Assessing Logos**: Logos is the logical aspect of persuasion. It involves the use of reasoning, evidence, and factual data. Critical thinkers must evaluate the strength, relevance, and validity of the logical arguments presented (Toulmin, 2003).

5. **Recognizing Rhetorical Devices and Fallacies**: Various rhetorical devices and fallacies can be used in persuasion, some of which may obscure logical analysis (Damer, 2009). Identifying and understanding these devices is crucial for critical analysis.

6. **The Role of Context and Audience**: The effectiveness of persuasion often depends on the context and the audience (Bitzer, 1968). Critical thinkers consider these factors when evaluating arguments.

7. **Developing Persuasive Arguments**: Critical thinkers not only analyze but also construct persuasive arguments. This involves effectively using ethos, pathos, and logos while maintaining logical coherence and ethical integrity (Aristotle, 1991).

In conclusion, the role of argumentation in the art of persuasion and rhetoric is a critical aspect of becoming a proficient critical thinker. It involves understanding and applying rhetorical strategies, evaluating the use of ethos, pathos, and logos, recognizing rhetorical devices and fallacies, and considering the context and audience. By mastering these skills, individuals can enhance their ability to analyze, construct, and deconstruct arguments, which is fundamental to effective communication and decision-making in various spheres of life.

Chapter 5: Emotional Intelligence and Critical Thinking

The integration of emotional intelligence into the development of critical thinking skills, particularly in the context of persuasion and rhetoric, represents a nuanced and sophisticated approach to argumentation and decision-making. Emotional intelligence (EI) involves the ability to recognize, understand, manage, and use emotions effectively in oneself and others (Mayer & Salovey, 1997). It plays a significant role in enhancing critical thinking, especially within the realms of persuasion and rhetoric.

Emotional Intelligence and Critical Thinking in Persuasion and Rhetoric

Recognizing Emotional Appeals (Pathos):

Emotional intelligence enables individuals to identify and understand emotional appeals (pathos) in rhetoric (Aristotle, 1991). EI helps in discerning whether these appeals are used manipulatively or genuinely add value to the argument.

To become an adept critical thinker in the realm of persuasion and rhetoric, particularly in recognizing emotional appeals (pathos), one must intertwine emotional intelligence (EI) with critical thinking skills. Emotional intelligence plays a critical role in identifying, understanding, and appropriately responding to the emotional dimensions in rhetoric and argumentation.

Recognizing Emotional Appeals (Pathos) in Persuasion and Rhetoric

1. **Understanding Pathos**: Pathos, one of Aristotle's three modes of persuasion, refers to the emotional appeal used in rhetoric (Aristotle, 1991). Recognizing pathos involves identifying emotional triggers in language, imagery, and the overall context of the argument.

2. **Role of Emotional Intelligence in Identifying Pathos**: Emotional intelligence aids in discerning the subtle use of emotions in arguments. It involves sensitivity to verbal and non-verbal emotional cues (Mayer & Salovey, 1997).

3. **Evaluating the Appropriateness of Emotional Appeals**: Critical thinkers use EI to assess whether emotional appeals are appropriate for the argument's context or whether they are manipulative or misleading (Goleman, 1995).

4. **Balancing Emotional and Logical Appeals**: While pathos can be powerful, it needs to be balanced with ethos (credibility) and logos (logic). EI helps in maintaining this balance, ensuring emotional appeals do not overshadow logical reasoning (Aristotle, 1991).

5. **Ethical Considerations in Using Emotional Appeals**: Emotional intelligence involves recognizing the ethical implications of using emotional appeals. EI guides the use of pathos in a way that is sincere and not exploitative (Kidwell, Hardesty, Murtha, & Sheng, 2011).

6. **Impact of Emotional Appeals on Audience**: Understanding how emotional appeals affect different audiences is a key aspect of EI. This understanding can guide the formulation of arguments that resonate with the audience's values and beliefs (Bar-On, 2006).

7. **Critical Reflection on Personal Emotional Responses**: A critical thinker reflects on their own emotional responses to arguments. This self-awareness, a component of EI, helps in separating personal biases or emotional reactions from the objective analysis of the argument (Goleman, Boyatzis, & McKee, 2002).

In conclusion, the integration of emotional intelligence with critical thinking skills is vital in recognizing and appropriately responding to emotional appeals in persuasion and rhetoric. Understanding and evaluating pathos, balancing emotional appeals with logic, considering the ethical implications of such appeals, and being aware of one's own emotional responses are crucial in effectively navigating and constructing arguments. This holistic approach allows for more nuanced, ethical, and effective communication and decision-making in various aspects of life.

Managing Personal Emotions in Argumentation:

Critical thinkers with high EI are better equipped to manage their emotions during debates or discussions, preventing emotional responses from clouding judgment (Goleman, 1995).

Becoming a critical thinker, particularly in the context of the art of persuasion and rhetoric, necessitates the ability to manage personal emotions effectively during argumentation. This skill, at the intersection of emotional intelligence (EI) and critical thinking, is crucial for engaging in rational discourse and making sound decisions.

Managing Personal Emotions in Argumentation

1. **Self-awareness in Emotional Responses**: Emotional intelligence begins with self-awareness, which involves recognizing one's emotional responses during argumentation (Goleman, 1995). This recognition allows critical thinkers to identify how emotions might influence their reasoning and argumentative strategies.

2. **Regulating Emotions for Objective Analysis**: The ability to regulate emotions is vital for maintaining objectivity in arguments (Mayer & Salovey, 1997). EI empowers individuals to control emotional biases or reactions that may cloud judgment or lead to irrational decisions.

3. **Stress and Emotional Management**: High-pressure situations in argumentation can trigger stress responses. EI involves managing stress to maintain composure and think clearly (Goleman, Boyatzis, & McKee, 2002).

4. **Empathy in Argumentation**: Understanding and considering the emotions of others is a component of EI. Empathy helps in formulating arguments that are considerate and respectful, fostering a more constructive discourse (Bar-On, 2006).

5. **Conflict Resolution Skills**: EI contributes to effective conflict resolution by enabling individuals to approach disagreements with a calm, composed demeanor, essential for resolving conflicts constructively (Mayer, Roberts, & Barsade, 2008).

6. **Communicating with Emotional Intelligence**: Effective communication, a key aspect of EI, involves expressing oneself clearly and calmly, especially when presenting or countering arguments (Salovey & Mayer, 1990).

7. **Impact of Emotional Tone on Persuasion**: The emotional tone used in argumentation can influence its persuasiveness. EI helps in adjusting this tone to be more effective in persuading others, while still maintaining logical coherence (Kidwell, Hardesty, Murtha, & Sheng, 2011).

In summary, managing personal emotions in argumentation is a critical skill for those aspiring to become effective critical thinkers in the art of persuasion and rhetoric. Emotional intelligence provides the tools to recognize and regulate one's emotions, empathize with others, and communicate effectively, all of which are essential for rational, effective, and ethical argumentation. By mastering emotional self-regulation and empathetic engagement, individuals can enhance their persuasive abilities and engage more constructively in various discourses.

Empathizing with the Audience:

EI aids in understanding and connecting with the audience's emotions. This empathy can be pivotal in tailoring arguments in a way that resonates emotionally with the audience, making persuasion more effective (Bar-On, 2006).

Empathizing with the audience is a fundamental aspect of emotional intelligence (EI) that significantly enhances critical thinking, especially in the context of the art of persuasion and rhetoric. Empathy, a core component of EI, involves the ability to understand and share the feelings of others. In persuasive communication, empathy enables a speaker or writer to connect more effectively with their audience, facilitating a deeper understanding and resonance with the message being conveyed.

Empathizing with the Audience in Persuasion and Rhetoric

1. **Understanding Audience Perspectives**: Empathy involves appreciating the audience's perspectives, beliefs, and emotions (Mayer, Caruso, & Salovey, 2016). This understanding is crucial for tailoring arguments that are relevant and compelling to the audience.

2. **Emotional Resonance**: Empathizing with the audience helps in creating emotional resonance, making arguments more persuasive and impactful (Bar-On, 2006). This involves aligning the message with the audience's values, concerns, and experiences.

3. **Building Trust and Credibility (Ethos)**: Demonstrating empathy can enhance the speaker's ethos, or credibility, as it shows respect and understanding towards the audience (Aristotle, 1991). This trust is pivotal in persuasive communication.

4. **Enhancing Communication Effectiveness**: Effective communication is not just about the content but also how it is received by the audience. Empathy allows for adjustments in communication style to ensure clarity and prevent misunderstandings (Goleman, 1995).

5. **Conflict Resolution in Rhetoric**: In persuasive contexts where opinions diverge, empathy can be instrumental in resolving conflicts and finding common ground (Goleman, Boyatzis, & McKee, 2002).

6. **Incorporating Feedback**: Empathy involves being open to and understanding feedback from the audience. This can provide insights into the audience's needs and perceptions, informing more effective future communication (Mayer & Salovey, 1997).

7. **Ethical Persuasion**: Empathy ensures that persuasive techniques are used ethically, respecting the audience's autonomy and emotions, rather than manipulating them (Kidwell, Hardesty, Murtha, & Sheng, 2011).

In conclusion, empathizing with the audience is a critical skill in the art of persuasion and rhetoric, deeply intertwined with emotional intelligence and critical thinking. Understanding and resonating with the audience's emotions, perspectives, and values enhances the effectiveness of persuasive communication. It builds trust, facilitates conflict resolution, and ensures ethical persuasion. By employing empathy effectively, communicators can create more impactful, meaningful, and ethical arguments, ultimately achieving more effective and harmonious outcomes in their persuasive efforts.

Ethical Considerations in Persuasion:

Emotional intelligence fosters ethical considerations in persuasion, ensuring that emotional appeals are not exploitative (Kidwell, Hardesty, Murtha, & Sheng, 2011).

In the pursuit of becoming a critical thinker, particularly in the context of the art of persuasion and rhetoric, ethical considerations play a paramount role. Integrating emotional intelligence (EI) with critical thinking is essential to ensure that persuasive tactics are employed responsibly and ethically.

Ethical Considerations in Persuasion

1. **Respect for Audience Autonomy**: Ethical persuasion respects the audience's right to make informed decisions. This involves providing truthful information and avoiding deception (Bok, 1978). Emotional intelligence aids in understanding and respecting the perspectives and autonomy of the audience.

2. **Avoiding Manipulation**: Ethical persuasion distinguishes itself from manipulation by ensuring that the intent behind the message is transparent and respects the audience's welfare (Cialdini, 2001). EI helps in recognizing and avoiding emotionally manipulative tactics.

3. **Balancing Emotional and Logical Appeals**: While emotional appeals (pathos) are a powerful aspect of persuasion, relying solely on them can be unethical if it overshadows logical reasoning (logos) and credibility (ethos) (Aristotle, 1991). Critical thinkers use EI to balance emotional appeals with factual and logical arguments.

4. **Responsibility of Influence**: Persuaders have a responsibility to use their influence ethically. This includes being aware of the potential impact of their arguments and ensuring that they contribute positively to the audience's understanding (Harris & Nelson, 2008).

5. **Consideration of Cultural and Contextual Factors**: Ethical persuasion requires sensitivity to cultural and contextual factors that may influence how messages are received and interpreted (Ting-Toomey, 1999). EI is critical in understanding and adapting to these factors.

6. **Transparency and Disclosure**: Ethical persuasion practices involve being transparent about any vested interests and disclosing relevant information that might affect the audience's decision-making process (Drumwright & Murphy, 2009).

7. **Promoting Fairness and Equity**: In persuasion, ethical considerations include promoting fairness and avoiding rhetoric that discriminates or marginalizes specific groups (Kidwell, Hardesty, Murtha, & Sheng, 2011).

Ethical considerations in persuasion and rhetoric are integral to becoming a critical thinker. They involve respecting the audience's autonomy, avoiding manipulation, balancing emotional and logical appeals, being responsible with influence, considering cultural and contextual factors, maintaining transparency, and promoting fairness. Emotional intelligence complements critical thinking by providing the sensitivity and awareness necessary to navigate these ethical considerations effectively, ensuring that persuasive efforts are not only effective but also responsible and respectful.

Critical Evaluation of Emotional Content:

EI combined with critical thinking skills allows for a more nuanced evaluation of the emotional content of arguments, assessing whether emotional elements are supporting or overshadowing logical elements (Perelman & Olbrechts-Tyteca, 1969).

The integration of emotional intelligence (EI) and critical thinking is particularly significant in the critical evaluation of emotional content within the art of persuasion and rhetoric. This integration enables an individual to not only understand and resonate with emotional appeals but also to scrutinize them critically to ensure they are used appropriately and effectively.

Critical Evaluation of Emotional Content in Persuasion and Rhetoric

1. **Understanding the Role of Emotions in Arguments**: Emotional content in rhetoric can significantly influence an audience's response. Critical thinkers must first understand the role and impact of emotions in persuasive contexts (Aristotle, 1991).

2. **Distinguishing between Emotional Manipulation and Genuine Appeal**: EI enables the distinction between emotional manipulation and genuine emotional appeal. This involves assessing whether emotions are used to deceive or genuinely connect with the audience (Bok, 1978).

3. **Evaluating the Relevance and Appropriateness of Emotions**: Critical thinkers evaluate whether the emotional content is relevant to the argument's context and whether it aligns ethically with the intended message (Kidwell, Hardesty, Murtha, & Sheng, 2011).

4. **Balancing Emotional and Rational Elements**: It's important to balance emotional appeals with rational arguments. EI aids in recognizing when emotions overshadow logic, potentially leading to fallacious reasoning (Goleman, 1995).

5. **Recognizing Emotional Biases**: Emotional intelligence helps in identifying personal and others' emotional biases that might affect the interpretation and construction of arguments (Mayer & Salovey, 1997).

6. **Impact of Emotions on Decision Making**: Understanding how emotions impact decision-making processes is crucial. EI combined with critical thinking helps in discerning when emotions are driving decisions inappropriately (Lazarus, 1991).

7. **Ethical Use of Emotional Appeals**: Critical evaluation involves ensuring that emotional content is used ethically, respecting the audience's intelligence and emotional state (Drumwright & Murphy, 2009).

The critical evaluation of emotional content in persuasion and rhetoric is a nuanced process that requires both emotional intelligence and critical thinking skills. It involves understanding the influence of emotions, distinguishing between manipulation and genuine appeal, evaluating the relevance and appropriateness of emotional content, balancing emotional and rational elements, recognizing emotional biases, understanding the impact of emotions on decision-making, and ensuring the ethical use of emotional appeals. By effectively combining EI and critical thinking, individuals can navigate complex emotional landscapes in persuasive contexts, leading to more informed, ethical, and effective communication and decision-making.

Communication Skills in Rhetoric:

Effective communication, a component of EI, is crucial in rhetoric and persuasion. It involves not just what is communicated but how it is communicated, which can significantly influence the effectiveness of the argument (Mayer, Roberts, & Barsade, 2008).

In the journey to becoming a critical thinker, the development of communication skills, particularly within the context of the art of persuasion and rhetoric, is significantly enriched by the application of emotional intelligence (EI). Communication in rhetoric is not just about the content delivered; it's equally about how it's delivered and perceived. EI plays a crucial role in this regard, enhancing both the understanding and expression of emotions in communication.

Communication Skills in Rhetoric

1. **Effective Expression of Ideas**: Communication in rhetoric involves clearly and effectively expressing ideas. EI contributes to this by enabling a speaker to convey messages in a way that resonates with the audience, considering their emotional states and expectations (Goleman, 1995).

2. **Active Listening and Empathy**: Effective communication is a two-way process. EI involves active listening and empathy, allowing for a deeper understanding of the audience's viewpoints and concerns (Bar-On, 2006). This facilitates more engaging and persuasive rhetoric.

3. **Non-Verbal Communication**: Non-verbal cues, such as body language and tone of voice, play a significant role in rhetoric. EI helps in both interpreting these cues from others and effectively using them to enhance verbal communication (Mehrabian, 1972).

4. **Adapting to Audience Feedback**: EI involves being sensitive to audience feedback, both verbal and non-verbal, and adjusting communication

strategies accordingly. This adaptability can make rhetoric more effective and audience-centric (Mayer, Roberts, & Barsade, 2008).

5. **Managing Emotional Tone**: The emotional tone of communication can greatly impact its persuasiveness. EI aids in managing this tone to align with the purpose of the rhetoric and the audience's mood (Kidwell, Hardesty, Murtha, & Sheng, 2011).

6. **Conflict Resolution in Communication**: EI is crucial in resolving conflicts that may arise during rhetorical exchanges. It involves using emotional information to guide thinking and behavior towards constructive solutions (Goleman, Boyatzis, & McKee, 2002).

7. **Ethical and Empathetic Persuasion**: EI drives ethical persuasion by enabling a balance between advocating for one's position and respecting the audience's emotions and viewpoints (Drumwright & Murphy, 2009).

Emotional intelligence significantly enhances communication skills in the art of persuasion and rhetoric. It involves effective expression, active listening, understanding non-verbal cues, adapting to audience feedback, managing emotional tone, resolving conflicts, and employing ethical and empathetic persuasion strategies. Mastery of these skills, facilitated by EI, allows critical thinkers to engage more effectively and ethically in persuasive communication, enhancing their ability to influence, engage, and understand their audience.

Conflict Resolution and Consensus Building:

EI is key in resolving conflicts and building consensus, especially in situations where differing views need to be reconciled through critical discussion (Goleman, Boyatzis, & McKee, 2002).

The fusion of emotional intelligence (EI) and critical thinking is particularly crucial in conflict resolution and consensus building within the art of persuasion and rhetoric. Persuasion, at its core, often involves addressing and resolving conflicts of ideas, beliefs, or positions. Emotional intelligence enhances the capacity to navigate these conflicts thoughtfully and to work towards consensus in a way that respects all parties involved.

Conflict Resolution and Consensus Building in Persuasion and Rhetoric

1. **Understanding and Managing Emotions**: Effective conflict resolution starts with understanding and managing one's own emotions

and recognizing the emotions of others involved (Goleman, 1995). Emotional intelligence allows for this by providing skills to identify and regulate emotional responses constructively.

2. **Active Listening and Empathy**: EI involves active listening and empathy, essential for understanding differing perspectives in a conflict (Bar-On, 2006). This understanding is key to finding common ground and building consensus.

3. **Effective Communication**: Communication skills, enhanced by EI, play a vital role in conflict resolution. This includes expressing thoughts clearly and respectfully, and ensuring that all parties feel heard and understood (Mayer, Caruso, & Salovey, 2016).

4. **Problem-Solving Skills**: Critical thinking contributes to effective problem-solving during conflicts. It involves analyzing the situation, identifying underlying issues, and developing creative solutions that can lead to consensus (Facione, 2015).

5. **Negotiation Skills**: EI and critical thinking together enhance negotiation skills. They enable individuals to negotiate differences with a balance of empathy and logical reasoning, aiming for solutions that are mutually beneficial (Thompson, 2009).

6. **Dealing with Emotional Biases**: Recognizing and managing emotional biases is crucial in conflict resolution. EI helps in identifying such biases in oneself and others, thus preventing them from derailing the process (Goleman, Boyatzis, & McKee, 2002).

7. **Ethical Considerations**: Ethical considerations are paramount in conflict resolution. EI and critical thinking together ensure that the process and outcomes are fair, respectful, and considerate of all parties' needs and values (Kidwell, Hardesty, Murtha, & Sheng, 2011).

The integration of emotional intelligence and critical thinking is vital in conflict resolution and consensus building within the realm of persuasion and rhetoric. This combination allows for a deeper understanding of emotions, effective communication, empathetic listening, ethical problem-solving, and effective negotiation, all of which are essential in resolving conflicts and building consensus. By employing both EI and critical thinking, individuals can navigate complex interpersonal dynamics more effectively, leading to more constructive and harmonious outcomes.

Incorporating emotional intelligence into critical thinking, especially in the context of persuasion and rhetoric, offers a more holistic approach to argumentation. It involves understanding and managing emotions, both one's own and others', to enhance the effectiveness of communication. EI provides a framework for ethically engaging in emotional appeals, understanding the audience, and resolving conflicts, all of which are essential in the art of persuasion and rhetoric. By marrying EI with critical thinking, individuals can navigate complex arguments and discussions more effectively, leading to more reasoned and empathetic outcomes.

Understanding Emotions in Reasoning:

Understanding emotions in reasoning is a crucial aspect of becoming a critical thinker, particularly when integrating emotional intelligence (EI) with critical thinking skills. This integration is essential for processing information, making decisions, and solving problems effectively.

Understanding Emotions in Reasoning

1. **Role of Emotions in Reasoning**: Emotions play a significant role in how individuals perceive and interact with the world. They can influence reasoning and decision-making processes, both positively and negatively (Damasio, 1994). Acknowledging the impact of emotions is a fundamental step in critical thinking.

2. **Emotional Intelligence and Cognitive Bias**: Emotional intelligence helps in recognizing and managing cognitive biases that can skew reasoning. EI involves being aware of how emotions can drive these biases and distort logical thinking (Goleman, 1995).

3. **Emotions as Information**: Emotions can provide valuable information that can aid in decision-making. For instance, intuitive feelings can serve as a form of rapid, experiential processing that supplements more analytical thought processes (Mayer & Salovey, 1997).

4. **Balancing Emotional and Logical Thinking**: Critical thinking involves balancing emotional responses with logical analysis. This balance ensures that decisions are not overly influenced by either excessive emotionality or cold logic (Lazarus, 1991).

5. **Empathy in Understanding Others' Perspectives**: Emotional intelligence enables individuals to understand and empathize with others' emotions. This skill is crucial in reasoning, especially in collaborative or group decision-making scenarios (Bar-On, 2006).

6. **Self-Regulation and Emotional Control**: Effective reasoning requires self-regulation and control over one's emotional responses. EI involves developing strategies to manage emotions, particularly in high-stress or emotionally charged situations (Goleman, Boyatzis, & McKee, 2002).

7. **Impact of Emotions on Communication and Persuasion**: Emotions significantly impact how messages are communicated and received. Understanding this impact is essential for effective persuasion and rhetoric (Kidwell, Hardesty, Murtha, & Sheng, 2011).

Understanding emotions in reasoning is a critical component of both emotional intelligence and critical thinking. Recognizing the influence of emotions on reasoning, balancing emotional and logical thinking, managing cognitive biases, and employing empathy are all vital in making informed and balanced decisions. This integration of EI and critical thinking enhances an individual's ability to process information, communicate effectively, and solve problems in a comprehensive and nuanced manner.

Bias and Heuristics:
To become a critical thinker, it's crucial to understand the interplay between emotional intelligence (EI) and critical thinking, especially in the context of biases and heuristics. Biases are systematic patterns of deviation from norm or rationality in judgment, while heuristics are simple, efficient rules which people often use to form judgments and make decisions. Both are deeply influenced by emotions and can significantly impact critical thinking processes.

Emotional Intelligence, Biases, and Heuristics in Critical Thinking

1. **Recognition of Cognitive Biases**: Emotional intelligence aids in the recognition of various cognitive biases, such as confirmation bias, where individuals favor information that confirms their preexisting beliefs (Nickerson, 1998). EI can help in identifying and regulating emotional responses that might lead to such biases.

2. **Impact of Heuristics on Decision Making**: Heuristics are mental shortcuts that reduce complex problem-solving demands. However, they can lead to errors in judgment. Emotional intelligence helps in understanding the emotional underpinnings of these heuristics and their impact on decision-making (Tversky & Kahneman, 1974).

3. **Balancing Emotion and Reason**: Emotional intelligence plays a crucial role in balancing emotional responses with logical reasoning, a key aspect in overcoming biases and the misuse of heuristics (Lazarus, 1991).

4. **Self-awareness in Decision Making**: Self-awareness, a component of EI, involves being conscious of one's own feelings, biases, and thought processes. This awareness is vital for critically evaluating one's own decisions and thought patterns (Goleman, 1995).

5. **Empathy and Perspective-Taking**: EI involves empathy and perspective-taking, which can mitigate biases like the fundamental attribution error – the tendency to attribute others' behaviors to their character rather than to external factors (Ross, 1977). Understanding others' perspectives can lead to more balanced and fair judgments.

6. **Managing Emotional Influences**: Emotional influences can lead to heuristic-driven biases like the affect heuristic, where decisions are unduly influenced by emotions. EI involves managing these influences to enable more rational decision-making (Slovic, Finucane, Peters, & MacGregor, 2002).

7. **Critical Evaluation of Information**: Critical thinking involves the rigorous evaluation of information and arguments, a process that can be compromised by emotional biases. EI assists in maintaining objectivity in evaluating evidence and arguments (Facione, 1990).

In conclusion, the integration of emotional intelligence with critical thinking is essential in understanding and mitigating the effects of biases and heuristics. Emotional intelligence provides the tools for recognizing and managing the emotional aspects of these cognitive processes, promoting a more balanced and rational approach to decision-making and problem-solving. This integration is key for individuals aiming to enhance their critical thinking skills in various aspects of personal and professional life.

The Balance of Emotion and Logic:

Achieving a balance between emotion and logic is a fundamental aspect of becoming a critical thinker, particularly when integrating emotional intelligence (EI) with critical thinking. This balance is crucial for making reasoned decisions, solving problems effectively, and communicating persuasively.

The Balance of Emotion and Logic:

1. **Role of Emotions and Logic in Decision-Making**: Emotions and logic both play vital roles in decision-making. While emotions can provide quick, intuitive guidance, logic offers a more analytical and structured approach

(Damasio, 1994). The key is to integrate these aspects for well-rounded decision-making.

2. **Emotional Intelligence in Understanding Emotions**: EI involves the ability to perceive, use, understand, and manage emotions (Salovey & Mayer, 1990). A high level of EI helps in recognizing and understanding both one's own emotions and those of others, which is essential in incorporating emotional insights into logical reasoning.

3. **Critical Thinking for Logical Analysis**: Critical thinking involves the objective analysis and evaluation of an issue in order to form a judgment (Facione, 1990). It helps in logically assessing information and arguments, independent of emotional biases.

4. **Overcoming Cognitive Biases**: Emotions can lead to cognitive biases, affecting logical reasoning. Critical thinkers use their understanding of emotions (through EI) to identify and mitigate these biases (Kahneman, 2011).

5. **Empathy and Perspective-Taking**: EI enhances empathy and perspective-taking, enabling individuals to understand and consider the emotional states and viewpoints of others. This empathetic understanding is crucial in logical problem-solving and decision-making, particularly in social contexts (Goleman, 1995).

6. **Emotion Regulation and Rational Thinking**: EI also involves emotion regulation, which is the ability to manage and respond to emotions appropriately (Gross, 1998). Effective emotion regulation is key to maintaining clarity of thought and preventing emotions from overpowering logical analysis.

7. **Integrating Emotional and Logical Intelligence**: The ultimate goal is to integrate emotional and logical intelligence. This means using emotions to enhance reasoning and applying logical analysis to understand and manage emotions (Mayer, Caruso, & Salovey, 2016).

In conclusion, the balance of emotion and logic is essential in the development of critical thinking skills. Emotional intelligence provides the tools to understand and regulate emotions, while critical thinking offers a framework for logical analysis and judgment. The effective integration of EI and critical thinking enables individuals to make more informed, rational, and empathetic decisions in both personal and professional contexts.

Chapter 6: Critical Thinking in the Digital Age

In the digital age, the landscape of information and communication has drastically changed, presenting new challenges and opportunities for critical thinking. The vast availability of information, the speed at which it spreads, and the diverse mediums through which it is presented necessitate a more nuanced approach to critical thinking.

Critical Thinking in the Digital Age

Evaluating Information Sources:

In the digital age, the ability to evaluate the credibility of various information sources has become paramount (Wineburg & McGrew, 2019). Critical thinkers must assess the reliability, bias, and purpose of digital content.

In the digital age, the skill of evaluating information sources becomes increasingly critical for effective critical thinking. The internet offers a vast array of information sources, ranging from academic journals and mainstream news outlets to personal blogs and social media posts. Distinguishing reliable information from misinformation or biased content is essential.

Evaluating Information Sources in the Digital Age

1. **Assessing Credibility of Sources**: The credibility of an information source is a fundamental aspect of its evaluation. This includes examining the author's credentials, the publication's reputation, and the source's track record for accuracy (Metzger, 2007).

2. **Understanding Source Bias**: All sources have some form of bias. Critical thinkers must identify these biases and understand how they might influence the information presented (Allcott & Gentzkow, 2017).

3. **Cross-Checking Information**: Verifying information across multiple reputable sources is crucial. This practice helps in identifying inconsistencies and ensuring that the information is not an isolated claim (Wineburg & McGrew, 2019).

4. **Analyzing the Purpose and Context**: Understanding why the information was created and its context is essential. This involves considering whether the source aims to inform, persuade, entertain, or sell something (Hobbs, 2011).

5. **Distinguishing Between Opinion and Fact**: Critical thinkers must distinguish between opinion and fact-based information. While opinions are subjective, facts should be objective and supported by evidence (Kahne & Bowyer, 2017).

6. **Evaluating the Quality of the Evidence**: The quality of evidence supporting a claim is a key factor. This includes assessing the reliability of the data, the methodologies used, and the presence of peer review or fact-checking (Facione, 1990).

7. **Digital Literacy Skills**: Digital literacy involves the ability to effectively find, interpret, evaluate, and create information using digital technology. It's a crucial skill for navigating the digital information landscape (Bawden, 2001).

Evaluating information sources in the digital age is a complex yet crucial component of critical thinking. It involves a combination of assessing credibility, understanding biases, cross-checking information, distinguishing between opinion and fact, evaluating the quality of evidence, and possessing digital literacy skills. By mastering these skills, individuals can navigate the vast digital information landscape more effectively, discerning reliable information from misleading content, and making informed decisions based on accurate data.

Dealing with Information Overload:

The sheer volume of information available online can be overwhelming. Critical thinking involves the ability to filter information effectively, focusing on quality rather than quantity (Bawden & Robinson, 2009).

In the digital age, one of the significant challenges to critical thinking is dealing with information overload. The immense volume of data available online can overwhelm individuals, making it difficult to discern what information is relevant and credible.

Dealing with Information Overload in the Digital Age

1. **Prioritizing Information**: One of the first steps in managing information overload is learning to prioritize information based on relevance and importance. This involves focusing on information that is directly related to one's goals or tasks at hand (Eppler & Mengis, 2004).

2. **Developing Filtering Strategies**: Developing effective strategies to filter out unnecessary or less important information is crucial. This might involve using specific tools or techniques, such as RSS feeds, to manage the flow of information (Bawden & Robinson, 2009).

3. **Critical Evaluation of Sources**: Evaluating the credibility and relevance of information sources can help in reducing the amount of data to be processed. It involves assessing the authority, accuracy, and purpose of the information (Wineburg & McGrew, 2017).

4. **Selective Attention**: Practicing selective attention involves focusing on information that is necessary and avoiding distractions. This includes being mindful of the tendency to engage in aimless web browsing or excessive social media use (Kirschner & De Bruyckere, 2017).

5. **Time Management**: Effective time management is key to dealing with information overload. Allocating specific times for information gathering and processing can prevent the feeling of being overwhelmed (Bell & Tang, 1998).

6. **Utilizing Technology Effectively**: Technology, when used effectively, can help manage information overload. Tools such as data aggregation and content management systems can streamline information processing (Sparrow, Liu, & Wegner, 2011).

7. **Developing Digital Literacy**: Digital literacy includes skills that enable individuals to find, evaluate, organize, and use information effectively. Developing these skills is essential in navigating the vast amount of information online (Gilster, 1997).

Dealing with information overload in the digital age requires a multifaceted approach. It involves prioritizing information, developing filtering strategies, critically evaluating sources, practicing selective attention, managing time effectively, utilizing technology, and developing digital literacy skills. By mastering these strategies, individuals can navigate through the vast amounts of information available online more efficiently, enhancing their ability to think critically and make informed decisions.

Recognizing and Overcoming Digital Biases:

The algorithms that govern what we see online often create echo chambers and reinforce biases. Critical thinking requires awareness of these digital biases and actively seeking diverse perspectives (Pariser, 2011).

In the digital age, the proliferation of online content has led to the emergence of digital biases that can significantly influence critical thinking. Recognizing and overcoming these biases is essential for ensuring that our understanding and decision-making processes are not unduly influenced by skewed or limited information.

Recognizing and Overcoming Digital Biases

1. **Understanding Digital Biases**: Digital biases refer to the predispositions and distortions that arise in the digital environment. These can stem from algorithmic filtering, echo chambers, and personalized content feeds that reinforce pre-existing beliefs (Pariser, 2011).

2. **Algorithmic Bias**: Algorithms, especially those used by search engines and social media platforms, play a significant role in determining what information we see. They can create a filter bubble that limits exposure to diverse viewpoints (Bakshy, Messing, & Adamic, 2015).

3. **Echo Chambers and Confirmation Bias**: Digital platforms often lead to the creation of echo chambers where users are exposed primarily to opinions and information that reinforce their existing beliefs, exacerbating confirmation bias (Sunstein, 2001).

4. **Critical Evaluation of Online Content**: To overcome digital biases, it's crucial to critically evaluate online content. This involves assessing the source's credibility, cross-referencing information, and seeking out diverse viewpoints (Wineburg & McGrew, 2017).

5. **Diversifying Information Sources**: Actively seeking information from a variety of sources, including those that offer differing viewpoints, is key to overcoming digital biases. This broadens perspective and reduces the risk of being trapped in an echo chamber (Brundidge, 2010).

6. **Developing Digital Literacy**: Digital literacy includes the ability to use digital technology, communication tools, and networks to access, manage, integrate, evaluate, and create information. Enhancing these skills is critical to identifying and mitigating digital biases (Gilster, 1997).

7. **Awareness of Personal Biases**: Self-awareness about one's own biases is crucial. Recognizing that personal biases can influence how we search for and process information can help in mitigating their impact (Nickerson, 1998).

In the digital age, recognizing and overcoming digital biases is essential for effective critical thinking. This requires understanding the nature of these biases, critically evaluating online content, diversifying information sources, enhancing digital literacy, and being aware of personal biases. By actively engaging in these practices, individuals can ensure that their critical thinking skills are not compromised by the biases inherent in digital environments, leading to more informed and well-rounded perspectives.

Critical Media Literacy:

This involves understanding how media messages are constructed and for what purposes. It includes the analysis of various media forms, understanding their contexts, and deciphering underlying messages (Hobbs, 2011).

Critical media literacy is an essential component of critical thinking in the digital age. As the media landscape continues to evolve rapidly, the ability to analyze, evaluate, and create media in a variety of forms becomes increasingly important. This skill set enables individuals to decipher the complex messages presented in various media and to understand the influence of media on culture and society.

Critical Media Literacy in the Digital Age

1. **Understanding Media Constructions**: Media messages are constructed with specific languages, techniques, and technologies. Critical media literacy involves understanding these constructions and recognizing the ways in which they can shape perceptions and beliefs (Kellner & Share, 2007).

2. **Analyzing Media Content**: This includes critically analyzing the content for biases, intended messages, and underlying assumptions. It's important to evaluate the purpose of the media message and the context in which it was created (Hobbs, 2011).

3. **Recognizing Media Influence**: Media has the power to influence public opinion and cultural norms. Critical thinkers in the digital age need to be aware of how media can influence their perceptions and behaviors (Potter, 2018).

4. **Distinguishing Between Different Types of Media**: Differentiating between various types of media (news, advertising, entertainment, etc.) and

understanding their unique conventions and purposes is crucial (Aufderheide, 1993).

5. **Evaluating Information Sources**: In the age of digital media, evaluating the credibility and reliability of information sources is vital. This includes distinguishing between credible news sources, propaganda, misinformation, and disinformation (Wineburg & McGrew, 2017).

6. **Developing Digital Literacy**: Digital literacy goes hand-in-hand with critical media literacy. It involves the ability to use digital technology, communication tools, and networks to access and evaluate media (Gilster, 1997).

7. **Creating Media Responsibly**: Critical media literacy also involves understanding the ethical implications of media creation and the responsibilities of media producers to the public (Hobbs & Frost, 2003).

Critical media literacy is a crucial skill in the digital age, enabling individuals to navigate the complex and rapidly changing media environment. It involves understanding how media messages are constructed, analyzing and evaluating media content, recognizing the influence of media, differentiating between types of media, assessing the credibility of sources, developing digital literacy, and understanding the ethics of media creation. By cultivating these skills, individuals can become more informed, reflective, and responsible media consumers and producers, enhancing their overall critical thinking abilities.

Navigating Misinformation and Disinformation:

The digital age has seen a rise in misinformation (false information shared without harmful intent) and disinformation (false information shared with harmful intent). Critical thinking skills are essential for identifying and challenging such content (Lewandowsky, Ecker, & Cook, 2017).

Navigating misinformation and disinformation is a crucial aspect of critical thinking in the digital age. The internet, while a valuable resource for information, is also rife with inaccurate and deliberately misleading information. Developing the skills to discern trustworthy information from false or misleading content is essential.

Navigating Misinformation and Disinformation

1. **Understanding Misinformation and Disinformation**: Misinformation refers to false or inaccurate information that is spread, regardless of an

intention to deceive. Disinformation, on the other hand, is deliberately misleading or biased information, manipulated narrative or facts, or propaganda (Wardle & Derakhshan, 2017).

2. **Developing a Critical Mindset**: A critical mindset involves questioning the validity of information, regardless of its source. This includes being skeptical of information that confirms personal biases and seeking evidence to support or refute it (Paul & Elder, 2006).

3. **Evaluating Source Credibility**: Assessing the credibility of information sources is vital. This involves examining the author's credentials, the source's reputation, and the presence of quality control measures such as fact-checking or peer review (Metzger, 2007).

4. **Cross-Checking Information**: Verifying information through cross-checking with multiple credible sources can help ascertain its accuracy. This practice is especially important in the case of breaking news or controversial topics (Wineburg & McGrew, 2017).

5. **Recognizing Bias and Perspective**: Understanding that all information sources have some form of bias is crucial. Critical thinkers should identify these biases and consider how they might influence the presentation of information (Allcott & Gentzkow, 2017).

6. **Digital Literacy Skills**: Digital literacy encompasses skills that enable individuals to effectively find, evaluate, and create digital content. It is crucial for navigating digital environments and discerning the reliability of various sources of information (Gilster, 1997).

7. **Using Fact-Checking Websites and Tools**: Utilizing fact-checking websites and digital tools can aid in verifying the accuracy of information. These resources are especially useful for checking the veracity of viral content and debunking false claims (Lewandowsky, Ecker, & Cook, 2017).

Navigating misinformation and disinformation in the digital age is a complex but essential skill for critical thinkers. It involves developing a critical mindset, evaluating source credibility, cross-checking information, recognizing bias, enhancing digital literacy, and using fact-checking tools. By mastering these skills, individuals can more effectively sift through the vast amounts of information available online, discerning accurate and reliable content from false or misleading information. This capability is crucial for informed decision-making and responsible participation in digital discourse.

Digital Empathy and Communication:

Online interactions lack many non-verbal cues that inform communication. Critical thinking in the digital age involves considering the context and potential misinterpretations in digital communications (Joinson, 2004).

In the digital age, the concept of digital empathy and effective communication plays a crucial role in critical thinking. As interactions increasingly occur in digital spaces, understanding and appropriately responding to the emotional content in these interactions is essential. This involves not only interpreting messages accurately but also conveying thoughts and feelings in ways that are considerate and clear.

Digital Empathy and Communication in Critical Thinking

1. **Understanding Digital Empathy**: Digital empathy refers to the ability to empathize with others in digital communication environments. It involves understanding and being sensitive to the emotional tone and content of digital communications, even in the absence of non-verbal cues (Wright & Akgun, 2021).

2. **Challenges in Digital Communication**: Digital communication often lacks the non-verbal cues (like facial expressions, tone of voice) that aid in understanding a speaker's intent and emotions. Critical thinkers must therefore be more attentive to the nuances of written communication and consider the potential for misinterpretation (Derks, Fischer, & Bos, 2008).

3. **Enhancing Communication Clarity**: In digital communication, conveying messages clearly and effectively is vital. This involves being concise, using unambiguous language, and where appropriate, using emoticons or explicit expressions of emotion to aid in conveying tone (Walther, 2012).

4. **Developing Listening Skills in Digital Spaces**: Active listening in digital spaces involves carefully reading or listening to digital content, asking clarifying questions, and reflecting back the content to ensure understanding. This is crucial in online discussions and collaborations (Tannen & Trester, 2013).

5. **Avoiding Digital Dehumanization**: There's a risk of dehumanization in digital interactions due to physical and emotional distance. Critical

thinkers practice digital empathy by remembering the human element behind digital screens, promoting respectful and thoughtful interactions (Suler, 2004).

6. **Responding Appropriately to Digital Content**: Responding to digital content requires not only understanding the content but also the emotional state and intent of the communicator. This involves thoughtful and empathetic engagement, considering the impact of responses on others (Turkle, 2015).

Digital empathy and effective communication are integral to critical thinking in the digital age. They involve understanding the unique challenges of digital communication, enhancing clarity, practicing active listening, avoiding dehumanization, and responding empathetically. By cultivating these skills, individuals can navigate digital interactions more effectively, fostering understanding and meaningful connections in an increasingly digital world.

Ethical Considerations in Digital Contexts*:*

Ethical thinking is a significant part of critical thinking. This includes understanding digital footprints, respecting privacy, and considering the ethical implications of digital actions (Koehler & Mishra, 2009).

Ethical considerations in digital contexts are a crucial aspect of critical thinking in the digital age. As digital technologies become increasingly integrated into daily life, ethical dilemmas arise related to privacy, data security, digital citizenship, and the responsible use of technology. Navigating these ethical challenges requires a nuanced understanding of both the digital landscape and the moral implications of actions within it.

Ethical Considerations in Digital Contexts

1. **Digital Privacy and Security**: Concerns about digital privacy and security are paramount. Critical thinkers must understand the implications of data sharing and the importance of protecting personal and sensitive information online (Acquisti, Brandimarte, & Loewenstein, 2015).

2. **Intellectual Property and Plagiarism**: The ease of accessing and sharing information online brings forward concerns about intellectual property rights and plagiarism. Ethical critical thinking involves recognizing and respecting these rights in digital environments (Moore & Vitale, 2016).

3. **Digital Footprint and Reputation**: Every digital interaction leaves a footprint. Critical thinkers must be aware of how their online actions can impact their reputation and the perceptions of others, and the long-term implications of their digital behaviors (Boyd, 2014).

4. **Ethics in Online Communication**: The anonymity and distance provided by digital communication can sometimes lead to unethical behavior, such as cyberbullying or hateful speech. Ethical critical thinking involves engaging respectfully and constructively in digital spaces (Patchin & Hinduja, 2012).

5. **Information Ethics**: In the digital age, the ethical use and distribution of information are key. This includes understanding the potential biases in algorithms and artificial intelligence and the ethical implications of these biases (Mittelstadt, Allo, Taddeo, Wachter, & Floridi, 2016).

6. **Social Responsibility and Digital Citizenship**: Digital citizenship encompasses understanding how to interact positively, responsibly, and safely in digital environments. Critical thinkers must consider the social responsibility they hold as digital citizens (Ribble & Bailey, 2007).

Ethical considerations in digital contexts are integral to critical thinking in the digital age. They involve understanding and navigating the complexities of digital privacy, intellectual property, digital footprints, online communication ethics, information ethics, and digital citizenship. By incorporating these ethical considerations into their decision-making processes, individuals can engage more responsibly and thoughtfully in digital environments, contributing positively to the digital ecosystem.

In conclusion, critical thinking in the digital age requires adapting traditional skills to a new context. This includes evaluating digital information sources, managing information overload, understanding digital biases, developing critical media literacy, navigating misinformation, practicing digital empathy, and considering ethical implications of digital actions. By honing these skills, individuals can navigate the complex and fast-paced digital landscape more effectively, making informed decisions and engaging in responsible digital citizenship.

Information Overload:

In the digital age, one of the significant challenges to critical thinking is managing information overload. With the exponential growth of digital content, individuals are constantly bombarded with vast amounts of information, making it difficult to process, analyze, and use this information effectively.

Understanding and managing information overload is, therefore, a critical skill in today's digital environment.

Information Overload in the Digital Age

1. **Definition and Implications of Information Overload**: Information overload occurs when the amount of input to a system exceeds its processing capacity. Decision-makers have fairly limited cognitive processing capacity. Consequently, when information overload occurs, it is likely that a reduction in decision quality will occur (Eppler & Mengis, 2004).

2. **Causes of Information Overload**: The digital age has exacerbated information overload due to the ease of access to vast quantities of data, constant connectivity, and the rapid dissemination of information through social media and other digital platforms (Bawden & Robinson, 2009).

3. **Impact on Critical Thinking**: Information overload can impair critical thinking by overwhelming cognitive resources, leading to difficulties in concentrating, making decisions, and thinking critically. It can result in hasty decisions, oversimplification of complex issues, and poor judgment (Klapp, 1986).

4. **Strategies to Manage Information Overload**:

-   **Prioritization of Information**: Learning to prioritize information based on relevance and importance is crucial (Edmunds & Morris, 2000).

-   **Selective Consumption**: Developing the skill to selectively consume information that is necessary and relevant can help manage the overload (Hargittai, Fullerton, Menchen-Trevino, & Thomas, 2010).

-   **Time Management**: Allocating specific times for information consumption and processing can mitigate the effects of overload (Bell & Tang, 1998).

-   **Use of Technology**: Utilizing technology tools, such as RSS feeds, data filters, and aggregation services, can assist in managing the flow of information (Sparrow, Liu, & Wegner, 2011).

5. **Developing Digital Literacy**: Digital literacy involves the ability to effectively find, evaluate, organize, and use information. Enhancing

these skills is critical to navigating the digital information landscape (Gilster, 1997).

Managing information overload is critical for maintaining effective critical thinking in the digital age. It involves understanding the causes and implications of overload, employing strategies like prioritization, selective consumption, time management, and the use of technology tools. Developing digital literacy skills is also crucial in navigating and processing the vast amounts of information available. By adopting these strategies, individuals can mitigate the challenges posed by information overload, thereby enhancing their ability to think critically and make informed decisions.

Evaluating Sources and Fake News:
Evaluating sources and discerning fake news are crucial skills for critical thinking in the digital age. The vast array of information available online makes it challenging to distinguish credible sources from misleading or false ones. Developing the ability to critically evaluate the reliability and accuracy of information is essential for informed decision-making and responsible digital citizenship.

Evaluating Sources and Fake News

1. **Understanding the Nature of Fake News**: Fake news refers to false or misleading information presented as news. It often aims to mislead, deceive, or manipulate the reader (Lazer et al., 2018). Understanding the intent and characteristics of fake news is crucial in combating its influence.

2. **Assessing Source Credibility**: Evaluating the credibility of a source is a key aspect of critical thinking. This involves considering the author's credentials, the publication's history of accuracy, and any potential biases or conflicts of interest (Metzger, 2007).

3. **Cross-Checking Information**: Verifying information through multiple reputable sources is an effective strategy for combating fake news. Cross-checking helps confirm the accuracy of information and reveals discrepancies in reporting (Wineburg & McGrew, 2017).

4. **Recognizing Bias**: Every source has some form of bias. Critical thinkers must identify these biases and understand how they might influence the information presented. This involves distinguishing between fact-based reporting and opinion or propaganda (Allcott & Gentzkow, 2017).

5. **Analyzing Content Quality**: The quality of the content, including writing style, language use, and the presence of supporting evidence, can indicate the reliability of a source. Reliable sources typically provide evidence for claims and avoid sensationalist language (Wardle & Derakhshan, 2017).

6. **Digital Literacy Skills**: Digital literacy encompasses skills that enable individuals to find, evaluate, and create digital content. Enhancing these skills is critical to identifying and mitigating the effects of fake news (Gilster, 1997).

7. **Using Fact-Checking Services**: Fact-checking websites and tools can be valuable resources for verifying the accuracy of news stories and claims. Utilizing these services can help in identifying false information (Lewandowsky, Ecker, & Cook, 2017).

Critical thinking in the digital age demands proficiency in evaluating sources and identifying fake news. This involves understanding the nature of fake news, assessing source credibility, cross-checking information, recognizing bias, analyzing content quality, developing digital literacy skills, and utilizing fact-checking services. By mastering these skills, individuals can navigate the complex digital information landscape more effectively, discerning credible information from misinformation and contributing to informed and responsible discourse.

Digital Literacy and Critical Thinking:

In the context of the digital age, digital literacy is intricately linked to critical thinking. Digital literacy goes beyond just the ability to use technological tools; it encompasses a range of competencies that include finding, evaluating, producing, and communicating information in digital formats. Critical thinking, in this framework, is the ability to analyze and evaluate information critically, especially in digital environments, to make reasoned decisions.

Digital Literacy and Critical Thinking

1. **Understanding Digital Literacy**: Digital literacy involves a set of skills necessary for effective and critical navigation, evaluation, and creation of content in the digital world (Gilster, 1997). It includes the ability to understand and use information in multiple formats from a wide range of sources.

2. **Evaluating Digital Information**: Critical thinking in the digital age requires the ability to evaluate the credibility, relevance, and accuracy of digital information. This includes distinguishing between reliable sources

and misinformation, and understanding the biases and agendas that might shape digital content (Wineburg & McGrew, 2017).

3. **Critical Consumption of Digital Content**: Digital literacy entails not just accessing information, but also critically analyzing and interpreting it. This means being skeptical of surface-level information, understanding the context in which the information is presented, and recognizing potential manipulations in digital content (Hobbs, 2011).

4. **Ethical Use of Digital Information**: Part of being digitally literate is understanding the ethical implications of using and sharing digital information. This includes respecting copyright laws, privacy rights, and considering the moral impacts of digital footprints (Ribble & Bailey, 2007).

5. **Navigating Digital Tools and Platforms**: Digital literacy also involves understanding how to navigate and utilize various digital tools and platforms effectively. This skill is essential for critical thinking as it allows individuals to access and synthesize information from diverse sources (Martin, 2008).

6. **Creating Digital Content**: Beyond consumption, digital literacy involves creating digital content responsibly. Critical thinking is applied in considering the accuracy, impact, and clarity of the content being produced (Jenkins, Clinton, Purushotma, Robison, & Weigel, 2006).

In summary, digital literacy and critical thinking are interdependent in the digital age. Digital literacy provides the tools and skills necessary to navigate the digital world, while critical thinking offers the framework to analyze, evaluate, and create digital content thoughtfully and ethically. Together, these skills enable individuals to engage effectively with the vast array of information and tools available in the digital landscape, making informed decisions and contributing responsibly to the digital community.

Chapter 7: Strategies for Effective Critical Thinking

Becoming a critical thinker involves developing a set of skills and strategies that allow for effective analysis, evaluation, and synthesis of information. Critical thinking is not just an innate ability but a skill that can be cultivated and improved over time. Here are some key strategies for effective critical thinking:

Strategies for Effective Critical Thinking

Asking Questions:

Critical thinkers consistently ask probing and analytical questions. This helps in exploring deeper meanings and challenging assumptions (Paul & Elder, 2006). Questions like "What is the evidence for this claim?" or "What are the alternative viewpoints?" are central to critical thinking.

Asking questions is a foundational strategy in developing effective critical thinking skills. This approach is not just about seeking answers, but about exploring possibilities, challenging assumptions, and deepening understanding. It's a dynamic process that encourages curiosity and fosters a more profound and nuanced exploration of ideas and issues.

Strategies for Effective Critical Thinking: Asking Questions

1. **The Role of Inquiry in Critical Thinking**: Inquiry is at the heart of critical thinking. By asking questions, critical thinkers engage in an active process of exploration and examination. This process helps in uncovering hidden assumptions, identifying biases, and understanding different perspectives (Paul & Elder, 2006).

2. **Types of Questions to Enhance Critical Thinking**:

- **Clarifying Questions**: Seek to understand the basics. E.g., "What do you mean by that?" or "Can you explain this further?"

- **Probing Assumptions**: These questions challenge the assumptions underlying statements or beliefs. E.g., "What assumption is this based on?" (Brookfield, 2012).

- **Probing Reasons and Evidence**: Aimed at understanding the foundation of arguments. E.g., "What evidence supports this view?" (Ennis, 1996).

- **Questioning Viewpoints and Perspectives**: These questions explore different angles and viewpoints. E.g., "What might be an alternative?" (King, 1995).

- **Implications and Consequences**: Look at the potential outcomes. E.g., "What are the implications if this is true?" (Facione, 1990).

3. **Developing a Habit of Questioning**: Cultivating a questioning mind is essential for critical thinking. This involves continuously asking questions in different contexts and not settling for easy answers (Dewey, 1933).

4. **Socratic Questioning**: This is a disciplined questioning method that can be used to pursue thought in many directions. It involves systematically questioning and breaking down a complex problem into fundamental elements (Paul & Elder, 2006).

5. **Open-Ended Questions**: Asking open-ended questions encourages deeper thought and discussion, as opposed to closed questions that often result in yes/no answers or factual responses (Dillon, 1988).

Asking questions is a vital strategy in cultivating critical thinking. It involves engaging in inquiry, probing assumptions, reasons, evidence, viewpoints, and implications. Developing a habit of questioning, utilizing Socratic questioning, and asking open-ended questions are essential practices in this regard. By embracing a questioning approach, individuals can enhance their critical thinking abilities, leading to more informed, reasoned, and comprehensive understanding and decision-making.

Analyzing and Evaluating Evidence:

Critical thinking involves analyzing and evaluating evidence critically. This means not taking information at face value and examining the quality, relevance, and validity of the evidence presented (Facione, 1990).

Analyzing and evaluating evidence is a fundamental strategy in effective critical thinking. This approach involves carefully examining information, data, and arguments to assess their validity, reliability, and relevance. In the process of critical thinking, evidence forms the backbone of reasoned arguments and rational decision-making.

Strategies for Effective Critical Thinking: Analyzing and Evaluating Evidence

1. **Understanding the Role of Evidence in Arguments**: Critical thinking requires recognizing that good reasoning is often supported by solid evidence. This involves identifying the types of evidence used in arguments and assessing their appropriateness and strength (Facione, 1990).

2. **Differentiating Types of Evidence**: Understanding the difference between empirical evidence, anecdotal evidence, and expert testimony is crucial. Each type of evidence has its own strengths and limitations and must be evaluated accordingly (Gilovich, Griffin, & Kahneman, 2002).

3. **Checking for Relevance and Adequacy of Evidence**: Not all evidence is relevant to the argument at hand. Critical thinkers must assess whether the evidence presented directly supports the claims made and whether it is sufficient to substantiate the argument (Bowell & Kemp, 2005).

4. **Evaluating the Source of Information**: The credibility of the evidence often depends on the reliability of its source. Evaluating the source includes considering the author's expertise, potential biases, and the methodological rigor with which the evidence was gathered (Metzger, 2007).

5. **Recognizing Biases and Fallacies**: Biases and fallacies can distort the interpretation and use of evidence. Critical thinkers must be aware of common logical fallacies and cognitive biases that can undermine the validity of arguments (Tversky & Kahneman, 1974).

6. **Applying Logical Reasoning**: Logical reasoning is used to determine whether the evidence logically supports the conclusion. This involves assessing the structure of the argument and the logical connection between evidence and conclusions (Copi, Cohen, & McMahon, 2016).

7. **Synthesizing Evidence from Multiple Sources**: Effective critical thinking often involves synthesizing evidence from various sources to form a comprehensive understanding of the topic. This requires comparing and contrasting different pieces of evidence and identifying patterns or inconsistencies (Bailin, Case, Coombs, & Daniels, 1999).

Analyzing and evaluating evidence is a critical component of effective critical thinking. It involves understanding the role of evidence in arguments, differentiating between types of evidence, assessing their relevance and adequacy, evaluating the credibility of sources, recognizing biases and fallacies, applying logical reasoning, and synthesizing evidence from multiple sources. By mastering these skills, individuals can enhance their ability to engage in reasoned analysis and make well-informed decisions.

Recognizing Biases and Prejudices:

It's important to recognize one's own biases and prejudices and understand how they can influence thinking. Being aware of cognitive biases, such as confirmation bias or availability heuristic, is crucial in objective thinking (Nickerson, 1998).

Recognizing biases and prejudices is an essential strategy for effective critical thinking. Biases, often unconscious, can skew our reasoning and decision-making processes, leading to flawed conclusions or unfair judgments. Critical thinkers need to identify and address these biases, both in themselves and in the arguments presented by others.

Strategies for Effective Critical Thinking: Recognizing Biases and Prejudices

1. **Understanding the Nature of Biases and Prejudices**: Biases are inclinations or prejudices for or against one person or group, especially in a way considered to be unfair. Prejudices are preconceived opinions that are not based on reason or actual experience. Acknowledging that everyone has biases and prejudices is the first step in addressing them (Nickerson, 1998).

2. **Self-Awareness**: Self-awareness is key in recognizing one's own biases and prejudices. This involves reflecting on one's beliefs and values, and understanding how they might influence perceptions and decisions (Banaji & Greenwald, 2013).

3. **Challenging Assumptions**: Critical thinkers challenge their own assumptions and those of others. This involves questioning the basis of beliefs and considering alternative viewpoints (Brookfield, 2012).

4. **Seeking Diverse Perspectives**: Actively seeking out and considering diverse perspectives is a powerful way to counteract personal biases and prejudices. Exposure to different viewpoints can challenge and broaden one's understanding (Sue, 2010).

5. **Critical Reflection**: Engaging in critical reflection helps in examining the influence of one's social background, experiences, and societal norms on

their thinking process. This reflective practice is essential for recognizing biases and prejudices (Mezirow, 1997).

6. **Educating Oneself**: Continuous education and learning about different cultures, societies, and perspectives can reduce biases and prejudices. Education fosters empathy and understanding of differences (Gorski, 2009).

7. **Cognitive De-biasing Strategies**: Employing cognitive strategies to de-bias one's thinking is crucial. This includes considering information that contradicts one's beliefs, thinking from others' perspectives, and seeking factual evidence (Lilienfeld, Ammirati, & Landfield, 2009).

Recognizing biases and prejudices is a critical aspect of effective critical thinking. It involves self-awareness, challenging assumptions, seeking diverse perspectives, critical reflection, continuous education, and employing de-biasing strategies. By actively working to identify and address biases and prejudices, critical thinkers can enhance their ability to reason more objectively and make more equitable decisions.

Developing Foresight:

Effective critical thinkers think ahead and consider the consequences of different actions or ideas. This strategic thinking involves evaluating the potential long-term outcomes of decisions (Sternberg, 1986).

Developing foresight is a key strategy in effective critical thinking. Foresight is the ability to anticipate potential outcomes and implications of actions or decisions. It involves looking beyond immediate situations and considering the long-term effects and possibilities. This forward-thinking approach is essential for making well-informed decisions and for planning and preparing for future challenges and opportunities.

Strategies for Effective Critical Thinking: Developing Foresight

1. **Understanding the Concept of Foresight**: Foresight is about predicting future trends and scenarios based on current knowledge and data. It involves thinking ahead to foresee possible consequences, opportunities, and challenges (Slaughter, 1995).

2. **Scenario Planning**: This strategy involves envisioning different future scenarios based on current trends and changes. Scenario planning helps in preparing for various possible futures, not just the most likely one (Schwartz, 1996).

3. **Long-Term Impact Analysis**: When making decisions, critically think about the long-term impacts rather than just short-term gains or results. This includes considering how actions will affect different areas over time (Godet, 2000).

4. **Systems Thinking**: Foresight requires understanding how different elements within a system interact with each other. Systems thinking helps in identifying potential unintended consequences of actions in complex systems (Senge, 1990).

5. **Critical Reflection on Past Decisions**: Analyzing past decisions and their outcomes can provide valuable insights for future decision-making. Reflecting on what worked or didn't work in the past helps in developing a better understanding of potential future outcomes (Argyris & Schön, 1978).

6. **Continuous Learning and Adaptability**: Staying informed about emerging trends, new technologies, and global changes is crucial for foresight. Continuously updating knowledge and being adaptable to change are key components of developing foresight (Bell, 2003).

7. **Consulting Diverse Perspectives**: Engaging with diverse viewpoints and disciplines can broaden one's understanding of possible future trends and scenarios. Diverse perspectives provide a more comprehensive view of potential future developments (Wilkinson, 2009).

Developing foresight is an integral part of effective critical thinking. It involves scenario planning, long-term impact analysis, systems thinking, critical reflection on past decisions, continuous learning, adaptability, and consulting diverse perspectives. By cultivating these skills, individuals can enhance their ability to anticipate future trends and scenarios, make more informed decisions, and prepare effectively for the future.

Engaging in Reflective Thinking:

Reflective thinking involves examining and reflecting on one's own thought processes and understanding. This meta-cognition is crucial for self-improvement in critical thinking (Dewey, 1933).

Engaging in reflective thinking is a vital strategy for effective critical thinking. Reflective thinking involves examining and considering your own thoughts, actions, and experiences in order to gain new insights or understandings. This process is crucial for personal growth and development in critical thinking skills.

Strategies for Effective Critical Thinking: Engaging in Reflective Thinking

1. **Definition and Importance of Reflective Thinking**: Reflective thinking is the process of internally examining and exploring an issue of concern, triggered by an experience, which creates and clarifies meaning in terms of self, and leads to a changed conceptual perspective (Boud, Keogh, & Walker, 1985). It is essential for critical thinking as it allows individuals to step back and think about how they approach problems and decisions.

2. **Models of Reflective Thinking**: Several models can guide reflective thinking. Schön's (1983) reflection-in-action and reflection-on-action, Dewey's (1933) model of reflective thought, and Gibbs' (1988) reflective cycle are some prominent frameworks. These models provide a structured approach to reflective thinking.

3. **Practicing Self-Awareness**: Self-awareness is the foundation of reflective thinking. It involves being conscious of one's thoughts, feelings, motivations, biases, and their impact on decisions and actions (Mezirow, 1997).

4. **Journaling as a Reflective Practice**: Keeping a reflective journal is a practical way to engage in reflective thinking. Writing about experiences and their personal and professional impacts can lead to deeper insights (Moon, 1999).

5. **Critical Incident Analysis**: This involves reflecting on significant events or 'critical incidents' to explore why they happened and what can be learned from them. It is a common practice in fields like education and healthcare (Flanagan, 1954).

6. **Feedback and Reflection**: Seeking and reflecting on feedback from others is another way to engage in reflective thinking. Feedback provides alternative perspectives on one's actions and thoughts (London, 2002).

7. **Mindfulness and Reflective Thinking**: Mindfulness practices, such as meditation, can enhance reflective thinking by promoting a focused and reflective state of mind (Kabat-Zinn, 1994).

Engaging in reflective thinking is a crucial aspect of developing effective critical thinking skills. It involves using various models and practices such as journaling, critical incident analysis, seeking feedback, and mindfulness to reflect on experiences and decisions. Through reflective thinking, individuals can gain deeper insights into their cognitive processes, biases, and decision-making strategies, leading to personal and professional growth.

Practicing Empathy and Open-Mindedness:

Understanding others' viewpoints is essential in critical thinking. Empathy and open-mindedness help in considering diverse perspectives and reduce the risk of narrow thinking (Halpern, 2003).

Practicing empathy and open-mindedness is a fundamental strategy for effective critical thinking. Empathy allows individuals to understand and share the feelings of others, fostering a more comprehensive perspective on issues. Open-mindedness involves being receptive to a wide range of ideas, arguments, and information, even those that contradict one's preconceived notions. These qualities are crucial for unbiased and holistic thinking.

Strategies for Effective Critical Thinking: Practicing Empathy and Open-Mindedness

1. **The Role of Empathy in Critical Thinking**: Empathy involves understanding others' perspectives and emotions. It is crucial for critical thinking as it allows one to consider different viewpoints and understand the reasoning behind others' thoughts and actions (Hoffman, 2000). This understanding can lead to more nuanced and balanced judgments.

2. **Developing Empathic Understanding**: Practicing active listening and putting oneself in others' shoes are ways to develop empathy. This means not only hearing but also understanding others' viewpoints, concerns, and emotions (Rogers, 1957).

3. **The Importance of Open-Mindedness**: Open-mindedness is the willingness to consider different ideas and opinions and to change one's own viewpoint based on new evidence or arguments. It is essential for critical thinking as it prevents one from becoming dogmatic and overly biased (King & Kitchener, 1994).

4. **Strategies to Cultivate Open-Mindedness:**

- **Challenging Personal Beliefs**: Actively challenging one's beliefs and assumptions helps in becoming more open-minded. This involves critically analyzing one's own viewpoints and considering their limitations (Baron, 1993).

- **Exposure to Diverse Perspectives**: Seeking out and engaging with diverse perspectives and ideas can broaden one's understanding and foster open-mindedness (Gurin, Dey, Hurtado, & Gurin, 2002).

5. **Avoiding Empathy Fatigue**: While empathy is crucial, it's also important to be aware of empathy fatigue, especially when dealing with emotionally charged issues. Balancing emotional involvement with a degree of emotional regulation is important for sustained empathetic engagement (Figley, 1995).

6. **Integrating Empathy in Argumentation**: Empathy in critical thinking also involves acknowledging others' emotions and perspectives in discussions and argumentation. This approach leads to more respectful and constructive dialogues (Galinsky & Moskowitz, 2000).

Practicing empathy and open-mindedness is vital for effective critical thinking. Empathy allows for a deeper understanding of diverse perspectives, while open-mindedness ensures receptiveness to new information and viewpoints. By cultivating these skills, individuals can enhance their ability to think critically, engage in constructive dialogue, and make well-informed, balanced decisions.

Logical Reasoning:

Applying logical reasoning to arguments and ideas is a fundamental aspect of critical thinking. This includes understanding logical connections between ideas, identifying fallacies, and constructing coherent arguments (Copi, Cohen, & McMahon, 2016).

Logical reasoning is a cornerstone of effective critical thinking. It involves the ability to analyze arguments in a disciplined, systematic way, and to construct arguments that are coherent and well-supported. The essence of logical reasoning is the ability to deduce valid conclusions from given premises, to identify logical fallacies, and to structure thoughts in a clear, linear manner.

Strategies for Effective Critical Thinking: Logical Reasoning

1. **Understanding Logical Reasoning**: Logical reasoning involves the application of systematic steps and principles to evaluate arguments and evidence. It's about reasoning consistently and coherently, based on established logical processes (Copi, Cohen, & McMahon, 2016).

2. **Deductive and Inductive Reasoning**:

*   **Deductive Reasoning**: This involves drawing specific conclusions from general principles or premises. If the premises are true and the reasoning is valid, the conclusion must be true (Baron, 2000).

*   **Inductive Reasoning**: This involves making generalizations based on specific observations or cases. The conclusion is probable, based on the evidence provided (Holland, Holyoak, Nisbett, & Thagard, 1986).

3. **Identifying Logical Fallacies**: A key aspect of logical reasoning is the ability to identify logical fallacies – errors in reasoning that weaken arguments. These include ad hominem attacks, false dichotomies, straw man arguments, and more (Tarski, 2002).

4. **Building Logical Arguments**: Constructing a logical argument involves presenting premises that logically lead to a conclusion. This includes ensuring that arguments are valid (the conclusion logically follows from the premises) and sound (the premises are true) (Salmon, 1984).

5. **Evaluating Evidence and Arguments**: Critical thinkers must evaluate both the evidence presented and the structure of arguments. This involves assessing the quality, relevance, and reliability of the evidence, and how logically it supports the conclusion (Facione, 1990).

6. **Developing Critical Thinking through Logic Training**: Engaging in exercises that enhance logical reasoning, such as solving logical puzzles or studying formal logic, can improve one's ability to think critically (Manktelow, 1999).

Logical reasoning is a fundamental strategy for effective critical thinking. It involves understanding the principles of logical reasoning, identifying and avoiding logical fallacies, constructing logical arguments, and evaluating evidence and arguments critically. By enhancing logical reasoning skills, individuals can improve their ability to analyze information critically, make sound decisions, and articulate well-reasoned arguments.

Continuous Learning and Curiosity:

A disposition towards continuous learning and staying curious is essential for critical thinkers. It involves a willingness to update beliefs and understandings in light of new evidence (Dweck, 2006).

Continuous learning and curiosity are pivotal strategies for effective critical thinking. The pursuit of lifelong learning and a curious mindset not only expands knowledge and skills but also fosters a deeper understanding of the world, encouraging open-mindedness and the questioning of established norms and beliefs.

Strategies for Effective Critical Thinking: Continuous Learning and Curiosity

1. **Importance of Continuous Learning**: Continuous learning refers to the ongoing pursuit of knowledge for personal and professional development. It is fundamental to critical thinking as it ensures that individuals do not become stagnant in their knowledge or thinking patterns. It helps in staying informed about new developments, theories, and perspectives (Merriam & Bierema, 2014).

2. **Cultivating Curiosity**: Curiosity drives the desire to explore, understand, and engage with the world. It leads to questioning, exploring new ideas, and being open to new experiences. Curiosity is crucial for critical thinking as it motivates individuals to seek out new knowledge and challenge existing assumptions (Kashdan, 2009).

3. **Engaging in Diverse Learning Opportunities**: Exposure to diverse sources of information and different learning environments can enhance critical thinking. This includes reading widely, attending workshops or lectures, participating in discussions, and engaging with various media forms (Hofstein & Lunetta, 2004).

4. **Reflective Practice**: Reflective practice involves critically analyzing one's own learning and experiences. This self-reflection enhances understanding and supports the integration of new knowledge with existing beliefs and knowledge (Schön, 1983).

5. **Application of Knowledge**: Applying new knowledge to real-world situations is a critical component of continuous learning. This practical application reinforces learning and encourages critical analysis of how theoretical concepts work in practice (Kolb, 1984).

6. **Embracing Intellectual Humility**: Intellectual humility involves acknowledging that one's knowledge is limited and being open to new information and perspectives. This trait is essential for continuous learning and effective critical thinking (Leary et al., 2017).

7. **Networking and Collaborative Learning**: Engaging with peers, mentors, and experts in various fields can facilitate continuous learning. Collaborative learning environments encourage the sharing of ideas and exposure to different viewpoints (Lave & Wenger, 1991).

Continuous learning and curiosity are essential for effective critical thinking. They involve a commitment to lifelong learning, cultivating curiosity, engaging in diverse educational experiences, reflective practice, applying knowledge practically, embracing intellectual humility, and participating in collaborative learning. These strategies ensure that critical thinking is dynamic and evolving, keeping pace with new information and changing contexts.

In conclusion, effective critical thinking involves a combination of skills and strategies, including asking insightful questions, analyzing and evaluating evidence, recognizing biases, practicing empathy, applying logical reasoning, and engaging in continuous learning. By cultivating these skills and adopting a mindset geared towards open-minded exploration and reflective thinking, individuals can enhance their capacity to think critically and make well-informed decisions.

Questioning Techniques:

Questioning techniques are a fundamental strategy in the development of effective critical thinking skills. The art of asking questions is not just about seeking answers but is a tool for deeper understanding, challenging assumptions, and stimulating thoughtful discussion. Effective questioning techniques can lead to improved problem-solving, decision-making, and learning.

Strategies for Effective Critical Thinking: Questioning Techniques

The Role of Questioning in Critical Thinking:

Asking questions is a key component of critical thinking as it stimulates curiosity, encourages deeper inquiry, and challenges existing beliefs and assumptions (Paul & Elder, 2006). Effective questioning can uncover new information, reveal gaps in knowledge, and lead to more comprehensive understanding.

The role of questioning in critical thinking is pivotal. Questioning is not just a matter of seeking answers but a crucial tool for exploration, understanding, and challenging established norms and beliefs. Effective questioning techniques stimulate deeper thought, encourage open dialogue, and foster a culture of inquiry and skepticism, which are essential elements of critical thinking.

The Role of Questioning in Critical Thinking

1. **Stimulating Intellectual Curiosity**: Questioning ignites intellectual curiosity and leads to a deeper investigation of ideas and issues. It encourages individuals to go beyond surface-level information and explore the underlying principles or assumptions (Paul & Elder, 2006).

2. **Challenging Assumptions**: Effective questioning challenges both the questioner's and others' assumptions. It enables individuals to uncover biases and preconceived notions that might color their understanding and judgments (Brookfield, 2012).

3. **Facilitating Learning and Understanding**: Questions drive learning and comprehension. By asking questions, individuals engage more actively with the material, leading to better understanding and retention of information (Chi, De Leeuw, Chiu, & LaVancher, 1994).

4. **Promoting Critical Analysis**: Questions are tools for analysis and evaluation. They help dissect arguments, assess the validity of claims, and evaluate the reliability of evidence (Bloom, 1956).

5. **Encouraging Open Communication**: Questioning encourages a more interactive and dialogic form of communication. It fosters an environment where ideas can be openly shared and critically examined (Dillon, 1988).

6. **Developing Problem-Solving Skills**: In problem-solving, questions help identify the problem's root, explore possible solutions, and consider their potential consequences (King, 1995).

The role of questioning in critical thinking is fundamental. It serves as a catalyst for intellectual curiosity, a tool for challenging assumptions, a means for enhancing learning and understanding, a method for promoting critical analysis, a facilitator for open communication, and a strategy for improving problem-solving skills. By mastering effective questioning techniques, individuals can significantly enhance their critical thinking capabilities, leading to more informed decision-making and a deeper understanding of complex issues.

Types of Questions for Critical Thinking:

➢ **Open-Ended Questions:**

These questions encourage expansive thinking and cannot be answered with a simple 'yes' or 'no'. They often begin with 'why', 'how', or 'what do you think about...' (Dillon, 1988).

Open-ended questions are a powerful tool in the arsenal of questioning techniques for effective critical thinking. Unlike closed questions, which typically elicit a limited response, open-ended questions encourage a more expansive, thoughtful, and detailed exploration of topics. These questions are fundamental in fostering deeper understanding, critical analysis, and creative thinking.

Types of Questions for Critical Thinking: Open-Ended Questions

1. **Characteristics of Open-Ended Questions**: Open-ended questions are designed to encourage a full, meaningful answer using the subject's own knowledge and/or feelings. They are broad and can lead to multiple pathways of thought, allowing for a wide range of responses (Dillon, 1988).

2. **Promoting Exploration and Discovery**: Open-ended questions are effective in promoting exploration and discovery. They allow individuals to think more deeply about a subject, explore different perspectives, and articulate their thoughts in a comprehensive manner (Bloom, 1956).

3. **Encouraging Elaboration and Explanation**: These questions require more than a simple yes or no answer. They encourage elaboration, justification, and explanation, thereby facilitating a deeper understanding of the subject matter (King, 1995).

4. **Examples of Open-Ended Questions in Critical Thinking**:

- "What are the potential impacts of...?"

- "How would you describe...?"

- "What evidence supports...?"

- "Can you explain why...?"

5. **Use in Diverse Contexts**: Open-ended questions are valuable in various contexts, including education, counseling, management, and research. They are instrumental in interviews, discussions, and whenever critical and creative thinking is required (Harvard Business Review, 2018).

6. **Developing Critical Thinking Skills**: Regularly posing and responding to open-ended questions helps develop essential critical thinking skills such as analysis, synthesis, and evaluation. It encourages learners to integrate and apply different types of knowledge (Paul & Elder, 2006).

7. **Challenges and Considerations**: While open-ended questions are valuable, they also require careful construction to ensure they are clear and truly open. It's important to avoid leading questions that might guide the respondent toward a particular answer (Wilen, 1991).

Open-ended questions are crucial in fostering effective critical thinking. They encourage exploration, elaboration, and comprehensive understanding. Regularly employing open-ended questions in various contexts can significantly enhance critical thinking skills, encouraging individuals to think deeply, analyze information, and articulate well-reasoned responses. While powerful, crafting effective open-ended questions requires skill to ensure they are clear, unbiased, and truly open to diverse perspectives and answers.

➢ **Clarifying Questions**:

These questions seek to understand and clear up confusion about the topic under discussion. They often ask for elaboration, examples, or definitions.

Clarifying questions play a vital role in the strategies for effective critical thinking, particularly within the scope of questioning techniques. These questions are designed to uncover more information, clarify ambiguities, and ensure understanding. They are instrumental in dissecting complex ideas, concepts, and arguments, making them clearer and more comprehensible.

Types of Questions for Critical Thinking: Clarifying Questions

1. **Purpose of Clarifying Questions**: The primary goal of clarifying questions is to eliminate confusion and reach a better understanding of the subject matter. They help in breaking down complex information into simpler, more digestible parts (Paul & Elder, 2006).

2. **Characteristics of Clarifying Questions**: Such questions are typically open-ended and non-threatening. They aim to elucidate, elaborate, and explain, rather than to challenge or critique (Brookfield, 2012).

3. **Examples of Clarifying Questions**:

- "Could you explain that point further?"

- "What do you mean by...?"

- "Can you provide an example of...?"

- "How does this relate to...?"

4. **Importance in Critical Thinking**: Clarifying questions are crucial in critical thinking as they prevent misunderstandings and misinterpretations. They ensure that discussions are based on a clear and accurate understanding of all aspects of the topic (Dillon, 1988).

5. **Use in Various Contexts**: These questions are valuable in educational settings, professional environments, and everyday interactions. They help in deepening understanding and fostering effective communication (King, 1995).

6. **Enhancing Listening Skills**: Clarifying questions also enhance active listening skills. They require the questioner to listen carefully to the speaker's words and then respond with a question that seeks deeper understanding (Rogers, 1957).

7. **Building on Existing Knowledge**: By clarifying concepts and ideas, individuals can build upon their existing knowledge base, connecting new information with what they already know (Vygotsky, 1978).

8. **Promoting Deeper Discussion**: These questions encourage further exploration and discussion. They open up new avenues of thought and inquiry, leading to a more profound engagement with the material (Bloom, 1956).

Clarifying questions are a fundamental component of effective critical thinking and questioning techniques. They serve to deepen understanding, eliminate confusion, and foster clearer communication. Employing clarifying questions enhances critical thinking by ensuring that discussions and analyses are grounded in a mutual and clear understanding of the subject matter. These questions are invaluable tools in education, professional settings, and daily interactions, aiding in the exploration and comprehension of complex ideas and concepts.

➢ **Probing Questions**:

Probing questions go deeper into the subject matter, challenging superficial responses and assumptions. They often ask for evidence, reasons, or explore the implications of what has been said (Browne & Keeley, 2007).

Probing questions are an essential aspect of questioning techniques within the framework of effective critical thinking. These types of questions delve deeper into the subject matter, challenging superficial answers and encouraging a more thorough and nuanced exploration of ideas and issues.

Types of Questions for Critical Thinking: Probing Questions

1. **Purpose of Probing Questions**: Probing questions are used to dig deeper into a topic, argument, or statement. They go beyond surface-level understanding and encourage a more comprehensive and critical examination of the issue at hand (Paul & Elder, 2006).

2. **Characteristics of Probing Questions**: These questions are designed to explore deeper meanings, motivations, and the evidence behind statements or beliefs. They often require detailed and thoughtful responses and cannot typically be answered with a simple 'yes' or 'no' (Browne & Keeley, 2007).

3. **Examples of Probing Questions**:

- "Can you provide further evidence for your claim?"

- "What are the reasons behind your statement?"

- "How does this relate to what we have learned before?"

- "Can you explain why you think this is the case?"

4. **Importance in Critical Thinking**: Probing questions are critical for developing higher-order thinking skills. They encourage individuals to analyze, synthesize, and evaluate information rather than just recalling facts (Bloom, 1956).

5. **Use in Various Contexts**: Probing questions are useful in educational settings, professional discussions, and everyday conversations. They are particularly valuable in discussions where critical analysis and problem-solving are required (King, 1995).

6. **Encouraging Reflective Thinking**: Probing questions often lead to reflective thinking, where individuals consider their own thought processes and the bases of their knowledge and beliefs (Schön, 1983).

7. **Challenging Assumptions**: These types of questions challenge the assumptions underlying statements or decisions. By probing these assumptions, individuals can uncover new insights and perspectives (Brookfield, 2012).

8. **Facilitating Deeper Discussion**: Probing questions can transform superficial discussions into more meaningful and substantial dialogues.

They encourage participants to think more deeply and critically about the topic (Dillon, 1988).

Probing questions are a vital component of effective critical thinking and questioning techniques. They play a crucial role in deepening understanding, challenging assumptions, encouraging reflective thinking, and facilitating more substantial and meaningful discussions. By mastering the art of asking probing questions, individuals can enhance their critical thinking skills, leading to more insightful and well-reasoned analyses and decisions.

Socratic Questioning:

This is a disciplined questioning approach that can be used to pursue thought in many directions and for many purposes. It is a systematic, disciplined approach to ask questions aimed at exploring complex ideas, uncovering assumptions, and revealing underlying truths (Paul & Elder, 2006).

Socratic questioning is a disciplined and systematic approach to questioning that is a central strategy in effective critical thinking. Named after the classical Greek philosopher Socrates, this method of questioning is designed to stimulate critical thinking and illuminate ideas. The essence of Socratic questioning is not to find a definitive answer but to foster a deeper understanding of issues through persistent inquiry and dialogue.

Socratic Questioning in Critical Thinking

1. **Definition and Principles of Socratic Questioning**: Socratic questioning is a form of disciplined questioning that can be used to pursue thought in many directions for many purposes. It is characterized by an open and inquisitive mind, a methodical and logical approach, and a focus on fundamental concepts and principles (Paul & Elder, 2006).

2. **Purpose and Goals**: The primary goal of Socratic questioning is to explore complex ideas, uncover assumptions, analyze concepts, and understand the implications of statements or beliefs. It aims to expose contradictions and stimulate deeper thought (Overholser, 1993).

3. **Techniques and Types of Socratic Questions**:

- **Clarifying Concepts**: Asking for definitions and examples to understand the concept better.

- **Probing Assumptions**: Challenging the assumptions that underlie beliefs and arguments.

126

- **Exploring Reasons and Evidence**: Seeking the rationale and evidence supporting a statement or viewpoint.

- **Questioning Perspectives and Viewpoints**: Encouraging consideration of alternative perspectives.

- **Examining Implications and Consequences**: Investigating the potential outcomes of an idea or action.

- **Questioning the Question**: Reflecting on the nature and intent of the questions being asked (Browne & Keeley, 2007).

4. **Importance in Critical Thinking**: Socratic questioning is essential for critical thinking because it encourages deep, analytical, and independent thinking. It moves beyond superficial understanding to a more profound exploration of issues (McComas & Abraham, 2004).

5. **Application Across Disciplines**: Socratic questioning is versatile and can be applied across various disciplines, including education, psychology, philosophy, and business. It is a powerful tool for teaching, counseling, and collaborative problem-solving (Wilberding, 2015).

6. **Challenges and Considerations**: While Socratic questioning is a powerful tool, it requires skill and practice to master. The questioner needs to be patient, open-minded, and ready to explore a range of possibilities. It's important to create a safe and respectful environment for Socratic dialogue (Jackson, 1992).

Socratic questioning is a vital component of effective critical thinking and questioning techniques. It fosters an environment of deep exploration, analytical thinking, and open dialogue. Mastering Socratic questioning can significantly enhance one's ability to think critically, leading to more profound insights, informed decisions, and intellectual growth.

Reflective Questioning:

Reflective questions encourage individuals to reflect on their own thinking and reasoning processes. They often involve asking oneself about the thought process used to reach conclusions (Dewey, 1933).

Reflective questioning is a pivotal strategy in effective critical thinking, emphasizing self-examination and introspection. This technique involves asking questions that prompt individuals to reflect on their beliefs, reasoning processes, and the basis of their knowledge. Reflective questioning is not just about seeking external answers but is focused on fostering a deeper understanding of one's thought processes and perspectives.

Reflective Questioning in Critical Thinking

1. **Definition and Purpose of Reflective Questioning**: Reflective questioning is a process that encourages individuals to think about their own thinking. This metacognitive approach helps individuals understand how they form ideas, opinions, and conclusions, and to critically examine their own reasoning processes (Dewey, 1933).

2. **Characteristics of Reflective Questions**: These questions often focus on the 'why' and 'how' of thinking. They prompt deeper analysis and encourage individuals to consider the origins and implications of their beliefs and assumptions (Schön, 1983).

3. **Examples of Reflective Questions**:

*   "Why do I believe this to be true?"

*   "What are the reasons behind my viewpoint?"

*   "How did I reach this conclusion?"

*   "What assumptions am I making?"

4. **Importance in Critical Thinking**: Reflective questioning is crucial in developing critical thinking as it promotes self-awareness and the evaluation of one's thought processes. This self-reflection leads to more deliberate and thoughtful reasoning and decision-making (Mezirow, 1997).

5. **Application in Learning and Development**: Reflective questioning is widely used in education, professional development, and counseling. It helps learners and professionals critically assess their experiences, integrate new knowledge, and apply it effectively in future situations (Boud, Keogh, & Walker, 1985).

6. **Enhancing Problem-Solving Skills**: By reflecting on their cognitive processes, individuals can improve their problem-solving skills. Reflective questioning helps identify biases, gaps in understanding, and areas for improvement (King, 1995).

7. **Challenges in Implementing Reflective Questioning**: One of the challenges in reflective questioning is the discomfort it may cause, as it

often challenges deeply held beliefs. Cultivating an environment of trust and openness is crucial for effective reflective questioning (Brookfield, 1998).

Reflective questioning is a vital strategy for effective critical thinking, focusing on internal dialogue and introspection. It aids in understanding and improving one's cognitive processes, leading to more informed and rational decision-making. By engaging in reflective questioning, individuals can enhance their ability to think critically, solve problems more effectively, and engage in continuous personal and professional development.

Critical Evaluation Questions:

These questions focus on evaluating information and arguments. They often involve asking about the source, context, relevance, and validity of the information presented (Ennis, 1996).

Critical evaluation questions are a significant component of questioning techniques in the context of effective critical thinking. These types of questions are designed to assess the credibility, relevance, and validity of information, arguments, and evidence. They play a crucial role in enabling individuals to scrutinize information critically and make informed judgments.

Critical Evaluation Questions in Critical Thinking

1. **Understanding Critical Evaluation Questions**: Critical evaluation questions are inquiries that focus on assessing the quality and reliability of information and arguments. They are essential for discerning the strength, relevance, and credibility of the evidence presented (Facione, 1990).

2. **Types of Critical Evaluation Questions**:

* **Assessing Source Credibility**: Questions like "What is the source of this information?" and "Does the source have any potential bias?"

* **Evaluating Evidence**: Inquiries such as "What evidence supports this claim?" and "Is the evidence current, relevant, and reliable?"

* **Identifying Assumptions**: Questions like "What assumptions underlie the argument?" and "Are these assumptions valid?"

* **Checking for Logical Consistency**: Questions such as "Are there any contradictions or inconsistencies in the argument?"

- **Determining Relevance**: Asking "How is this information relevant to the issue at hand?" or "Does this information address the core problem?"

3. **Purpose of Critical Evaluation Questions**: The primary purpose of these questions is to engage in a deeper level of thinking and analysis. They help in breaking down complex information, distinguishing facts from opinions, and recognizing flawed reasoning or biases (Browne & Keeley, 2007).

4. **Application in Various Contexts**: Critical evaluation questions are applicable in a wide range of contexts, including academic research, professional decision-making, and everyday information processing. They are fundamental in areas where critical analysis and evidence-based reasoning are required (Paul & Elder, 2006).

5. **Developing Skills for Asking Critical Evaluation Questions**: This involves cultivating a habit of skepticism and inquiry, being mindful of cognitive biases, and continuously practicing the art of questioning in various scenarios (Halpern, 2003).

6. **Challenges and Considerations**: One challenge is ensuring that the questioning does not become adversarial or confrontational. The aim should be to seek clarity and understanding rather than to disprove or undermine others (Brookfield, 2012).

Critical evaluation questions are integral to the practice of effective critical thinking. They enable individuals to rigorously assess the quality and reliability of information and arguments, leading to more informed and rational conclusions. Developing the skill to ask and answer critical evaluation questions enhances one's ability to engage in deep analysis, recognize biases, and make decisions based on sound evidence and reasoning.

Developing a Questioning Mindset:

Cultivating a mindset that continually asks questions is essential for critical thinking. This involves being inquisitive and skeptical, not taking things at face value, and being willing to question widely accepted beliefs (King, 1995).

Developing a questioning mindset is a vital strategy in the pursuit of effective critical thinking. This approach involves cultivating an attitude that is continually inquisitive, skeptical, and open to exploring new questions and challenges. A questioning mindset encourages ongoing inquiry and deepens understanding, playing a crucial role in enhancing critical thinking abilities.

Developing a Questioning Mindset in Critical Thinking

1. **Concept of a Questioning Mindset**: A questioning mindset refers to a mental attitude that prioritizes inquiry and skepticism over passive acceptance of information (Paul & Elder, 2006). It involves a propensity to ask thoughtful, probing questions about beliefs, arguments, and evidence.

2. **Characteristics of a Questioning Mindset**:

- **Curiosity and Inquisitiveness**: A natural curiosity and desire to understand the world more deeply.

- **Skepticism and Critical Inquiry**: A tendency to question the validity, reliability, and source of information.

- **Openness to New Ideas**: Willingness to consider and explore diverse perspectives and viewpoints.

- **Self-Reflection**: Regularly reflecting on one's own beliefs, values, and thought processes.

3. **Strategies to Develop a Questioning Mindset**:

- **Active Engagement with Information**: Engaging actively with texts, discussions, and experiences, and asking questions that foster deeper understanding (Brookfield, 2012).

- **Encouraging Intellectual Curiosity**: Seeking out new experiences, ideas, and knowledge areas to broaden one's understanding (King, 1995).

- **Practicing Socratic Questioning**: Using disciplined questioning methods to explore complex ideas and uncover assumptions (Overholser, 1993).

- **Challenging Assumptions**: Regularly questioning and reassessing one's assumptions and the assumptions of others.

4. **Benefits of a Questioning Mindset**:

- **Enhanced Problem-Solving Skills**: Better ability to analyze problems and think through solutions.

- **Deeper Learning**: Greater engagement with material leads to a more profound and lasting understanding.

- **Improved Decision Making**: More informed and well-considered decisions based on thorough questioning and analysis.

5. **Challenges in Cultivating a Questioning Mindset:**

- **Overcoming Intellectual Comfort Zones**: Moving beyond familiar ways of thinking and challenging long-held beliefs.

- **Balancing Skepticism with Openness**: Maintaining a balance between being critically skeptical and open to new ideas.

Developing a questioning mindset is a fundamental aspect of effective critical thinking. It involves fostering curiosity, practicing skepticism, embracing new ideas, and engaging in self-reflection. By cultivating a mindset that consistently questions and analyzes, individuals can enhance their problem-solving skills, deepen their learning, and make more informed decisions. This approach requires moving beyond comfort zones and balancing skepticism with openness, but it is invaluable in achieving a more comprehensive and critical understanding of the world.

In conclusion, effective questioning techniques are integral to critical thinking. They involve employing a variety of questioning types, including open-ended, clarifying, probing, reflective, and critical evaluation questions. The use of Socratic questioning and the development of a questioning mindset are also key to deepening understanding and fostering critical analysis. Through the strategic use of questions, individuals can enhance their ability to think critically, engage in thoughtful dialogue, and make well-informed decisions.

Creative and Lateral Thinking

Creative and lateral thinking are integral strategies for effective critical thinking. While critical thinking often involves logical and structured approaches to problem-solving, incorporating creative and lateral thinking can lead to more innovative solutions and a broader perspective on issues. These approaches involve thinking outside the conventional frameworks and challenging established norms.

Creative and Lateral Thinking in Critical Thinking

1. **Understanding Creative and Lateral Thinking:**

- **Creative Thinking**: This refers to the ability to think in novel ways and to come up with unique solutions to problems. It involves divergent thinking, which is the capacity to generate multiple, varied ideas on a topic (Guilford, 1956).

- **Lateral Thinking**: Coined by Edward de Bono, lateral thinking involves solving problems through an indirect and creative approach. It emphasizes looking at things from different angles, rather than following traditional step-by-step logic (de Bono, 1970).

2. **Importance in Critical Thinking**:

- Creative and lateral thinking enhance critical thinking by providing alternative ways to approach problems and encouraging the exploration of unconventional solutions.

- These approaches can lead to more innovative and effective outcomes, especially in complex situations where traditional methods may not be sufficient (Cropley, 2006).

3. **Techniques for Fostering Creative and Lateral Thinking**:

- **Brainstorming**: Generating a large number of ideas without immediate judgment or analysis.

- **Mind Mapping**: Visualizing problems and their potential solutions in a non-linear format.

- **Analogical Thinking**: Drawing parallels between unrelated domains to gain insights.

- **Challenging Assumptions**: Deliberately questioning and overturning conventional beliefs.

- **Provocation Techniques**: Intentionally introducing absurd or provocative ideas to disrupt conventional thinking patterns (de Bono, 1992).

4. **Application in Problem Solving**:

- Creative and lateral thinking are particularly useful in problem-solving where traditional approaches are ineffective.

- These methods can be applied in a range of fields, from business and education to scientific research and technology development (Friedel, 2005).

5. **Challenges and Considerations**:

- While valuable, creative and lateral thinking strategies may initially be met with resistance due to their deviation from traditional methods.

- It requires an environment where risk-taking and non-conventional approaches are encouraged and where there is a tolerance for ambiguity and failure (Runco, 2004).

Creative and lateral thinking are essential components of effective critical thinking. They complement traditional analytical methods by introducing novel and diverse perspectives, challenging the status quo, and fostering innovative problem-solving. These approaches require a supportive environment that encourages experimentation, open-mindedness, and the exploration of unconventional ideas. By integrating creative and lateral thinking strategies, individuals and organizations can enhance their ability to tackle complex problems and generate groundbreaking solutions.

Problem-solving Strategies:

Problem-solving strategies are a crucial aspect of effective critical thinking. These strategies provide a systematic approach to identifying, analyzing, and resolving problems. By employing these strategies, critical thinkers can address complex issues in a structured and efficient manner, leading to more effective solutions.

Problem-solving Strategies in Critical Thinking

1. **Identifying and Defining the Problem**: The first step in problem-solving involves accurately identifying and defining the problem. This step requires a clear understanding of the issue at hand, distinguishing between symptoms and root causes (Jonassen, 2000).

2. **Gathering and Analyzing Information**: Critical thinkers gather relevant information and analyze it to understand the problem better. This involves seeking diverse sources of information, evaluating the credibility of data, and using analytical skills to interpret and synthesize information (Facione, 1990).

3. **Generating Possible Solutions**: Once the problem is understood, the next step is to generate a range of possible solutions. This phase benefits from creative thinking techniques such as brainstorming, mind mapping, or lateral thinking, encouraging the exploration of innovative and unconventional solutions (de Bono, 1970).

134

4. **Evaluating Alternatives**: After generating potential solutions, each option is evaluated based on its feasibility, potential impact, and alignment with goals or objectives. This step requires critical judgment and often involves weighing pros and cons, considering short-term and long-term consequences, and assessing risks (Halpern, 2003).

5. **Making Decisions**: Based on the evaluation, a decision is made regarding the best course of action. Decision-making in critical thinking is informed, deliberate, and often involves selecting from among various alternatives (Baron, 2000).

6. **Implementing the Solution**: The chosen solution is then implemented. Effective implementation requires planning, organization, and sometimes, the coordination of resources and people (Lussier & Achua, 2015).

7. **Monitoring and Reviewing**: After implementation, the solution is monitored for effectiveness. This includes reviewing outcomes, analyzing whether the problem has been resolved, and making adjustments if necessary (Paul & Elder, 2006).

8. **Reflective Thinking and Learning from Experience**: Problem-solving is an ongoing process that includes reflective thinking and learning from experiences. Reflective practice helps in understanding what worked or didn't work and why, which is crucial for continuous improvement in problem-solving skills (Schön, 1983).

In conclusion, problem-solving strategies are an essential component of effective critical thinking. These strategies involve a sequence of steps including identifying the problem, gathering and analyzing information, generating and evaluating solutions, making decisions, implementing solutions, and reviewing outcomes. Incorporating reflective practice and learning from experiences enhances the problem-solving process. By applying these strategies, critical thinkers can tackle complex problems more effectively, leading to well-reasoned and practical solutions.

Chapter 8: Critical Thinking in Everyday Life

Critical thinking in everyday life involves applying the principles of critical analysis, reasoning, and problem-solving to daily decisions and interactions. This skill is not just limited to academic or professional settings but is equally important in personal life, enabling individuals to make informed, rational, and reflective decisions.

Critical Thinking in Everyday Life

Making Informed Decisions:

Critical thinking helps in evaluating options more effectively and making informed decisions in everyday situations, from financial choices to health-related decisions (Halpern, 2003).

Making informed decisions is a key aspect of applying critical thinking in everyday life. This process involves systematically evaluating information, weighing options, and considering potential outcomes before reaching a conclusion. Informed decision-making is essential for navigating the complexities of daily life, from personal choices to professional judgments.

Critical Thinking in Everyday Life: Making Informed Decisions

1. **Understanding Informed Decision-Making**: Informed decision-making involves making choices based on a thorough understanding of the relevant information, potential risks, and benefits. It entails a careful analysis of options and their consequences (Facione, 1990).

2. **Gathering and Analyzing Information**: The first step in making informed decisions is to gather relevant information. This involves seeking out reliable sources, critically evaluating the credibility and relevance of the information, and understanding the context (Halpern, 2003).

3. **Identifying Biases and Assumptions**: Critical thinkers recognize their own biases and assumptions and how these might influence their decisions. They strive to approach decision-making with an open mind and consider alternative viewpoints (Paul & Elder, 2006).

4. **Evaluating Options and Outcomes**: Critical thinking in decision-making involves comparing the potential outcomes of different options. This includes considering short-term and long-term effects, as well as possible unintended consequences (King & Kitchener, 1994).

5. **Applying Logical Reasoning**: Logical reasoning is used to systematically process the gathered information and to evaluate the pros and cons of each option. This helps in arriving at a conclusion that is logically sound and supported by evidence (Baron, 2000).

6. **Reflecting on Past Decisions**: Reflective thinking is a component of critical thinking that involves analyzing past decisions, learning from experiences, and applying these lessons to future decisions (Schön, 1983).

7. **Involving Others in Decision Making**: Sometimes, particularly in complex decisions, it is beneficial to involve others. Discussions with trusted individuals can provide different perspectives and insights, further informing the decision-making process (Brookfield, 2012).

Making informed decisions is a fundamental application of critical thinking in everyday life. It involves a structured approach to gathering and analyzing information, evaluating options, applying logical reasoning, and learning from past experiences. By practicing informed decision-making, individuals can enhance the quality of their choices, leading to more successful and satisfying outcomes in various aspects of life.

Problem-Solving in Daily Life:

It involves using logical and structured approaches to solve everyday problems, whether they're simple issues like planning a day's schedule or more complex family or work-related challenges (Facione, 1990).

Problem-solving in daily life is a practical application of critical thinking, involving the ability to address everyday challenges with effective solutions. This skill is essential for navigating various aspects of personal and professional life, from simple tasks to complex issues. Critical thinking enhances problem-solving by providing a structured approach to identifying, analyzing, and resolving problems.

Critical Thinking in Everyday Life: Problem-Solving in Daily Life

1. **Understanding Problem-Solving with Critical Thinking**: Problem-solving involves identifying a problem, generating potential solutions, evaluating these solutions, and implementing the most effective one. Critical thinking contributes to this process by enabling logical analysis, systematic organization of information, and evaluation of evidence (Jonassen, 2000).

2. **Identifying and Defining the Problem**: The first step in problem-solving is to accurately identify and define the problem. Critical thinking skills are used to distinguish between symptoms and root causes and to articulate the problem clearly (Paul & Elder, 2006).

3. **Gathering and Analyzing Relevant Information**: Critical thinkers gather relevant data and information about the problem. They apply analytical skills to understand the problem's context and implications (Facione, 1990).

4. **Generating Creative and Logical Solutions**: Critical thinking aids in generating a range of solutions by combining creativity with logical evaluation. Brainstorming and lateral thinking techniques can be employed to come up with innovative solutions (de Bono, 1970).

5. **Evaluating and Prioritizing Solutions**: After generating possible solutions, critical thinking is used to evaluate the feasibility, effectiveness, and potential impact of each option. This involves considering both short-term and long-term consequences (Halpern, 2003).

6. **Implementing and Monitoring the Solution**: Implementing the chosen solution requires planning and organization, skills enhanced by critical thinking. Monitoring the solution's effectiveness and making adjustments as necessary is also part of the critical thinking process (Schön, 1983).

7. **Learning from Experience**: Critical thinking in problem-solving involves reflecting on the solution's outcomes and the problem-solving process. This reflection helps in learning from experience and improving future problem-solving abilities (King & Kitchener, 1994).

Problem-solving in daily life is significantly enhanced by critical thinking. It involves a systematic process of identifying and defining problems, gathering and analyzing information, generating solutions, evaluating and implementing these solutions, and learning from outcomes. By applying critical thinking skills, individuals can tackle daily challenges more effectively, leading to more successful and practical solutions in various aspects of life.

Evaluating Media and Information:

In the age of information overload, critical thinking is essential for evaluating the credibility and reliability of information encountered daily, including news sources, social media, and advertisements (Paul & Elder, 2006).

Evaluating media and information critically is a fundamental aspect of applying critical thinking in everyday life. In an era characterized by information overload and the prevalence of digital media, the ability to discern reliable information from misinformation is crucial. This skill involves analyzing the credibility, bias, and validity of the information we encounter daily.

Critical Thinking in Everyday Life: Evaluating Media and Information

1. **Understanding the Need for Critical Evaluation of Media and Information**: In the digital age, individuals are bombarded with a vast array of information from various sources, including social media, news outlets, blogs, and advertisements. The ability to critically evaluate this information is essential for making informed decisions and forming accurate perceptions (Wineburg & McGrew, 2017).

2. **Assessing Source Credibility**: One of the key components of evaluating media and information is assessing the credibility of the source. This involves looking at the author's qualifications, the reputation of the publication, and the presence of any potential biases or conflicts of interest (Metzger, 2007).

3. **Analyzing Content Objectively**: Critical thinkers analyze the content objectively, focusing on the evidence presented and the logic of the arguments. They look for signs of bias, propaganda, or misleading information and distinguish between opinion and factual information (Paul & Elder, 2006).

4. **Understanding Confirmation Bias**: Critical evaluation also involves being aware of one's own confirmation biases – the tendency to favor information that confirms existing beliefs. Recognizing this bias is important in approaching media and information with an open mind (Nickerson, 1998).

5. **Cross-Checking Information**: Verifying information from multiple reliable sources is a crucial strategy. Cross-checking helps to confirm the accuracy of the information and provides a broader perspective on the issue (Kahne & Bowyer, 2017).

6. **Evaluating Information in Context**: Contextual evaluation of information is important. This includes understanding the historical, social, and political context in which the information was produced and considering its relevance (Hodgin & Kahne, 2018).

7. **Educating Oneself About Media Literacy**: Continuous learning and educating oneself about media literacy is important for effectively evaluating media and information. This includes understanding how media messages are created and learning to read media critically (Hobbs, 2011).

Evaluating media and information critically is an essential skill in everyday life, especially in the digital age. It involves assessing source credibility, analyzing content objectively, understanding personal biases, cross-checking information, and considering context. By developing these skills, individuals can navigate the complex media landscape more effectively, discerning credible information from misinformation and contributing to a more informed and discerning society.

Interpersonal Relationships:

Critical thinking contributes to healthier interpersonal relationships by enabling individuals to understand perspectives, negotiate conflicts, and communicate more effectively (King & Kitchener, 1994).

Critical thinking plays a vital role in interpersonal relationships in everyday life. It involves the ability to think clearly and rationally about what to do or what to believe in social interactions. This skill is crucial in understanding and responding to the thoughts, emotions, and behaviors of others, as well as in communicating one's own ideas and feelings effectively.

Critical Thinking in Everyday Life: Interpersonal Relationships

1. **Empathetic Listening and Understanding**: Empathy, a key component of critical thinking, involves trying to see situations from another person's perspective. This skill is vital in interpersonal relationships for understanding where others are coming from, which is essential for effective communication and conflict resolution (Hoffman, 2000).

2. **Evaluating Emotional Responses**: Critical thinking in relationships includes the evaluation of emotional responses. This means not just reacting impulsively to what others say or do but rather analyzing the reasons behind these emotions and responding thoughtfully (Goleman, 1995).

3. **Effective Communication**: Critical thinking enhances communication skills by encouraging clarity and precision in expressing thoughts. It involves organizing thoughts logically, presenting arguments coherently, and considering the best way to convey messages to others (Riggio, 2010).

4. **Conflict Resolution**: Critical thinking is essential in resolving conflicts. It involves identifying the underlying issues in a conflict, evaluating different viewpoints, and finding a rational, fair solution that respects all parties involved (Wilmot & Hocker, 2011).

5. **Decision Making in Relationships**: In relationships, critical thinking aids in making joint decisions. It involves weighing the pros and cons, considering both short-term and long-term consequences of decisions, and ensuring that decisions are mutually beneficial (Johnson & Johnson, 2005).

6. **Understanding and Respecting Differences**: Critical thinking allows individuals to recognize and respect differences in opinions, beliefs, and values. It involves being open-minded and tolerant of different viewpoints, which is crucial for healthy and diverse relationships (Halpern, 2003).

7. **Building Trust and Rapport**: Critical thinking contributes to building trust and rapport in relationships. It involves being honest, transparent, and consistent in interactions, and showing respect for others' thoughts and feelings (Solomon & Flores, 2001).

Critical thinking is essential in fostering healthy and effective interpersonal relationships. It enhances empathetic understanding, emotional intelligence, communication skills, conflict resolution, decision-making, and respect for differences. Applying critical thinking in everyday interactions leads to more meaningful, respectful, and fulfilling relationships, both personally and professionally.

Self-Reflection and Personal Growth:

Regular self-reflection, a key aspect of critical thinking, promotes personal growth and self-improvement. It involves questioning one's own beliefs, values, and biases, leading to more mindful and intentional living (Mezirow, 1997).

Self-reflection and personal growth are integral aspects of critical thinking in everyday life. They involve introspection and the continual reassessment of one's beliefs, values, and behaviors. Engaging in self-reflection helps individuals understand their motivations, biases, and the impact of their actions, leading to personal growth and improved decision-making.

Critical Thinking in Everyday Life: Self-Reflection and Personal Growth

1. **Understanding Self-Reflection in Critical Thinking**: Self-reflection in critical thinking refers to the process of consciously analyzing and evaluating one's thoughts, beliefs, and actions. It involves questioning why we think and behave the way we do and considering how our mental models shape our understanding of the world (Mezirow, 1997).

2. **Importance of Self-Reflection for Personal Growth**:

- **Enhanced Self-Awareness**: Self-reflection leads to greater self-awareness, helping individuals understand their strengths, weaknesses, and underlying motivations (Schön, 1983).

- **Identification and Challenge of Biases**: Through self-reflection, individuals can identify personal biases and cognitive errors, working towards overcoming them (Halpern, 2003).

- **Improved Decision-Making**: Reflecting on past decisions, their outcomes, and the reasoning behind them enhances future decision-making capabilities (Facione, 1990).

3. **Strategies for Effective Self-Reflection**:

- **Keeping a Reflection Journal**: Writing about experiences and reactions can provide insights into one's thought processes and behaviors (Moon, 1999).

- **Engaging in Mindfulness Practices**: Mindfulness meditation and other practices can enhance self-reflection by focusing on present experiences and thoughts without judgment (Kabat-Zinn, 1994).

- **Seeking Feedback**: Constructive feedback from others can offer new perspectives and aid in self-reflection (London, 2002).

4. **Challenges in Self-Reflection**:

- Overcoming Defensive Reactions: Acknowledging personal flaws or mistakes can be difficult, and individuals may react defensively to self-critique (Argyris, 1991).

- Maintaining Consistency: Regular self-reflection requires discipline and commitment, and it can be challenging to maintain over time.

5. **Role of Critical Thinking in Personal Growth**:

- Critical thinking through self-reflection leads to personal growth by fostering a deeper understanding of oneself and promoting continual learning and development (King & Kitchener, 1994).

Self-reflection and personal growth are critical components of critical thinking in everyday life. They enable individuals to gain deeper self-awareness, challenge personal biases, and improve decision-making skills. By engaging in regular self-reflection and being open to feedback and new perspectives, individuals can foster continuous personal and intellectual growth, leading to more thoughtful and informed actions and decisions.

Consumer Decisions:

It aids in making smarter consumer decisions by analyzing products and services critically, considering factors like cost, quality, and necessity (Brookfield, 2012).

Applying critical thinking to consumer decisions is an essential aspect of everyday life. In a world filled with endless choices and pervasive marketing, the ability to make well-informed, rational, and ethical purchasing decisions is crucial. Critical thinking in this context involves analyzing products and services, considering the credibility of advertising, assessing personal needs and values, and understanding the broader impact of consumer choices.

Critical Thinking in Everyday Life: Consumer Decisions

1. **Analyzing Product Information and Claims**: Critical thinking enables consumers to analyze product information and advertising claims critically. This includes evaluating the reliability and accuracy of the information, distinguishing between factual data and marketing hype, and understanding the potential biases behind promotional materials (Harris & Mowen, 2004).

2. **Assessing Needs versus Wants**: Critical thinking involves distinguishing between what is needed and what is wanted. This distinction helps in making purchasing decisions that are not solely based on impulse or external influences but are aligned with genuine needs and priorities (Kasser & Kanner, 2004).

3. **Evaluating Cost versus Benefit**: Consumers use critical thinking to assess the cost versus the benefit of a product or service. This evaluation goes

beyond price, considering factors such as quality, durability, utility, and long-term value (Schiffman & Wisenblit, 2015).

4. **Considering Ethical and Environmental Impacts**: Critical thinking in consumer decisions also involves considering the ethical and environmental impacts of purchases. This includes thinking about the sustainability of products, the ethics of labor practices involved in production, and the ecological footprint of consumption (Peattie & Charter, 2003).

5. **Avoiding Impulse Purchases and Consumer Biases**: Critical thinking helps consumers avoid impulse purchases and recognize common consumer biases, such as the bandwagon effect or the influence of brand reputation on purchasing decisions (Kahneman & Tversky, 1979).

6. **Comparing and Contrasting Alternatives**: Critical thinkers compare and contrast different products or services, examining their features, prices, reviews, and overall value propositions (Solomon, 2014).

7. **Seeking Out and Evaluating Reviews and Recommendations**: Critical consumers seek out and critically evaluate reviews and recommendations from various sources, understanding that some reviews may be biased or unrepresentative (Chevalier & Mayzlin, 2006).

Applying critical thinking to consumer decisions is a vital skill in modern consumer culture. It enables individuals to make informed, rational, and ethical choices, considering a broad range of factors such as cost, benefit, needs, wants, ethical implications, and environmental impact. By employing critical thinking, consumers can navigate the complex marketplace more effectively, making decisions that align with their values and contribute to their well-being.

Civic Engagement and Social Awareness:

Critical thinking is vital for informed civic engagement and social awareness. It encourages individuals to engage with social and political issues thoughtfully and to understand the complexities of societal challenges (Parker & Ritson, 2005).

Critical thinking is a vital skill for civic engagement and social awareness in everyday life. It involves the ability to engage thoughtfully and responsibly in community and societal matters. Critical thinking in this context means analyzing social issues, understanding the complexities of civic life, and making informed decisions about social and political issues.

144

Critical Thinking in Everyday Life: Civic Engagement and Social Awareness

1. **Understanding Issues in Depth**: Critical thinking allows individuals to understand social, political, and civic issues in depth. It involves analyzing different aspects of an issue, understanding its historical and cultural contexts, and recognizing the underlying complexities (Parker & Hess, 2001).

2. **Evaluating Sources and Information**: In an era of information overload, critical thinking is key to evaluating the credibility and bias of information sources, especially in the context of social and political issues. This skill is crucial for discerning fact from opinion and for understanding the agendas behind information sources (Wineburg & McGrew, 2017).

3. **Recognizing and Challenging Assumptions**: Critical thinkers are adept at recognizing and challenging societal and personal assumptions. They question traditional beliefs and consider alternative viewpoints, leading to a more nuanced understanding of social issues (Giroux, 1989).

4. **Engaging in Informed Discussions and Debates**: Critical thinking enables individuals to participate effectively in discussions and debates on social and civic issues. It involves articulating viewpoints clearly, presenting arguments logically, and engaging with opposing viewpoints constructively (Hess, 2009).

5. **Making Informed Decisions in Civic Life**: Critical thinking contributes to informed decision-making in civic life, including voting, advocacy, and community participation. It involves weighing the implications of policies and decisions and understanding their impact on different groups in society (Delli Carpini & Keeter, 1996).

6. **Promoting Social Justice and Equity**: Critical thinkers are often driven by concerns for social justice and equity. They examine issues such as inequality, discrimination, and injustice, and consider how they can contribute to positive social change (Freire, 1970).

7. **Developing Empathy and Cultural Sensitivity**: Critical thinking in civic engagement involves understanding and empathizing with diverse perspectives, especially those from different cultural or socioeconomic backgrounds (Gay, 2010).

Critical thinking is essential for effective civic engagement and social awareness. It enables individuals to understand complex societal issues, engage in informed discussions, make reasoned decisions in civic life, and advocate for social justice and equity. By applying critical thinking skills, individuals can contribute to a more informed, empathetic, and equitable society.

In conclusion, critical thinking in everyday life is a multifaceted skill that enhances decision-making, problem-solving, information evaluation, interpersonal relationships, self-reflection, consumer choices, and civic engagement. By integrating critical thinking into daily life, individuals can approach situations more rationally, communicate more effectively, and make decisions that are more informed and reflective. The application of critical thinking skills in everyday contexts contributes significantly to personal development, effective citizenship, and overall life satisfaction.

Personal Decision Making:

Personal decision-making is an everyday application of critical thinking, encompassing the process of making choices about one's life and circumstances. Critical thinking enhances personal decision-making by providing a structured and reflective approach to evaluating options and their potential outcomes. This process leads to more informed, rational, and effective decisions in various aspects of life, from career choices to personal relationships.

Critical Thinking in Everyday Life: Personal Decision Making

Incorporating Logical Analysis:

Critical thinking in personal decision-making involves the use of logical analysis to assess situations and options. This includes identifying the key elements of a decision, organizing relevant information, and systematically evaluating the options (Facione, 1990).

Incorporating logical analysis is a key element in personal decision making, especially within the framework of critical thinking in everyday life. Logical analysis involves using clear, reasoned thought processes to evaluate information, assess options, and make decisions. It helps individuals avoid impulsive conclusions, instead leading to more considered and rational outcomes.

Personal Decision Making: Incorporating Logical Analysis

1. **Understanding Logical Analysis**: Logical analysis in decision making refers to the process of applying reasoned and structured thinking to evaluate information and options. This method involves identifying premises, assessing the validity of arguments, and deducing conclusions based on evidence (Baron, 2000).

2. **Identifying Key Elements of a Decision**: The first step in logical analysis is to clearly identify the problem or decision at hand. This involves breaking down the decision into its fundamental components and understanding the criteria for a successful outcome (Facione, 1990).

3. **Gathering and Organizing Information**: Collecting relevant information is crucial. Logical analysis requires organizing this information systematically to understand the various aspects of the decision and the relationships between them (Paul & Elder, 2006).

4. **Evaluating Evidence and Arguments**: Assessing the quality and relevance of the evidence supporting different options is a core part of logical analysis. This involves questioning the source of the information, looking for biases, and evaluating the strength of the arguments presented (Halpern, 2003).

5. **Avoiding Logical Fallacies**: Part of logical analysis in decision making is being aware of and avoiding common logical fallacies, such as ad hominem attacks, false dilemmas, hasty generalizations, and slippery slope arguments, which can lead to flawed conclusions (Tversky & Kahneman, 1981).

6. **Considering Multiple Perspectives and Consequences**: Logical analysis involves considering various viewpoints and potential consequences of each decision. This includes thinking through the short-term and long-term effects of each option (King & Kitchener, 1994).

7. **Making Reasoned Judgments**: The culmination of logical analysis in decision making is arriving at a reasoned judgment. This involves synthesizing the gathered information and analyses to make a decision that is logically sound and aligned with one's goals and values (Schön, 1983).

Incorporating logical analysis in personal decision making is a crucial aspect of critical thinking in everyday life. It ensures that decisions are not based on impulsive, emotional reactions but on reasoned, systematic evaluation of information and options. By applying logical analysis, individuals can make decisions that are more informed, rational, and aligned with their personal goals and values.

Recognizing and Evaluating Personal Biases: A critical aspect of personal decision-making is recognizing and evaluating one's own biases and prejudices. Critical thinking helps to identify these biases and consider how they might affect decision-making processes (Nickerson, 1998).

Weighing Risks and Benefits:

Critical thinkers evaluate the risks and benefits associated with each option in a decision. This involves considering both the short-term and long-term consequences of each potential choice (Baron, 2000).

Weighing risks and benefits is a crucial component of personal decision making, particularly within the scope of critical thinking in everyday life. This process involves carefully evaluating the potential positive and negative outcomes of different choices and actions. By assessing the risks and benefits, individuals can make more informed, balanced, and prudent decisions that align with their goals and values.

Personal Decision Making: Weighing Risks and Benefits

1. **Understanding Risk-Benefit Analysis**: Risk-benefit analysis in personal decision making is a critical thinking process where individuals evaluate the potential advantages and disadvantages of different options. This involves assessing the likelihood of various outcomes and the impact they may have (Baron, 2000).

2. **Identifying Potential Outcomes**: The first step in weighing risks and benefits is to identify all possible outcomes of a decision. This includes both the intended and unintended consequences, as well as short-term and long-term effects (Facione, 1990).

3. **Assessing Probability and Impact**: Critical thinking involves evaluating the probability of each potential outcome and its possible impact. This includes considering how likely certain outcomes are and how significantly they would affect one's life (Halpern, 2003).

4. **Balancing Risks and Benefits**: After identifying and assessing outcomes, the next step is to balance the risks and benefits. This means comparing the

potential gains against the possible losses or negative consequences of each option (Paul & Elder, 2006).

5. **Considering Personal Values and Goals**: Weighing risks and benefits is not solely a logical process; it also involves considering one's personal values and goals. Decisions should align with what individuals value most in their lives (King & Kitchener, 1994).

6. **Consulting Others and Seeking Advice**: Often, seeking advice from others can provide additional perspectives in the risk-benefit analysis. Consulting with trusted friends, family, or experts can offer insights that one might not have considered (Schön, 1983).

7. **Applying Critical Judgment**: The final step involves applying critical judgment to make a decision. This means synthesizing all the gathered information, insights, and analyses to make a choice that seems most balanced and prudent (Tversky & Kahneman, 1981).

Weighing risks and benefits is an essential aspect of personal decision making in everyday life, facilitated by critical thinking. It involves a comprehensive evaluation of the potential outcomes, considering their probabilities and impacts, and balancing them against one's values and goals. By thoroughly weighing risks and benefits, individuals are better equipped to make decisions that are judicious, well-informed, and aligned with their long-term objectives and well-being.

Reflective Thinking:

Reflective thinking is an integral part of critical thinking in decision-making. It involves reflecting on one's values, experiences, and knowledge, and how these influence decisions. Reflective thinking also entails considering the impact of decisions on one's life and on others (Schön, 1983).

Reflective thinking is a significant aspect of personal decision-making, particularly within the broader context of critical thinking in everyday life. It involves a deeper level of thinking where individuals examine their own beliefs, experiences, and reasoning processes. This introspective practice is crucial for making more informed and thoughtful decisions.

Personal Decision Making: Reflective Thinking

1. **Understanding Reflective Thinking**: Reflective thinking in personal decision-making refers to the process of introspectively examining one's

thoughts, beliefs, and experiences. It involves considering how these elements influence decision-making processes and outcomes (Schön, 1983).

2. **Importance of Reflective Thinking in Decision Making**:

- **Enhanced Self-Awareness**: Reflective thinking contributes to heightened self-awareness, enabling individuals to understand their motivations, biases, and values (Mezirow, 1997).

- **Improved Decision Quality**: By reflecting on past decisions, individuals can learn from previous experiences, which enhances the quality of future decisions (Dewey, 1933).

3. **Strategies for Engaging in Reflective Thinking**:

- **Journaling**: Writing about experiences, decisions, and their outcomes can provide valuable insights and foster deeper self-understanding (Moon, 1999).

- **Mindfulness Practices**: Engaging in mindfulness and meditation can enhance reflective thinking by fostering a focused and contemplative state of mind (Kabat-Zinn, 1994).

- **Seeking Feedback**: Gathering perspectives from others can offer new insights and aid in the reflective process (London, 2002).

4. **Challenges in Practicing Reflective Thinking**:

- **Overcoming Discomfort**: Reflective thinking can be uncomfortable as it may involve confronting personal flaws or mistakes (Argyris, 1991).

- **Consistency**: Maintaining a regular practice of reflective thinking requires discipline and commitment.

5. **Application in Everyday Life**:

- **Personal Growth**: Regular reflective thinking contributes to ongoing personal development and self-improvement.

- **Adaptability and Resilience**: Reflective thinking helps individuals adapt to new situations and challenges by learning from past experiences.

Reflective thinking is a vital component of personal decision-making in the context of critical thinking in everyday life. It enables individuals to gain a deeper understanding of their decision-making processes, learn from past experiences, and make more informed choices in the future. Engaging in regular reflective thinking practices such as journaling, mindfulness, and seeking feedback can significantly enhance an individual's ability to make thoughtful, well-informed decisions.

Seeking and Evaluating Diverse Perspectives:

In personal decision-making, critical thinkers seek out and evaluate different perspectives and sources of advice. They recognize that their own knowledge and experience may be limited and that other viewpoints can provide valuable insights (King & Kitchener, 1994).

Seeking and evaluating diverse perspectives is an essential component of personal decision-making within the context of critical thinking in everyday life. This approach involves actively pursuing different viewpoints and critically assessing their validity and relevance to enhance decision-making processes.

Personal Decision Making: Seeking and Evaluating Diverse Perspectives

1. **Importance of Diverse Perspectives in Decision Making**:

- **Broader Understanding**: Seeking diverse perspectives leads to a more comprehensive understanding of the issue at hand. It exposes individuals to a range of ideas, experiences, and knowledge that they might not have considered otherwise (King & Kitchener, 1994).

- **Reducing Bias**: Engaging with a variety of viewpoints helps in identifying and mitigating personal biases, leading to more balanced and impartial decisions (Nickerson, 1998).

2. **Strategies for Seeking Diverse Perspectives**:

- **Engaging with Different Sources**: Actively seeking information from a range of sources, including those that challenge one's own beliefs or standpoints (Paul & Elder, 2006).

- **Collaboration and Discussion**: Participating in discussions with individuals from diverse backgrounds or with differing opinions to gain new insights and understandings (Gurin, Dey, Hurtado, & Gurin, 2002).

3. **Evaluating the Credibility of Perspectives**:

- **Critical Analysis of Information**: Assessing the credibility, relevance, and reliability of the information obtained from different sources (Metzger, 2007).

- **Understanding the Context**: Considering the context in which different perspectives are formed, including cultural, social, and personal factors (Gay, 2010).

4. **Challenges in Seeking and Evaluating Perspectives**:

- **Confirmation Bias**: Being aware of the tendency to favor information that confirms pre-existing beliefs (Nickerson, 1998).

- **Overcoming Comfort Zones**: Pushing oneself beyond intellectual comfort zones to consider perspectives that may be contrary or challenging to one's own views (Brookfield, 2012).

5. **Application in Personal Decision Making**:

- **Informed Decision Making**: Utilizing diverse perspectives leads to more informed and well-rounded decision-making.

- **Enhancing Problem-Solving**: Different viewpoints can provide creative and innovative solutions to problems.

Seeking and evaluating diverse perspectives is a critical strategy in personal decision-making within the framework of everyday critical thinking. It enriches decision-making processes, broadens understanding, reduces bias, and fosters more inclusive and well-informed choices. By embracing diverse viewpoints and critically assessing their credibility and relevance, individuals can enhance their problem-solving abilities and make more balanced and effective decisions.

Emotional Intelligence in Decision-Making:

Critical thinking in personal decisions also involves emotional intelligence. This includes understanding and managing one's emotions and considering the emotional aspects of decisions, such as how choices align with one's feelings and values (Goleman, 1995).

Emotional intelligence plays a significant role in personal decision-making within the scope of critical thinking in everyday life. Emotional intelligence (EI) refers to the ability to recognize, understand, and manage one's own emotions, as well as to recognize, understand, and influence the emotions of others. Integrating emotional intelligence into decision-making processes enhances critical thinking by balancing rational analysis with emotional awareness, leading to more comprehensive and effective decision-making.

Personal Decision Making: Emotional Intelligence in Decision-Making

1. **Understanding Emotional Intelligence in Decision-Making**:

- Emotional intelligence in decision-making involves acknowledging and understanding the emotional aspects of decision-making processes. It's about considering how emotions influence thinking and behavior and using this understanding to make decisions (Goleman, 1995).

2. **Self-Awareness**:

- One of the key components of EI is self-awareness, which is the ability to recognize and understand one's own emotions. In decision-making, self-awareness helps individuals understand how their emotions can affect their choices and judgments (Salovey & Mayer, 1990).

3. **Self-Regulation**:

- Self-regulation involves managing one's emotions, especially in stressful or challenging situations. In decision-making, self-regulation helps in maintaining objectivity and prevents emotions from clouding judgment (Goleman, 1995).

4. **Empathy in Decision-Making**:

- Empathy, or the ability to understand and share the feelings of others, is crucial in decision-making. It helps in considering the impact of decisions on others and in understanding different perspectives, leading to more ethical and effective decisions (Mayer, Caruso, & Salovey, 2016).

5. **Balancing Emotion and Reason**:

- Effective decision-making involves balancing emotional responses with rational analysis. While emotions provide valuable insights, critical thinking ensures that decisions are not solely based on emotional reactions (Bar-On, 2006).

6. **Social Skills in Collaborative Decision-Making**:

- Emotional intelligence also encompasses social skills, which are essential in collaborative decision-making scenarios. These skills facilitate effective communication, conflict resolution, and negotiation (Goleman, 1998).

7. **Challenges and Considerations**:

- One of the challenges in integrating EI into decision-making is ensuring that emotions do not dominate the rational aspects of decision-making. It requires the development of skills to recognize and manage emotional influences appropriately (Brackett & Salovey, 2006).

Emotional intelligence is a crucial aspect of personal decision-making, enhancing critical thinking by providing a balanced approach between emotional awareness and rational analysis. By understanding and managing emotions, empathizing with others, and effectively applying social skills, individuals can make decisions that are not only rational but also considerate of the emotional dimensions of situations. Developing emotional intelligence skills is essential for making well-rounded, effective decisions in everyday life.

Avoiding Cognitive Shortcuts and Fallacies:

Critical thinking helps to avoid cognitive shortcuts and logical fallacies that can lead to poor decisions. It encourages a thorough examination of assumptions and reasoning behind choices (Halpern, 2003).

Avoiding cognitive shortcuts and fallacies is an essential aspect of personal decision-making, especially when applying critical thinking in everyday life. Cognitive shortcuts, or heuristics, are mental strategies that simplify decision-making processes, but they can often lead to errors in judgment. Fallacies are flawed patterns of reasoning that can mislead our thinking. Being aware of and avoiding these cognitive pitfalls is crucial for making well-reasoned and rational decisions.

Personal Decision Making: Avoiding Cognitive Shortcuts and Fallacies

1. **Understanding Cognitive Shortcuts and Fallacies**:

- Cognitive shortcuts are often automatic, unconscious processes used for making quick decisions. While they can be efficient, they can also lead to systematic errors or biases (Tversky & Kahneman, 1974).

- Fallacies are mistakes in reasoning, often due to incorrect logic or misinterpretations of evidence. Recognizing common fallacies like ad hominem attacks, false dilemmas, and straw man arguments is important for critical thinking (Walton, 1995).

2. **Types of Cognitive Shortcuts and Fallacies:**

- **Confirmation Bias**: The tendency to favor information that confirms existing beliefs while ignoring contradictory evidence (Nickerson, 1998).

- **Anchoring Bias**: Relying too heavily on the first piece of information encountered when making decisions (Tversky & Kahneman, 1974).

- **Hasty Generalization**: Making a rushed conclusion without considering all of the variables (Walton, 1995).

3. **Strategies for Avoiding Cognitive Shortcuts and Fallacies:**

- **Awareness and Education**: Being aware of common heuristics and fallacies is the first step in avoiding them. Education and training in critical thinking can enhance this awareness (Halpern, 2003).

- **Reflective Thinking**: Taking time to reflect on decisions and considering them from multiple perspectives can help avoid impulsive conclusions based on cognitive shortcuts (Schön, 1983).

- **Seeking Diverse Perspectives**: Consulting with others and considering different viewpoints can provide a check against personal biases and fallacies (King & Kitchener, 1994).

4. **Challenges in Overcoming Cognitive Shortcuts and Fallacies:**

- Cognitive shortcuts and fallacies are often ingrained and automatic, making them difficult to recognize and avoid (Kahneman, 2011).

- Overcoming these requires conscious effort and practice, as well as a willingness to question one's own thinking and assumptions.

5. **Application in Personal Decision Making:**

- Being mindful of cognitive shortcuts and fallacies can lead to more thoughtful and accurate decision-making in various aspects of life, from financial choices to interpersonal relationships.

Avoiding cognitive shortcuts and fallacies is vital for effective personal decision-making within the realm of everyday critical thinking. By understanding and being vigilant about these mental traps, individuals can enhance their decision-making processes, leading to more rational and well-considered choices. This requires continuous effort, education, and the willingness to critically assess one's own thinking patterns.

In conclusion, critical thinking is essential for effective personal decision-making. It involves logical analysis, recognizing and evaluating personal biases, weighing risks and benefits, reflective thinking, considering diverse perspectives, understanding emotional influences, and avoiding cognitive biases. By applying critical thinking skills to personal decisions, individuals can make choices that are more informed, rational, and aligned with their values and goals.

In the Workplace

Critical thinking in the workplace is a vital skill that enhances problem-solving, decision-making, and effective communication among employees and management. In a rapidly evolving business environment, the ability to think critically is crucial for adapting to change, innovating, and maintaining a competitive edge.

Critical Thinking in the Workplace

1. **Problem-Solving and Decision-Making**:

- Critical thinking is essential for effective problem-solving and decision-making in the workplace. It involves analyzing complex problems, synthesizing information from various sources, and generating innovative solutions (Facione, 1990).

- Decision-making, a key aspect of professional environments, benefits greatly from critical thinking. It helps in evaluating options, assessing risks, and making choices that are beneficial for the organization (Halpern, 2003).

2. **Enhancing Communication and Collaboration**:

- Critical thinking contributes to clearer and more effective communication. It involves articulating thoughts clearly, interpreting messages accurately, and engaging in reasoned dialogue with others (Rudinow & Barry, 2004).

- Collaboration in the workplace is enhanced by critical thinking as it encourages respect for diverse viewpoints and fosters constructive discussions that lead to better team decisions (West, Toplak, & Stanovich, 2008).

3. **Strategic Planning and Innovation**:

- In strategic planning, critical thinking aids in the analysis of market trends, the assessment of business opportunities, and the anticipation of future challenges (Browne & Keeley, 2007).

- Critical thinking is a driver of innovation, as it involves questioning the status quo, challenging existing paradigms, and thinking creatively to develop new ideas and solutions (Florida, 2002).

4. **Developing Leadership Skills**:

- Critical thinking is a core competency for effective leadership. It enables leaders to make well-informed decisions, foresee potential problems, and devise strategic plans for their teams and the organization (Kouzes & Posner, 2012).

5. **Fostering a Critical Thinking Culture**:

- Creating a workplace culture that values and fosters critical thinking can lead to increased efficiency, productivity, and employee satisfaction (Paul & Elder, 2006).

- Employers can promote a critical thinking culture by providing training, encouraging open discussions, and rewarding innovative thinking and problem-solving skills.

Critical thinking in the workplace is indispensable for navigating the complexities of the modern business world. It enhances problem-solving, decision-making, strategic planning, innovation, and communication. By fostering a culture that values critical thinking, organizations can improve their adaptability, efficiency, and overall success. Employees who hone their critical thinking skills can contribute significantly to their personal development and the organization's growth.

Social and Ethical Implications

Critical thinking in everyday life extends beyond individual decision-making and problem-solving; it also encompasses the social and ethical implications of our actions and beliefs. Critical thinkers consider how their decisions and actions affect others and society as a whole, emphasizing ethical reasoning and social responsibility.

Social and Ethical Implications of Critical Thinking

1. **Understanding the Impact on Society**:

- Critical thinkers recognize that their actions and decisions have broader implications beyond their immediate context. They consider how their choices affect community welfare, social justice, and environmental sustainability (Gardner, 2007).

2. **Ethical Reasoning**:

- Ethical reasoning is a crucial component of critical thinking. It involves reflecting on moral principles, such as fairness, equity, and respect for others, and applying these principles in decision-making processes (Kidder, 2009).

- Critical thinkers strive to make choices that are not only beneficial to themselves but also ethically sound and beneficial to others (Paul & Elder, 2006).

3. **Analyzing the Consequences of Actions**:

- Part of critical thinking is assessing the short-term and long-term consequences of actions. This includes considering potential negative outcomes and striving to minimize harm (Ruggiero, 2011).

4. **Promoting Social Justice**:

- Critical thinking encourages advocacy for social justice. It involves questioning social norms and power structures, challenging injustices, and advocating for the rights and well-being of marginalized groups (Freire, 1970).

5. **Encouraging Civic Engagement**:

- Critical thinking fosters informed and active civic engagement. It includes understanding political and social issues, participating in democratic processes, and engaging in community service (Parker, 2003).

6. **Balancing Personal Beliefs with Social Responsibility**:

- Critical thinkers balance their personal beliefs and values with a sense of social responsibility. They strive to be aware of their biases and prejudices and consider how these might impact others (Kahne & Westheimer, 2006).

7. **Developing Empathy and Cultural Sensitivity**:

- Critical thinking involves empathy and cultural sensitivity. Understanding and respecting diverse perspectives and experiences are vital for ethical interactions and decision-making in a globalized world (Gay, 2010).

In conclusion, critical thinking in everyday life involves not only analyzing and evaluating information for personal decision-making but also considering the social and ethical implications of our actions. It encompasses ethical reasoning, social responsibility, empathy, and cultural sensitivity. By applying critical thinking skills to the broader social context, individuals can contribute positively to society, promote social justice, and engage ethically with the world around them.

Chapter 9: Critical Thinking in Academia

Critical thinking in academia is fundamental to the educational process, playing a pivotal role in students' intellectual development and academic success. It involves the ability to think clearly, rationally, and independently, critically assess information and arguments, and articulate reasoned and coherent responses. This skill is essential across disciplines and levels of education.

Critical Thinking in Academia

Promoting Independent Thought and Inquiry:

Promoting independent thought and inquiry is a fundamental goal of critical thinking in academia. This objective involves encouraging students to think for themselves, ask questions, and engage in their own intellectual exploration and analysis. The development of independent thought is crucial for academic success and lifelong learning.

Promoting Independent Thought and Inquiry in Academia

1. **Encouraging Intellectual Autonomy:**

- Independent thought in academia is about fostering intellectual autonomy, where students are encouraged to develop their own ideas, opinions, and conclusions rather than relying solely on external authority or tradition (Paul & Elder, 2006).

- Intellectual autonomy involves teaching students to think critically about information presented to them, question assumptions, and form their own educated opinions (Brookfield, 2012).

2. **Creating a Conducive Learning Environment:**

- A learning environment that promotes inquiry and independence is crucial. This includes classrooms where questioning is encouraged, diverse perspectives are valued, and students feel safe to express their ideas (Bain, 2004).

- Such environments often involve active learning strategies, such as discussions, debates, and problem-based learning, where students are active participants in their learning process (Bonwell & Eison, 1991).

3. **Developing Critical Thinking Skills**:

- Critical thinking skills such as analysis, evaluation, and synthesis are integral to independent thought and inquiry. Educators focus on teaching these skills through various pedagogical approaches, including Socratic questioning and critical reading and writing exercises (Bean, 2011).

4. **Encouraging Exploration and Curiosity**:

- Curiosity and a desire for exploration are at the heart of independent thought. Academia aims to cultivate a sense of wonder and a quest for knowledge in students, motivating them to explore topics deeply and broadly (Kashdan & Steger, 2007).

5. **Teaching Information Literacy**:

- Information literacy, the ability to find, evaluate, and use information effectively, is key to independent inquiry. It enables students to research independently, discern credible sources, and gather information to support their arguments (Association of College & Research Libraries, 2016).

6. **Challenges in Promoting Independent Thought**:

- One challenge is balancing the need for foundational knowledge with opportunities for independent exploration. Students often need guidance to develop the skills necessary for effective inquiry (Meyers, 1986).

- Another challenge is overcoming the passive learning habits that students may have developed in prior educational experiences.

Promoting independent thought and inquiry in academia is essential for cultivating critical thinkers who are intellectually autonomous, curious, and capable of rigorous analysis. By creating an environment that encourages questioning, exploration, and active learning, and by teaching critical thinking and information literacy skills, educators can empower students to become independent thinkers and lifelong learners. This approach not only benefits students academically but also prepares them to be engaged and informed citizens.

Critical Analysis of Sources and Evidence:

Critical analysis of sources and evidence is a key component of critical thinking in academia. This process involves scrutinizing the information and data presented in various academic sources, assessing their credibility, reliability, and relevance to the subject matter. Effective critical analysis is crucial for academic research, writing, and learning, as it enables students and scholars to develop well-informed, logical, and substantiated arguments.

Critical Analysis of Sources and Evidence in Academia

1. **Evaluating Source Credibility**:

- Critical analysis in academia requires evaluating the credibility of sources. This involves considering the author's qualifications, expertise, and potential biases, as well as the publication's reputation (Willingham, 2007).

- Scholars and students must assess whether the source is peer-reviewed, its date of publication, and its alignment with other works in the field (Association of College & Research Libraries, 2016).

2. **Analyzing the Quality of Evidence**:

- Critical thinkers analyze the quality of evidence presented in sources. This includes assessing the methodology, data collection, and analysis techniques used in research studies (Bowell & Kemp, 2015).

- The strength of the evidence is evaluated based on its relevance, sufficiency, and representativeness for the argument or hypothesis it supports (Paul & Elder, 2006).

3. **Identifying Biases and Assumptions**:

- A critical analysis involves identifying and challenging the biases and assumptions underlying a source or piece of evidence. This includes recognizing personal, cultural, and theoretical biases that may color the interpretation of data (Brookfield, 2012).

4. **Distinguishing Fact from Opinion**:

- In academic work, distinguishing between factual information and opinion is essential. Critical thinkers scrutinize sources to separate objective data from subjective viewpoints (Facione, 1990).

5. **Synthesizing Information from Multiple Sources**:

- Critical analysis also involves synthesizing information from multiple sources. This means integrating diverse perspectives and findings to form a comprehensive understanding of the topic (Bloom, 1956).

6. **Developing Critical Reading Skills**:

- Developing critical reading skills is integral to effective source analysis. This includes active reading, annotating texts, questioning content, and seeking out further information to deepen understanding (Graff & Birkenstein, 2010).

7. **Challenges in Analyzing Sources and Evidence**:

- Students and academics may face challenges in distinguishing credible sources from unreliable ones, especially with the proliferation of information available online. Developing information literacy is crucial to overcome this challenge (Wineburg, 2018).

Critical analysis of sources and evidence is essential in academic contexts for cultivating a deep and accurate understanding of various subjects. It involves evaluating the credibility of sources, assessing the quality of evidence, identifying biases, and synthesizing information from multiple perspectives. These skills are indispensable for academic success and form the foundation for rigorous scholarly work. Developing proficiency in critical analysis enables students and academics to contribute valuable insights and knowledge to their fields of study.

Developing Argumentation Skills:

Developing argumentation skills is a crucial aspect of critical thinking in academia. Argumentation is the process of constructing, presenting, and defending a coherent and logical argument on a specific issue or topic. These skills are fundamental for academic success across various disciplines, as they enable students to engage in scholarly discourse, advance their ideas, and critically evaluate the arguments of others.

Developing Argumentation Skills in Academia

1. **Understanding the Elements of Argumentation**:

- Argumentation in academic contexts involves understanding and applying the elements of a strong argument, which includes a clear thesis, supporting evidence, counterarguments, and a conclusion (Toulmin, 2003).

- It also entails recognizing the structure of arguments, including premises, conclusions, and the logical connections between them (Govier, 2010).

2. **Critical Analysis of Evidence**:

- Effective argumentation requires the ability to critically analyze and select appropriate evidence. This involves evaluating the relevance, credibility, and strength of evidence in supporting the argument (Paul & Elder, 2006).

- It also includes the skill to integrate evidence smoothly and logically into the argument (Ramage, Bean, & Johnson, 2016).

3. **Recognizing and Countering Fallacies**:

- Identifying common logical fallacies and avoiding them in one's arguments is an essential skill. Fallacies such as ad hominem attacks, straw man arguments, and false dilemmas can undermine the validity of an argument (Walton, 1995).

4. **Balancing Emotional Appeal and Logical Reasoning**:

- While emotional appeals (pathos) can be powerful, effective argumentation in academia primarily relies on logical reasoning (logos) and ethical credibility (ethos) (Aristotle, trans. 1991).

- The ability to balance emotional appeal with logical reasoning is crucial for persuasive and credible arguments.

5. **Developing Critical Writing Skills**:

- Argumentation skills are closely linked with academic writing skills. Writing critically involves presenting ideas in a structured, coherent, and persuasive manner (Graff & Birkenstein, 2010).

6. **Engaging in Academic Debates and Discussions**:

- Participation in academic debates and discussions helps in honing argumentation skills. It provides opportunities to present arguments, respond to counterarguments, and refine thinking (Damer, 2009).

7. **Challenges in Developing Argumentation Skills**:

- One challenge for students is differentiating between asserting opinions and constructing well-reasoned arguments.

- Another challenge is developing the confidence to express and defend one's ideas, especially in the face of opposing viewpoints.

Developing argumentation skills is integral to critical thinking in academia. These skills involve constructing clear, logical, and well-supported arguments, critically analyzing evidence, recognizing and countering fallacies, and effectively balancing emotional and logical appeals. Proficiency in argumentation enables students to participate meaningfully in academic discourse, contributing to scholarly debates and advancing their own academic and intellectual growth.

Fostering Analytical Writing and Communication Skills:

Fostering analytical writing and communication skills is a vital aspect of critical thinking in academia. Analytical writing and communication involve the ability to articulate thoughts and arguments in a clear, concise, and logical manner. These skills are essential for academic success, as they enable students to effectively convey their ideas, engage in scholarly discourse, and demonstrate their understanding and analysis of complex topics.

Fostering Analytical Writing and Communication Skills in Academia

1. **Importance of Analytical Writing and Communication**:

- Analytical writing and communication skills are critical for success in academic environments. They allow students to effectively express their ideas, arguments, and research findings (Bean, 2011).

- These skills are not only essential for academic assignments and research papers but also for effective participation in discussions and presentations (Graff & Birkenstein, 2010).

2. **Developing a Clear Thesis and Argument Structure**:

- Central to analytical writing is the development of a clear thesis statement or central argument. This involves formulating a specific, arguable point that guides the content of the writing (Lunsford, 2015).

- Structuring arguments logically and coherently is essential. Each part of the argument should support the thesis and be clearly connected to the overall narrative (Toulmin, 2003).

3. **Critical Analysis and Synthesis of Information**:

- Analytical writing requires the critical analysis and synthesis of information. This includes evaluating sources, integrating evidence, and drawing reasoned conclusions based on the analysis (Paul & Elder, 2006).

- Synthesizing information from multiple sources to support an argument or thesis is a key skill in academic writing (Bloom, 1956).

4. **Clarity and Precision in Writing**:

- Clear and precise writing is crucial in analytical communication. This involves using specific and unambiguous language and avoiding vagueness or generalizations (Strunk & White, 2000).

- Attention to grammar, punctuation, and style also contributes to the clarity and effectiveness of academic writing (Williams & McEnerney, 2010).

5. **Developing Effective Communication Skills**:

- In addition to writing, verbal communication skills are essential in academia. This includes the ability to articulate ideas clearly in discussions, presentations, and academic debates (Hirschberg, 2017).

6. **Challenges in Developing Analytical Writing and Communication Skills**:

- Students often face challenges such as identifying appropriate evidence, organizing their thoughts coherently, and articulating complex ideas effectively.

- Overcoming these challenges requires practice, feedback, and a willingness to revise and improve (Sommers, 1980).

Fostering analytical writing and communication skills is fundamental in academic settings. These skills are essential for the clear and effective expression of ideas and arguments. Developing a clear thesis, structuring arguments logically, critically analyzing information, and conveying ideas with clarity and precision are key aspects of these skills. Continuous practice, along with seeking feedback and being open to revising and refining one's work, are crucial for mastering analytical writing and communication in academia.

Encouraging Intellectual Curiosity and Creativity:

Encouraging intellectual curiosity and creativity is a central aspect of fostering critical thinking in academia. Intellectual curiosity drives the desire to explore, ask questions, and seek out new knowledge and understanding. Creativity, on the other hand, involves thinking innovatively and developing original ideas. Both are crucial for academic growth and the advancement of knowledge.

Encouraging Intellectual Curiosity and Creativity in Academia

1. **Promoting a Culture of Inquiry and Exploration**:

- Academic environments that promote intellectual curiosity and creativity encourage students to pursue their interests and explore new ideas. This involves creating a culture that values questioning, open-mindedness, and the pursuit of knowledge for its own sake (Bain, 2004).

2. **Integrating Inquiry-Based Learning**:

- Inquiry-based learning approaches, where students are active participants in their learning process, can stimulate curiosity and creativity. This includes methods like problem-based learning, where students tackle complex, real-world problems (Savery, 2006).

3. **Fostering a Growth Mindset**:

- Encouraging a growth mindset, the belief that intelligence and abilities can be developed through effort and learning, is key to fostering curiosity and creativity. This perspective motivates students to embrace challenges and persist in the face of setbacks (Dweck, 2006).

4. **Emphasizing the Value of Questions**:

- In academia, emphasizing the value of asking questions – not just answering them – is crucial for intellectual curiosity. This involves teaching students how to ask effective, probing questions and encouraging them to explore these questions in depth (Rothstein & Santana, 2011).

5. **Encouraging Diverse Perspectives and Interdisciplinary Learning**:

- Exposure to diverse perspectives and interdisciplinary learning can enhance creativity. It helps students make novel connections between ideas and develop a more comprehensive understanding of complex issues (Jacobs, 2010).

6. **Providing Opportunities for Creative Expression**:

- Opportunities for creative expression, such as through writing, research projects, or artistic endeavors, allow students to explore and develop their creative abilities (Robinson, 2011).

7. **Challenges in Fostering Curiosity and Creativity**:

- One challenge in academia is balancing the need for structured learning with opportunities for free exploration. Overemphasis on standardized testing and rigid curricula can stifle curiosity and creativity (Zhao, 2012).

- Another challenge is overcoming the fear of failure, which can inhibit creative risk-taking and exploration (Kaufman & Beghetto, 2009).

Encouraging intellectual curiosity and creativity is essential in academia for fostering critical thinking. By promoting a culture of inquiry, integrating inquiry-based learning, fostering a growth mindset, and providing opportunities for creative expression, educational institutions can stimulate students' intellectual curiosity and creativity. These efforts not only enhance individual learning and development but also contribute to the advancement of knowledge and innovation in various fields.

Enhancing Problem-Solving Abilities*:*

Enhancing problem-solving abilities is a key objective of fostering critical thinking in academia. Problem-solving is an essential skill that involves identifying issues, analyzing complex information, generating solutions, and making reasoned decisions. In the academic context, developing these abilities prepares students for intellectual challenges both within and beyond their educational environments.

Enhancing Problem-Solving Abilities in Academia

1. **Defining and Understanding Problems**:

- Critical thinking in academia begins with the ability to accurately define and understand problems. This involves analyzing the problem's context, identifying its root causes, and clarifying its parameters (Jonassen, 2000).

- Students are taught to differentiate between symptoms and underlying problems, a skill that is crucial for effective problem-solving (Paul & Elder, 2006).

2. **Research and Information Gathering**:

- Effective problem-solving requires thorough research and information gathering. Students must learn to seek out relevant information, evaluate its credibility, and integrate it effectively into their problem-solving process (Facione, 1990).

3. **Analytical and Creative Thinking**:

168

- Problem-solving in academia involves both analytical and creative thinking. Analytical thinking is used to break down complex problems and analyze their components, while creative thinking generates innovative and out-of-the-box solutions (Sternberg, 2003).

4. **Critical Evaluation of Solutions**:

- Once solutions are generated, critical thinking skills are applied to evaluate these solutions in terms of their feasibility, potential impact, and ethical implications (Halpern, 2003).

- This evaluation also involves considering the short-term and long-term consequences of each solution (Baron, 2000).

5. **Implementing and Reflecting on Solutions**:

- Implementing solutions and reflecting on their outcomes are crucial steps in the problem-solving process. This includes monitoring the results and adapting strategies as necessary (Schön, 1983).

- Reflection helps students learn from their successes and mistakes, enhancing their problem-solving skills over time (Dewey, 1933).

6. **Challenges in Developing Problem-Solving Skills**:

- One challenge is ensuring students have opportunities to practice these skills in real-world or simulated scenarios.

- Another challenge is fostering a mindset that views problems as opportunities for learning rather than obstacles.

7. **Interdisciplinary Approaches**:

- Interdisciplinary approaches in problem-solving expose students to various perspectives and methods, enriching their problem-solving toolkit (Newell, 2001).

Enhancing problem-solving abilities through critical thinking is a vital component of academic education. It involves understanding and defining problems, conducting thorough research, applying analytical and creative thinking, critically evaluating solutions, and learning from the implementation of these solutions. By developing these skills, students are better equipped to tackle complex problems, both in their academic pursuits and in their future professional and personal lives.

Preparing for Professional and Civic Life:

Critical thinking in academia plays a pivotal role in preparing students for professional and civic life. The abilities honed through academic critical thinking are not confined to scholarly pursuits; they are transferable skills essential for success in a wide range of professional fields and for active, informed participation in civic life.

Preparing for Professional and Civic Life through Critical Thinking in Academia

1. **Transferable Skills for the Professional World**:

- Critical thinking develops skills such as problem-solving, analytical thinking, effective communication, and decision-making, which are highly valued in the workplace (Bok, 2006).

- These skills enable graduates to adapt to various professional environments, tackle complex challenges, and innovate in their respective fields (Arum & Roksa, 2011).

2. **Enhancing Communication and Collaboration**:

- In academia, students learn to articulate their thoughts clearly and persuasively, a skill crucial in any professional setting. Effective communication facilitates collaboration, negotiation, and leadership (Morreale, Osborn, & Pearson, 2000).

- Teamwork and collaborative skills developed through group projects and discussions in academic settings are directly applicable to professional teamwork and collaboration (Johnson & Johnson, 2009).

3. **Ethical Reasoning and Integrity**:

- Critical thinking involves ethical reasoning, which is essential for navigating professional and civic responsibilities. It helps individuals to make decisions that are not only effective but also ethically sound (Paul & Elder, 2006).

- Academic experiences that emphasize ethical considerations prepare students to address ethical dilemmas they may encounter in their careers and civic life (Colby & Sullivan, 2008).

4. **Informed Civic Engagement**:

- Critical thinking skills are vital for active and informed participation in civic life. They enable individuals to understand complex social and political issues, evaluate information critically, and engage in reasoned public discourse (Parker, 2003).

- These skills are crucial for voting, participating in community activities, and understanding the implications of public policies (Galston, 2001).

5. **Lifelong Learning and Adaptability**:

- Critical thinking fosters a mindset of lifelong learning, essential in a rapidly changing world. This adaptability is crucial for professional development and staying informed as a responsible citizen (Mezirow, 1997).

6. **Challenges in Bridging Academic and Practical Realms**:

- One challenge is ensuring that the critical thinking skills developed in academia are applicable and relevant to real-world scenarios (Bridgstock, 2009).

- Another challenge is creating academic experiences that accurately simulate professional and civic situations (Kuh, 2008).

Critical thinking in academia is instrumental in preparing students for the diverse challenges of professional and civic life. The skills developed through critical thinking – such as problem-solving, ethical reasoning, effective communication, and informed civic engagement – are highly transferable and necessary for success in a rapidly evolving global landscape. By bridging academic learning with practical application, educational institutions play a crucial role in shaping well-rounded, adaptable, and responsible professionals and citizens.

In conclusion, critical thinking is a cornerstone of academic success and intellectual growth. It equips students with vital skills such as independent thinking, critical analysis of sources, argumentation, communication, and problem-solving. These skills not only enhance academic performance but also prepare students for effective engagement in their professional and civic lives. Cultivating critical thinking in academic settings fosters a more informed, reflective, and capable society.

Critical Reading and Writing:

Preparing for critical reading and writing is a fundamental aspect of developing critical thinking skills in academia. Critical reading involves analyzing, evaluating, and synthesizing information from various texts, while critical writing requires expressing ideas clearly, logically, and effectively. These skills are essential for academic success, as they enable students to engage deeply with course material, construct well-reasoned arguments, and contribute meaningfully to academic discourse.

Preparing for Critical Reading and Writing in Academia

1. **Developing Critical Reading Skills**:

- Critical reading is an active process of interrogating texts, questioning the author's purpose, perspective, and arguments (Graff & Birkenstein, 2010).

- Students are encouraged to identify the main ideas, themes, and arguments in texts and evaluate the evidence supporting them (Bean, 2011).

- Annotating texts, summarizing content, and reflecting on the reading's implications and connections to other knowledge are crucial practices in critical reading (Lunsford, 2015).

2. **Engaging in Critical Writing**:

- Critical writing involves the expression of complex ideas and arguments in a clear, structured, and persuasive manner (Williams & McEnerney, 2010).

- It requires students to develop a strong thesis statement, organize their ideas coherently, and support their arguments with evidence (Toulmin, 2003).

- Critical writing also entails anticipating and addressing counterarguments, thus demonstrating a comprehensive understanding of the topic (Ramage, Bean, & Johnson, 2016).

3. **Interpreting and Evaluating Sources**:

- Critical thinkers in academia learn to assess the credibility and relevance of sources. This includes understanding the context in which the source was produced and its potential biases (Metzger, 2007).

- This skill is essential for both critical reading, where it informs the understanding of texts, and critical writing, where it guides the integration of sources into one's work (Gilroy, 2008).

172

4. **Enhancing Argumentation Skills**:

- Critical reading and writing involve developing strong argumentation skills. This includes understanding how to construct logical, coherent, and persuasive arguments and to critique the arguments presented by others (Govier, 2010).

5. **Challenges in Critical Reading and Writing**:

- Students may initially struggle with the depth of analysis required in critical reading and the clarity and coherence needed in critical writing.

- Overcoming these challenges involves practice, feedback, and guidance in developing these skills (Sommers, 1980).

6. **Integrating Critical Reading and Writing in Coursework**:

- Many academic courses integrate critical reading and writing assignments to help students apply these skills in context. This includes writing essays, research papers, and reports based on critical readings (Bean, 2011).

Preparing for critical reading and writing is integral to the cultivation of critical thinking in academia. These skills enable students to engage rigorously with academic materials and to articulate their ideas and arguments effectively. Through practice, guidance, and an integration of these skills into coursework, students can enhance their ability to think critically and contribute meaningfully to academic discourse.

Research Methodologies:

Understanding and applying research methodologies is a crucial aspect of critical thinking in academia. Research methodologies encompass the methods and techniques used to conduct research, including the formulation of hypotheses, data collection, analysis, and interpretation. Mastery of these methodologies is essential for students and scholars to conduct rigorous and credible research, contributing to the advancement of knowledge in their respective fields.

Research Methodologies in Critical Thinking in Academia

1. **Fundamentals of Research Design**:

- Research design involves planning and structuring a research study to address specific questions or hypotheses. It includes choosing the appropriate research method (qualitative, quantitative, or mixed methods) based on the research objectives (Creswell, 2014).

- Understanding the strengths and limitations of different research designs is crucial for critical evaluation of research (Bryman, 2016).

2. **Developing Research Questions and Hypotheses**:

- Critical thinking in academia involves formulating clear, concise, and researchable questions or hypotheses. This requires identifying gaps in existing literature and understanding the significance of the research question (Punch, 2016).

- Hypotheses should be testable and grounded in theoretical frameworks or previous research findings (Kerlinger & Lee, 2000).

3. **Data Collection and Analysis Techniques**:

- Selecting appropriate data collection methods (e.g., surveys, experiments, interviews) and understanding their implications is key to conducting effective research (Silverman, 2016).

- Data analysis techniques, whether qualitative or quantitative, should be chosen based on the nature of the data and the research questions. Critical thinking is required to interpret data accurately and avoid misinterpretations (Field, 2013).

4. **Ethical Considerations in Research**:

- Ethical considerations, including informed consent, confidentiality, and avoidance of harm, are paramount in research methodology. Researchers must critically evaluate the ethical implications of their studies (Resnik, 2015).

5. **Evaluating Sources and Evidence**:

- In academia, critical thinking involves the evaluation of sources and evidence used in research. This includes assessing the credibility of sources, the quality of evidence, and the validity of the researchers' interpretations (Metzger, 2007).

6. **Critical Review of Research Literature**:

- Conducting a critical review of existing literature is an integral part of research methodology. It involves analyzing and synthesizing previous studies to establish a foundation for new research (Hart, 2018).

7. **Challenges in Research Methodologies**:

- One challenge in academia is staying updated with evolving research methods and adapting to advancements in research technology.

- Another challenge is developing the ability to critically assess one's own research methodology and to be open to constructive critique from peers and mentors.

In conclusion, research methodologies are a fundamental component of critical thinking in academia. They involve a systematic approach to research design, data collection, analysis, and ethical considerations. Developing proficiency in these methodologies enables students and scholars to conduct robust, credible research and to critically evaluate the research of others. These skills are essential for contributing to the body of knowledge in their respective disciplines and for advancing scholarly and scientific inquiry.

Debate and Discussion in the Classroom:
Debate and discussion in the classroom are key practices in promoting critical thinking in academia. These interactive and dialogical approaches encourage students to analyze, evaluate, and articulate ideas while engaging with diverse perspectives. Through debates and discussions, students develop essential critical thinking skills, such as reasoning, argumentation, and the ability to consider and respond to different viewpoints.

Debate and Discussion in the Classroom for Critical Thinking

1. **The Role of Debate in Enhancing Critical Thinking**:

- Debates in the academic setting foster critical thinking by requiring students to research topics, formulate arguments, and consider counterarguments (Kennedy, 2007).

- Participating in debates helps students develop skills in building and defending positions, as well as understanding and refuting opposing views (Zare & Othman, 2015).

2. **Discussion as a Tool for Critical Engagement**:

- Classroom discussions encourage students to engage critically with the course material, articulate their thoughts, and listen to and evaluate the ideas of others (Brookfield & Preskill, 2016).

- Discussions often involve analyzing complex issues, synthesizing diverse viewpoints, and reflecting on personal beliefs and values (Garside, 1996).

3. **Developing Argumentation and Reasoning Skills**:

- Both debates and discussions require students to develop argumentation skills, where they learn to support their ideas with evidence and logical reasoning (Toulmin, 2003).

- These activities also enhance students' ability to think on their feet and articulate thoughts coherently and persuasively (Daly, 2013).

4. **Encouraging Active Listening and Empathy**:

- Engaging in debates and discussions in the classroom encourages active listening, where students must understand and consider the viewpoints of others (Johnson, 2009).

- This practice fosters empathy and the ability to appreciate and engage with perspectives different from one's own (Hess, 2009).

5. **Facilitating Diverse Perspectives and Critical Inquiry**:

- Classroom debates and discussions expose students to a variety of perspectives, which is crucial for broadening understanding and fostering critical inquiry (Parker & Hess, 2001).

- Educators play a key role in moderating discussions and ensuring that multiple viewpoints are represented and respected (Gurin, Dey, Hurtado, & Gurin, 2002).

6. **Challenges in Implementing Debates and Discussions**:

- Challenges include ensuring a respectful and inclusive environment where all students feel comfortable participating.

- Another challenge is balancing the need to cover course content with providing ample time for in-depth discussion and debate (Barkley & Major, 2014).

In conclusion, debates and discussions are powerful pedagogical tools in academia for fostering critical thinking. They provide dynamic platforms for students to practice and enhance various critical thinking skills, including argumentation, reasoning, empathy, and active listening. These activities also promote the appreciation of diverse perspectives and the development of effective communication skills. Successfully implementing debates and discussions requires thoughtful planning and facilitation to ensure an inclusive and productive learning environment.

Chapter 10: Continuing Your Journey

Continuing the journey to become a critical thinker is an ongoing process that extends beyond formal education and into various aspects of life. This lifelong pursuit involves constantly refining and applying critical thinking skills in personal, professional, and civic contexts. It is about cultivating a mindset of inquiry, skepticism, and reflection.

Continuing Your Journey to Become a Critical Thinker

Embracing Lifelong Learning:

Embracing lifelong learning is a fundamental principle in the journey to becoming and remaining a critical thinker. Lifelong learning involves a continuous commitment to acquiring new knowledge, skills, and understanding, both formally and informally, throughout one's life. This commitment is essential for maintaining and enhancing critical thinking abilities over time.

1. **The Concept of Lifelong Learning:**

- Lifelong learning is the ongoing, voluntary, and self-motivated pursuit of knowledge for personal or professional reasons (Jarvis, 2004). It extends beyond formal education to include informal learning experiences throughout one's life.

- This approach to learning emphasizes the development of knowledge, skills, and competencies in a wide range of contexts (Merriam & Bierema, 2013).

2. **Lifelong Learning and Critical Thinking:**

- Lifelong learning contributes to the enhancement of critical thinking skills. It involves constantly questioning, reflecting upon, and integrating new information and experiences (Paul & Elder, 2006).

- Engaging in diverse learning experiences exposes individuals to different perspectives and ways of thinking, which is crucial for critical thinking (Mezirow, 1997).

3. **Strategies for Lifelong Learning:**

- Actively seeking new learning opportunities, such as attending workshops, conferences, or online courses, helps maintain and develop critical thinking skills (Candy, 1991).

- Engaging with a variety of informational sources, including books, journals, and media, to expand one's knowledge base and understanding of different subjects (Dewey, 1938).

4. **Reflective Practice in Lifelong Learning**:

- Reflective practice is a key component of lifelong learning. It involves critically reflecting on one's experiences and learning to gain deeper insights and understanding (Schön, 1983).

- Keeping a learning journal can be an effective way to engage in reflective practice, allowing individuals to track their learning and development over time (Moon, 1999).

5. **Challenges in Lifelong Learning**:

- One challenge is finding the time and resources to engage in continuous learning amidst other life responsibilities.

- Another challenge is overcoming the comfort of established beliefs and being open to new ideas and perspectives (Brookfield, 2012).

Embracing lifelong learning is essential for the continuous development of critical thinking skills. It involves a proactive approach to seeking knowledge and understanding, reflecting on experiences, and remaining open to new ideas and perspectives. By committing to lifelong learning, individuals can continually enhance their critical thinking abilities, adapt to change, and make informed decisions in various aspects of their lives.

Applying Critical Thinking in Everyday Life:

Applying critical thinking in everyday life is a key aspect of continuing your journey as a critical thinker. This practice involves utilizing critical thinking skills not just in academic or professional settings, but in the day-to-day decisions and challenges one faces. The ability to think critically in everyday life enhances problem-solving abilities, decision-making quality, and the capacity to navigate complex situations effectively.

1. **Everyday Decision-Making**:

- Critical thinking plays a crucial role in everyday decision-making. It involves analyzing situations, evaluating options, considering potential outcomes, and making informed choices based on logical reasoning (Halpern, 2003).

- This process includes assessing the credibility of information, recognizing biases, and avoiding hasty conclusions (Paul & Elder, 2006).

2. **Problem-Solving in Real-Life Situations**:

- In daily life, individuals face various problems ranging from simple to complex. Critical thinking aids in breaking down these problems, identifying their root causes, and developing practical solutions (Facione, 1990).

- It also involves considering multiple perspectives and solutions, which can lead to more effective and creative problem-solving (Sternberg, 2003).

3. **Interpersonal Relationships**:

- Critical thinking is valuable in interpersonal relationships. It enables individuals to understand and empathize with others' perspectives, communicate effectively, and resolve conflicts constructively (Goleman, 1995).

- It also helps in navigating social dynamics, understanding others' motivations, and making sound judgments in personal interactions (Baron, 2000).

4. **Media Literacy and Information Consumption**:

- In an era of information overload, critical thinking is essential for media literacy. It involves critically evaluating the information consumed from various media sources, discerning between facts and opinions, and recognizing potential biases and misinformation (Hobbs, 2011).

- This skill is crucial for staying informed and making sense of the world in a balanced and informed way (Wineburg, 2018).

5. **Reflective Practice**:

- Engaging in reflective practice is a part of applying critical thinking in everyday life. It involves reflecting on one's experiences, beliefs, and decisions, and considering how they can be improved or adjusted in the future (Schön, 1983).

6. **Challenges in Applying Critical Thinking**:

- One challenge is the tendency to fall back on intuitive or habitual ways of thinking, especially under pressure or in familiar situations.

- Overcoming this requires mindfulness and a conscious effort to apply critical thinking skills consistently (Brookfield, 2012).

The application of critical thinking skills in everyday life is a vital aspect of being a well-rounded critical thinker. It enhances decision-making, problem-solving, interpersonal relationships, and media literacy. Continuously applying these skills in daily life situations fosters a habit of thoughtful analysis and reflection, leading to more informed, balanced, and effective decisions and interactions.

Engaging in Reflective Practice:

Engaging in reflective practice is a vital component of continuing your journey to become a critical thinker. Reflective practice involves regularly examining and evaluating one's thoughts, decisions, and actions to gain deeper insights and improve future performance. This self-examination leads to personal and professional growth, enhancing one's critical thinking skills.

1. **Concept of Reflective Practice**:

- Reflective practice is a process of self-examination and learning from one's experiences. It involves thinking about what happened, analyzing how it was handled, and considering what could be done differently in the future (Schön, 1983).

- This practice is considered crucial for continuous learning and development in various professions and personal life (Boud, Keogh, & Walker, 1985).

2. **Reflective Practice in Critical Thinking**:

- In the context of critical thinking, reflective practice involves questioning one's assumptions, beliefs, and values. It helps individuals understand their thinking patterns and how these influence their decisions and actions (Brookfield, 2012).

- Reflective practice also includes evaluating the effectiveness of one's problem-solving strategies and decision-making processes (Moon, 1999).

3. **Methods of Reflective Practice**:

- **Journaling**: Keeping a reflective journal is a practical way to engage in reflective practice. Writing about experiences, thoughts, and feelings helps in processing and analyzing them more deeply (Williams & Wessel, 2004).

- **Feedback Seeking**: Actively seeking feedback from others can provide new perspectives and insights, enhancing the reflective process (London, 2002).

- **Critical Incidents Analysis**: Reflecting on critical incidents or significant events can be particularly enlightening in understanding one's responses and learning from them (Flanagan, 1954).

4. **Benefits of Reflective Practice**:

- Reflective practice enhances self-awareness and emotional intelligence, which are key components of critical thinking (Goleman, 1995).

- It promotes continuous learning and adaptability, essential skills in an ever-changing world (Mezirow, 1997).

5. **Challenges in Reflective Practice**:

- One challenge is making time for reflection in a busy schedule. Reflective practice requires dedicated time and focus.

- Another challenge is confronting uncomfortable truths about oneself, which can be difficult but is essential for genuine growth and learning (Fook & Gardner, 2007).

Engaging in reflective practice is a crucial aspect of continuing the journey toward becoming a more effective critical thinker. It involves a consistent and honest examination of one's experiences, decisions, and thought processes. This practice not only fosters personal and professional growth but also enhances one's capacity for critical thinking by promoting self-awareness, emotional intelligence, and a deeper understanding of one's cognitive and decision-making processes.

Seeking Diverse Perspectives:

Continuing your journey to become a critical thinker crucially involves seeking diverse perspectives. This practice is about exposing oneself to a variety of viewpoints, cultures, and experiences, which broadens understanding, challenges preconceived notions, and strengthens critical thinking skills.

1. **Importance of Diverse Perspectives**:

- Engaging with diverse perspectives helps to challenge and refine one's thinking by exposing biases and assumptions (Gurin, Dey, Hurtado, & Gurin, 2002).

- It encourages the consideration of alternative viewpoints and ideas, which is essential for comprehensive and balanced critical thinking (Cotton, 1988).

2. **Cognitive Benefits of Diversity**:

- Diverse perspectives contribute to cognitive complexity. They encourage deeper information processing and critical evaluation, leading to more thorough and creative problem-solving (Phillips, 2014).

- Exposure to diversity enhances cognitive skills such as analytical thinking, adaptability, and the ability to synthesize conflicting information (Antonio et al., 2004).

3. **Strategies for Seeking Diversity**:

- **Active Engagement**: Actively seek out and engage with people, ideas, and cultures that are different from one's own. This can involve participating in cultural events, joining diverse groups or clubs, or reading literature from different viewpoints (Stephan & Stephan, 2013).

- **Critical Media Consumption**: Consume a wide range of media sources, especially those that challenge one's current beliefs or perspectives (Hobbs, 2011).

- **Educational Opportunities**: Take courses or attend lectures and seminars on topics outside of one's usual interests or expertise (Zúñiga, Williams, & Berger, 2005).

4. **Challenges in Seeking Diverse Perspectives**:

- One challenge is overcoming the comfort of the familiar. It can be easier and more comfortable to engage with like-minded individuals or familiar cultures (Pettigrew & Tropp, 2006).

- Another challenge is the potential for experiencing cognitive dissonance when encountering conflicting viewpoints, which requires an open and flexible mindset to navigate (Festinger, 1957).

5. **Developing Cultural Competence**:

- Seeking diverse perspectives is also part of developing cultural competence – the ability to understand, communicate with, and effectively interact with people across cultures (Sue, 2001).

Seeking diverse perspectives is a key component of continuing your journey as a critical thinker. It involves stepping out of one's comfort zone to engage with different ideas, cultures, and viewpoints. This practice not only enhances critical thinking skills but also fosters empathy, cultural competence, and a deeper understanding of the complex world we live in. By embracing diversity in thoughts and experiences, individuals can develop a more nuanced, comprehensive, and informed approach to thinking and decision-making.

Practicing Intellectual Humility:

Practicing intellectual humility is an essential step in continuing your journey as a critical thinker. Intellectual humility involves recognizing the limits of one's knowledge and being open to new ideas and perspectives. It is a fundamental trait for critical thinkers, as it fosters open-mindedness, encourages a willingness to revise one's beliefs, and enhances the ability to engage in rational discourse.

1. **Understanding Intellectual Humility**:

- Intellectual humility is the acknowledgment that one's knowledge and understanding are limited and fallible (Leary et al., 2017). It involves being open to the possibility of being wrong and valuing truth over one's ego or beliefs.

- This trait is not about doubting one's intelligence or abilities but about understanding that one's perspective is not the only or infallible one (Whitcomb et al., 2017).

2. **Intellectual Humility and Critical Thinking**:

- Intellectual humility is integral to critical thinking. It encourages individuals to question their assumptions, consider evidence objectively, and be open to changing their opinions based on new evidence or reasoning (Krumrei-Mancuso & Rouse, 2016).

- It also fosters a balanced approach to evaluating arguments, reducing the impact of biases and preconceptions (Porter & Schumann, 2018).

3. **Developing Intellectual Humility**:

- Engaging with diverse viewpoints and ideas is key to developing intellectual humility. This exposes individuals to different ways of thinking and challenges their existing beliefs (Hess, 2009).

- Reflective practices, such as journaling or meditation, can help individuals recognize their biases and limitations (Schön, 1983).

- Seeking feedback and constructive criticism from others can also promote intellectual humility by providing external perspectives on one's beliefs and thought processes (London, 2002).

4. **Benefits of Intellectual Humility**:

- Intellectual humility contributes to more effective communication and collaboration, as it promotes respect for others' viewpoints (Spiegel, 2012).

- It enhances lifelong learning, as individuals with intellectual humility are more likely to seek out new knowledge and experiences (Mezirow, 1997).

5. **Challenges in Practicing Intellectual Humility**:

- A common challenge is overcoming the natural tendency to defend one's existing beliefs or to interpret information in a way that confirms these beliefs (Nickerson, 1998).

- Cultivating intellectual humility requires continuous effort and self-awareness, as it goes against the common desire to appear certain or infallible (Kahneman, 2011).

Practicing intellectual humility is a key aspect of continuing the journey as a critical thinker. It involves recognizing and embracing the limitations of one's knowledge, being open to new evidence and arguments, and valuing truth over personal beliefs or ego. By cultivating intellectual humility, individuals enhance their ability to engage in open-minded and rational discourse, contribute to collaborative endeavors, and pursue lifelong learning.

Participating in Intellectual Communities:

Practicing intellectual humility is an essential step in continuing your journey as a critical thinker. Intellectual humility involves recognizing the limits of one's knowledge and being open to new ideas and perspectives. It is a fundamental trait for critical thinkers, as it fosters open-mindedness, encourages a willingness to revise one's beliefs, and enhances the ability to engage in rational discourse.

1. **The Role of Intellectual Communities**:

- Intellectual communities, such as academic conferences, workshops, discussion groups, and online forums, provide environments where individuals can exchange ideas, debate viewpoints, and gain new insights (Lave & Wenger, 1991).

- These communities act as incubators for critical thinking, where members challenge each other's ideas, leading to deeper understanding and knowledge creation (Brown & Duguid, 2001).

2. **Benefits of Participation**:

- Engagement in intellectual communities exposes individuals to a variety of perspectives and disciplines, enhancing their ability to think critically and approach problems from multiple angles (Wenger, 1998).

- Such participation promotes continuous learning and intellectual growth, as members are often exposed to the latest research, theories, and practices in their fields (Booth, Colomb, & Williams, 2008).

3. **Building Professional Networks**:

- Participation in intellectual communities enables the building of professional networks, which can provide support, mentorship, and collaborative opportunities (Granovetter, 1977).

- Networking with peers and experts can lead to the exchange of ideas, experiences, and resources, further enriching one's understanding and critical thinking abilities (Burt, 2004).

4. **Enhancing Communication Skills**:

- Engaging in intellectual communities enhances communication skills, particularly the ability to articulate ideas clearly, listen actively, and engage in constructive debate (De Janasz, Dowd, & Schneider, 2002).

- It also develops the skill of presenting complex information in accessible ways to different audiences (Gallo, 2014).

5. **Challenges and Considerations**:

- One challenge is finding and integrating into the right intellectual community, particularly for those new to a field or with interdisciplinary interests (Fischer, 2005).

- Ensuring that the community is inclusive and open to diverse viewpoints is important to avoid echo chambers or groupthink (Janis, 1972).

6. **Continued Engagement and Contribution**:

- Long-term benefits come from not just participating but actively contributing to these communities, such as through presenting work, providing feedback, or leading discussions (Johnson, 2001).

Participating in intellectual communities is a vital aspect of continuing the development as a critical thinker. These communities provide valuable opportunities for exposure to diverse ideas, professional networking, and skill enhancement. Actively engaging and contributing to such communities fosters a culture of learning, dialogue, and intellectual growth, essential for ongoing critical thinking development.

Overcoming Challenges and Obstacles:

Continuing your journey to become a critical thinker often involves overcoming various challenges and obstacles. These challenges can stem from cognitive biases, environmental factors, emotional influences, and the complexities of the information age. Recognizing and addressing these hurdles is crucial for the development and maintenance of critical thinking skills.

1. **Recognizing and Overcoming Cognitive Biases**:

    - Cognitive biases, such as confirmation bias, can significantly impede critical thinking. They lead to the selective gathering of information or interpretation that confirms pre-existing beliefs or ideas (Nickerson, 1998).

    - Overcoming these biases involves conscious efforts to seek out and consider information that contradicts one's beliefs and to regularly question one's assumptions (Kahneman, 2011).

2. **Dealing with Information Overload**:

- The vast amount of information available today can be overwhelming and can lead to difficulties in discerning credible information. This phenomenon, known as information overload, can impede critical thinking (Eppler & Mengis, 2004).

- Developing strategies for effective information management, such as prioritizing information sources and practicing selective focusing, is essential (Hargittai, Fullerton, Menchen-Trevino, & Thomas, 2010).

3. **Emotional Influences on Decision Making**:

- Emotions can significantly influence decision-making and judgment. While emotions are an important aspect of human experience, they can sometimes lead to irrational or biased decisions (Loewenstein & Lerner, 2003).

- Practicing emotional regulation and being aware of how emotions impact one's thinking can help mitigate their negative influence on critical thinking (Gross, 2002).

4. **Navigating Social and Group Dynamics**:

- Social pressures and group dynamics can also pose challenges to critical thinking. Phenomena such as groupthink can lead to conformity and discourage independent thinking (Janis, 1972).

- Cultivating independence in thought and being mindful of the influence of social dynamics are important in maintaining critical thinking in group settings (Nemeth, 1986).

5. **Challenges of the Digital Age**:

- The digital age presents unique challenges, such as the prevalence of fake news and echo chambers. These can distort one's understanding and impede critical thinking (Sunstein, 2001).

- Developing digital literacy skills, such as the ability to evaluate the credibility of online sources, is crucial in the digital age (Hobbs, 2011).

The journey to becoming a critical thinker involves navigating and overcoming various challenges and obstacles. Addressing cognitive biases, managing information overload, understanding the impact of emotions, and navigating social dynamics and digital complexities are all integral to this process. Developing strategies to counter these challenges is essential for maintaining and enhancing critical thinking abilities, enabling individuals to make more informed, rational, and unbiased decisions.

Lifelong Learning:

Lifelong learning is a key component in the journey of becoming a critical thinker. It is the ongoing, voluntary, and self-motivated pursuit of knowledge for both personal and professional reasons. Lifelong learning enhances an individual's understanding of the world around them, offers a more profound sense of fulfillment, and provides a framework for making better and more informed decisions throughout life.

Definition and Importance of Lifelong Learning:

Lifelong learning is a fundamental concept for those on the journey of becoming and remaining a critical thinker. This concept encompasses the continuous, self-initiated pursuit of knowledge for personal and professional reasons. In the context of critical thinking, lifelong learning is not just about accumulating information; it's about developing a mindset that is curious, questioning, and open to new ideas and perspectives.

1. **Definition of Lifelong Learning:**

- Lifelong learning is the ongoing, voluntary, and self-motivated pursuit of knowledge, skills, and competencies. It extends beyond formal education to encompass a broad range of learning activities, from informal learning experiences to structured courses (Jarvis, 2004).

- It involves actively seeking new skills, understanding, and wisdom in response to evolving personal interests, societal needs, and technological advancements (Field, 2000).

2. **Importance in Critical Thinking:**

- Lifelong learning is integral to critical thinking as it fosters an environment where questioning, reflection, and evaluation are routine. This continuous learning process helps in refining and updating one's thinking processes, making them more adaptive and nuanced (Mezirow, 1997).

- It contributes to the development of a well-informed and open-minded individual who is capable of analyzing information critically and making well-reasoned decisions (Facione, 1990).

3. **Personal and Professional Growth**:

- On a personal level, lifelong learning contributes to self-fulfillment, cognitive resilience, and personal satisfaction. It encourages individuals to explore new interests and develop new skills, leading to greater personal fulfillment and enhanced life experiences (Kolb, 1984).

- Professionally, it ensures that individuals remain competitive and competent in their fields, as it equips them with the latest knowledge and skills necessary in an ever-changing job market (Candy, 1991).

4. **Societal Benefits**:

- Lifelong learning has broader societal benefits as well. An informed and educated populace is crucial for the health of democratic societies. It leads to more civic engagement, informed decision-making, and a better understanding of global issues (Longworth, 2003).

- It also contributes to social inclusion and cultural diversity, as individuals learn about and understand different perspectives and cultures (Field, 2009).

Lifelong learning is a critical aspect of critical thinking. It involves a continuous effort to gain knowledge and understand a rapidly evolving world. This process of ongoing learning not only enhances personal and professional growth but also contributes significantly to societal well-being. By embracing lifelong learning, individuals ensure that their critical thinking skills remain sharp, relevant, and effective in various contexts throughout their lives.

Lifelong Learning and Knowledge Expansion:

Lifelong learning is crucial in the continual expansion of knowledge, an essential element for those dedicated to becoming adept critical thinkers. This ongoing process of learning is not confined to formal education; it encompasses a broad spectrum of learning opportunities that contribute to the constant development of knowledge and skills.

1. **Broadening Knowledge through Lifelong Learning**:

- Lifelong learning involves actively pursuing diverse educational opportunities, which broadens and deepens one's knowledge base beyond formal education (Jarvis, 2004). This can include self-study, online courses, workshops, seminars, and engaging with new experiences.

- Expanding knowledge through lifelong learning allows individuals to approach problems and decisions with a more informed and holistic perspective (Merriam & Bierema, 2013).

2. **Enhancing Critical Thinking Skills**:

- Continuous learning contributes to the enhancement of critical thinking skills. It involves not only acquiring information but also synthesizing, analyzing, and applying this knowledge in various contexts (Facione, 1990).

- Lifelong learning encourages individuals to remain curious, ask questions, and be open to new ideas, which are key components of critical thinking (Paul & Elder, 2006).

3. **Adapting to Changing Environments**:

- In a rapidly changing world, lifelong learning is vital for adapting to new challenges, technologies, and information. It helps individuals remain relevant and capable in their personal and professional lives (Field, 2000).

- This adaptability is especially important in the face of technological advancements and evolving societal needs (Siemens, 2005).

4. **Cultivating a Love for Learning**:

- Lifelong learning fosters a love for learning, encouraging individuals to pursue knowledge for both personal fulfillment and professional development (Tough, 1971).

- This intrinsic motivation for learning drives continuous personal growth and intellectual development (Deci & Ryan, 1985).

5. **Integrating Diverse Learning Sources**:

- Lifelong learning involves integrating knowledge from diverse sources and disciplines. This includes formal education, practical experiences, cultural exposure, and interdisciplinary studies (Kolb, 1984).

- Such integration leads to a more comprehensive understanding of complex issues and enhances problem-solving abilities (Boyd & Fales, 1983).

Lifelong learning is a pivotal element in the ongoing expansion of knowledge and skills essential for critical thinkers. It encompasses a variety of learning forms and sources, fostering adaptability, intellectual curiosity, and a comprehensive understanding of complex issues. By embracing lifelong learning, individuals not only enhance their critical thinking abilities but also prepare themselves to navigate an ever-evolving world effectively.

Strategies for Lifelong Learning:

Strategies for lifelong learning are pivotal in the ongoing journey of becoming a critical thinker. Lifelong learning transcends traditional education, encompassing a continuous commitment to acquire, refine, and apply knowledge throughout one's life. Effective strategies help individuals to engage actively in this process, ensuring that their critical thinking skills remain sharp and relevant.

1. **Setting Learning Goals**:

- Establish clear, attainable goals for your learning journey. These goals should be specific, measurable, achievable, relevant, and time-bound (Doran, 1981).

- Goals could range from learning a new skill, keeping abreast of developments in a specific field, or deepening understanding of a particular subject (Locke & Latham, 2002).

2. **Engaging in Reflective Practice**:

- Reflective practice involves regularly evaluating one's experiences and the knowledge gained from them. This helps in understanding how learning impacts thinking and behavior (Schön, 1983).

- Keeping a learning journal can be an effective way of facilitating this reflective practice (Moon, 1999).

3. **Seeking Diverse Sources of Information**:

- Diversify the sources of your information. This includes reading books, academic journals, attending workshops, seminars, and conferences, and engaging with online courses and webinars (Kolb, 1984).

- Engaging with a variety of perspectives encourages critical thinking and helps prevent the formation of echo chambers (Sunstein, 2007).

4. **Applying Knowledge Practically**:

- Apply the knowledge gained in practical settings. This could involve volunteering, working on new projects, or experimenting with new ideas in your professional or personal life (Billett, 1996).

- Practical application helps in consolidating learning and understanding its real-world implications (Eraut, 2000).

5. **Building a Learning Network**:

- Create or join learning communities, such as study groups, professional associations, or online forums. These networks provide support, resources, and diverse perspectives (Wenger, 1998).

- Peer discussions and collaborations can enhance understanding and provide different viewpoints on various topics (Johnson & Johnson, 1999).

6. **Embracing Technology**:

- Utilize technology for learning. This includes educational apps, online databases, e-books, and virtual reality experiences (Siemens, 2005).

- Online platforms can offer flexibility and access to a plethora of resources and learning communities (Anderson, 2008).

7. **Continual Self-Assessment**:

- Regularly assess your learning progress and adjust your strategies as needed. Self-assessment tools and feedback from others can provide insights into areas of improvement (Boud, 1995).

Adopting effective strategies for lifelong learning is crucial in the continuous development of critical thinking skills. These strategies include setting learning goals, engaging in reflective practice, diversifying information sources, applying knowledge practically, building learning networks, embracing technology, and regularly assessing one's progress. By implementing these strategies, individuals can ensure that their journey in lifelong learning and critical thinking is dynamic, informed, and responsive to the evolving demands of the personal, professional, and societal spheres.

Challenges in Lifelong Learning:

Engaging in lifelong learning is an integral part of becoming a critical thinker, but it is not without its challenges. Recognizing and understanding these challenges is crucial for individuals who are committed to continuous learning and personal development. Addressing these hurdles effectively can enhance one's ability to maintain and grow their critical thinking skills over time.

1. **Maintaining Motivation**:

- One of the primary challenges in lifelong learning is sustaining motivation, especially in a self-directed learning environment. Without the structured environment of formal education, individuals may struggle with maintaining the discipline required for continuous learning (Knowles, Holton III, & Swanson, 2005).

- Strategies like setting specific goals, establishing a routine, and joining learning communities can help maintain motivation (Locke & Latham, 2002).

2. **Information Overload**:

- The vast availability of information, especially online, can lead to information overload, making it challenging to discern what is relevant or credible (Eppler & Mengis, 2004).

- Developing critical literacy skills, such as evaluating sources and prioritizing information, is essential to navigate this challenge (Hobbs, 2011).

3. **Balancing Learning with Other Responsibilities**:

- Balancing the demands of lifelong learning with work, family, and other responsibilities is a significant challenge. Time management becomes a crucial skill in juggling these various aspects of life (Covey, 1989).

- Creating a structured yet flexible learning schedule can aid in managing this balance effectively (Macan, Shahani, Dipboye, & Phillips, 1990).

4. **Keeping Up with Rapid Technological Changes**:

- The rapid pace of technological advancement can make it difficult to stay updated with the latest developments and learning tools (Siemens, 2005).

- Continuous engagement with technological advancements and willingness to learn and adapt to new tools are necessary to overcome this challenge.

5. **Overcoming Educational Barriers**:

- Financial constraints, limited access to resources, and geographical barriers can impede the pursuit of lifelong learning (Cross, 1981).

- Online courses, open educational resources, and community-based learning opportunities can help mitigate these barriers (Khan, 2012).

6. **Dealing with Age-Related Challenges**:

- For older learners, there can be additional challenges such as age-related cognitive changes and societal stereotypes about learning in later life (Illeris, 2002).

- Strategies such as engaging in mentally stimulating activities and leveraging the rich experiences of older learners can help address these challenges (Schooler, 1984).

While lifelong learning is essential for continual development as a critical thinker, it presents several challenges, including maintaining motivation, managing information overload, balancing responsibilities, keeping up with technology, overcoming educational barriers, and dealing with age-related issues. Recognizing and strategically addressing these challenges is key to successful lifelong learning and the ongoing development of critical thinking skills.

Critical Thinking and Lifelong Learning:

The relationship between critical thinking and lifelong learning is integral to the continuous development and application of higher-order cognitive skills. Lifelong learning, defined as the ongoing, voluntary, and self-directed pursuit of knowledge, plays a crucial role in fostering and sustaining critical thinking abilities. This relationship is rooted in the idea that the constant acquisition and application of knowledge encourages a dynamic, reflective, and analytical approach to understanding and interacting with the world.

1. **Mutual Reinforcement of Critical Thinking and Lifelong Learning**:

- Critical thinking and lifelong learning are mutually reinforcing concepts. The skills gained through lifelong learning enhance critical thinking, while effective critical thinking skills facilitate deeper and more meaningful learning experiences (Facione, 1990).

- Lifelong learning provides the knowledge base and context necessary for critical thinking, and critical thinking, in turn, enables learners to assess, integrate, and apply this knowledge effectively (Paul & Elder, 2006).

2. **Adaptability and Flexibility in Thinking**:

- Lifelong learning contributes to adaptability and flexibility in thinking. As individuals encounter new information and experiences, critical thinking skills are required to evaluate and integrate this information effectively (Mezirow, 1997).

- This adaptability is crucial in a rapidly changing world, where individuals must continually reassess and update their understanding of new developments and challenges (Siemens, 2005).

3. **Enhancing Problem-Solving and Decision-Making Skills**:

- Lifelong learning equips individuals with a diverse range of knowledge and perspectives, enhancing their ability to approach problems and make decisions in nuanced and informed ways (Halpern, 2003).

- Critical thinking skills are essential in applying this knowledge to real-world situations, enabling individuals to analyze complex problems, identify solutions, and make well-reasoned decisions (Glaser, 1941).

4. **Cultivating Intellectual Curiosity and Openness**:

- A key component of lifelong learning is intellectual curiosity – a desire to explore new ideas and understand different perspectives. Critical thinking complements this curiosity by providing the tools to question, analyze, and critically assess new information (Dewey, 1933).

- Lifelong learning fosters an openness to new experiences and ideas, and critical thinking ensures that this openness does not lead to uncritical acceptance of information (Brookfield, 1987).

5. **Continuous Personal and Professional Development**:

- Engaging in lifelong learning and critical thinking contributes to continuous personal and professional development. It encourages individuals to reflect on their beliefs, challenge their assumptions, and grow intellectually (Schön, 1983).

- In professional contexts, these skills enhance one's ability to adapt to new roles, technologies, and industry developments (Eraut, 2000).

The synergy between critical thinking and lifelong learning is essential for personal and professional growth. Lifelong learning provides the content and context for critical thinking, while critical thinking offers the analytical framework for effective learning. Together, they create a dynamic cycle of growth, adaptation, and reflective understanding, enabling individuals to navigate an increasingly complex and information-rich world.

Lifelong learning is integral to the development and sustenance of critical thinking skills. It requires a commitment to continuous education, reflective practice, and the openness to constantly challenge and expand one's knowledge and beliefs. Lifelong learning not only enriches personal and professional life but also fosters a critical mindset essential for navigating the complexities of the modern world. By embracing lifelong learning, individuals can maintain cognitive agility, adaptability, and a deeper understanding of the ever-evolving global landscape.

Resources and Further Reading:
Continuing your journey in becoming a critical thinker can be greatly enhanced by utilizing a variety of resources and engaging in further reading. These resources provide deeper insights into critical thinking theories, strategies, and applications, offering continuous learning opportunities for those committed to developing their critical thinking skills.

1. **Books on Critical Thinking:**

- **"Thinking, Fast and Slow" by Daniel Kahneman (2011)**: This book explores the dichotomy between two modes of thought: "fast, instinctive and emotional" versus "slower, more deliberative, and more logical" and provides insights into how these modes influence our decision-making (Kahneman, 2011).

- **"Critical Thinking: A Concise Guide" by Tracy Bowell and Gary Kemp (2015)**: A guide that provides the essential tools for readers to become critical thinkers. It covers the basics of argumentation and critical reasoning (Bowell & Kemp, 2015).

2. **Online Courses and Workshops:**

- Various online platforms like Coursera, Udemy, and Khan Academy offer courses on critical thinking. These courses cover topics like logical reasoning, argument analysis, and cognitive biases.

- Workshops and webinars conducted by educational institutions or professional organizations often provide interactive opportunities to practice and refine critical thinking skills.

3. **Academic Journals and Articles**:

- Journals such as "Critical Thinking and Learning" and "Informal Logic" publish peer-reviewed articles on various aspects of critical thinking.

- Research articles can offer in-depth analyses of specific critical thinking topics, methodologies, and case studies.

4. **Educational Podcasts and Videos**:

- Podcasts like "The Critical Thinker" and YouTube channels dedicated to logic and reasoning can provide accessible ways to explore critical thinking concepts.

- TED Talks also feature a range of speakers discussing topics related to critical thinking and decision-making.

5. **Critical Thinking Tools and Apps**:

- Tools like the "Critical Thinking Wheel" and apps such as "Think Critically" offer practical ways to apply critical thinking skills in everyday scenarios.

- These tools can provide quick references and reminders to engage in critical thinking processes.

6. **Professional Organizations**:

- Organizations such as The Foundation for Critical Thinking and The Critical Thinking Community offer resources, conferences, and seminars for those interested in deepening their understanding of critical thinking.

A wide array of resources and further reading options are available for those seeking to enhance their critical thinking skills. These resources offer varied approaches to learning and understanding critical thinking, from academic literature to interactive tools and courses. Engaging with these resources can provide ongoing support and development for individuals at any stage of their journey in becoming proficient critical thinkers.

Developing a Personal Critical Thinking Plan:

Developing a personal critical thinking plan is an essential step in continuing your journey as a critical thinker. This plan involves setting clear goals, identifying strategies, and determining resources to enhance your critical thinking skills. A structured approach helps in tracking progress and maintaining focus on this ongoing developmental journey.

1. **Setting Goals for Critical Thinking**:

- The first step is to define clear, specific goals related to critical thinking. Goals could range from improving argumentation skills to enhancing decision-making or problem-solving abilities (Zimmerman, 2002).

- These goals should be SMART (Specific, Measurable, Achievable, Relevant, and Time-bound) to ensure they are effective and achievable (Doran, 1981).

2. **Self-Assessment of Current Skills**:

- Conducting a self-assessment helps in identifying current strengths and areas needing improvement in critical thinking (Facione, 1990). This could involve reflecting on past decisions, problem-solving instances, or discussions.

- Tools like critical thinking tests or reflective journals can be useful in this self-assessment process (Moon, 1999).

3. **Strategies for Skill Development**:

- Based on the self-assessment, develop strategies that target specific areas for improvement. For example, if improving analytical skills is a goal, strategies could include studying logical fallacies or practicing data analysis (Halpern, 2003).

- Incorporating diverse methods such as reading, workshops, courses, and practical exercises can cater to different learning styles and enhance skill development (Kolb, 1984).

4. **Allocating Resources and Time**:

- Allocate specific resources, such as books, courses, or mentorship opportunities, that can support your critical thinking development.

- Time management is crucial; setting aside dedicated time for practicing and learning new critical thinking skills is essential (Covey, 1989).

5. **Monitoring Progress and Reflecting**:

- Regularly monitor your progress towards your critical thinking goals. This could involve periodic self-assessments or seeking feedback from others (Drucker, 1954).

- Reflect on what strategies are working or not and adjust your plan accordingly. Reflective practice is key to continual improvement in critical thinking (Schön, 1983).

6. **Challenges and Adaptability**:

- Be prepared to encounter challenges, such as difficulty in changing ingrained thinking patterns or balancing time. Adaptability and resilience are important in overcoming these challenges (Dweck, 2006).

Developing a personal critical thinking plan is a strategic approach to enhancing one's critical thinking abilities. It involves setting specific goals, assessing current skills, strategizing for improvement, allocating resources, and regularly monitoring progress. This structured approach, combined with adaptability and reflective practice, ensures continual growth and development in the journey of becoming a proficient critical thinker.

In conclusion, the journey to becoming a critical thinker is a continuous and dynamic process that involves lifelong learning, reflective practice, and openness to diverse perspectives. It requires the application of critical thinking skills in various aspects of life and the cultivation of intellectual humility. By engaging in these practices and overcoming inherent challenges, individuals can maintain and enhance their critical thinking abilities throughout their lives, making more informed, reflective, and reasoned decisions.

Appendix

Exercises and Case Studies:

Creating an appendix with exercises and case studies in a guide on "How to Become a Critical Thinker" is an excellent way to reinforce learning and provide practical application of the concepts discussed. This approach allows readers to engage actively with the material, test their understanding, and apply critical thinking skills in varied contexts.

1. **Foundations of Critical Thinking**:

    - **Exercises**: Include activities like identifying logical fallacies in arguments, distinguishing between facts and opinions, or analyzing the structure of a well-constructed argument.

    - **Case Studies**: Present scenarios or historical cases that demonstrate effective or flawed critical thinking. For example, a case study on a scientific discovery or a historical decision-making process.

2. **Logical Reasoning**:

    - **Exercises**: Tasks could involve solving logical puzzles, constructing syllogisms, or identifying assumptions in arguments.

    - **Case Studies**: Analyze real-life examples where logical reasoning was pivotal, such as in legal cases or scientific research breakthroughs.

3. **Argumentation and Persuasion**:

    - **Exercises**: Develop exercises where readers must create their own persuasive arguments on given topics or critically analyze persuasive speeches or writings.

    - **Case Studies**: Include analyses of famous speeches, marketing campaigns, or political debates, highlighting the use of rhetorical strategies and argumentative techniques.

4. **Chapter on Emotional Intelligence and Critical Thinking**:

   - **Exercises**: Activities to recognize emotional influences in decision-making, such as reflecting on past decisions influenced by emotions or role-playing scenarios.

   - **Case Studies**: Present situations from business, politics, or personal relationships where emotional intelligence significantly impacted the outcomes.

5. **Critical Thinking in the Digital Age**:

   - **Exercises**: Include tasks like evaluating the credibility of online sources, identifying biases in media, or navigating misinformation.

   - **Case Studies**: Analyze instances of digital misinformation campaigns or explore how digital media can both hinder and enhance critical thinking.

6. **Strategies for Effective Critical Thinking**:

   - **Exercises**: Activities that involve practicing different critical thinking strategies, like brainstorming, mind mapping, or conducting a root cause analysis on a problem.

   - **Case Studies**: Explore real-world problems, such as a business challenge or a public policy issue, where strategic thinking led to effective solutions.

7. **Critical Thinking in Everyday Life**:

   - **Exercises**: Tasks could include analyzing everyday decisions, practicing reflective journaling, or conducting self-assessments on personal biases.

   - **Case Studies**: Offer real-life examples where individuals applied critical thinking in personal decision-making, conflict resolution, or lifestyle changes.

Each exercise and case study should be closely aligned with the key learnings of this book. This alignment ensures that readers can apply theoretical knowledge in practical, real-world scenarios, thereby reinforcing their understanding and skills in critical thinking. Such hands-on engagement not only enhances comprehension but also prepares readers to apply critical thinking skills in various aspects of their personal and professional lives.

Glossary of Key Terms:

Creating a glossary of key terms in an appendix for a guide on "How to Become a Critical Thinker" is essential for readers to quickly reference and understand important concepts related to critical thinking. This glossary should include definitions of terms that are central to the subject, explained in a clear and concise manner.

1. **Analytical Thinking**:

   The process of logically breaking down a problem or issue into smaller parts to understand its structure and underlying principles.

2. **Argumentation**:

   The process of forming reasons, drawing conclusions, and applying them to a case in discussion; the rationale and logical reasoning behind an argument.

3. **Cognitive Bias**:

   A systematic error in thinking that affects the decisions and judgments that people make, often leading to perceptual distortion, inaccurate judgment, or illogical interpretation.

4. **Critical Thinking**:

   The intellectually disciplined process of actively and skillfully conceptualizing, applying, analyzing, synthesizing, and evaluating information gathered from observation, experience, reflection, reasoning, or communication.

5. **Deductive Reasoning**:

   A logical process in which a conclusion is based on the concordance of multiple premises that are generally assumed to be true.

6. **Emotional Intelligence**:

   The ability to recognize, understand, and manage our own emotions and to recognize, understand, and influence the emotions of others.

7. **Fallacy**:

   An erroneous argument dependent upon an unsound or illogical contention.

8. **Heuristics**:

   Mental shortcuts or rules of thumb that simplify decision making; often useful, but sometimes leading to inaccurate judgments or cognitive biases.

9. **Inductive Reasoning**:

   A logical process in which multiple premises, all believed true or found true most of the time, are combined to obtain a specific conclusion.

10. **Intellectual Humility**:

    The recognition that one's knowledge and understanding are limited and fallible, and being open to new ideas, evidence, and viewpoints.

11. **Logical Fallacies**:

    Flaws in reasoning that undermine the logical validity of an argument, often through irrelevant, misleading, or oversimplified information.

12. **Metacognition**:

    Awareness and understanding of one's own thought processes; thinking about one's thinking.

13. **Socratic Questioning**:

    A method of questioning designed to stimulate critical thinking and to draw out ideas and underlying presuppositions.

14. **Systematic Thinking**:

    An approach to problem-solving that uses a step-by-step, logical process to analyze a complex situation or issue.

15. **Reflective Practice**:

    The act of routinely analyzing and reflecting on one's thoughts and actions for the purpose of learning and improving.

This glossary serves as a quick reference tool for readers, aiding their comprehension of essential terms related to critical thinking. By familiarizing themselves with these terms, readers can better understand the concepts discussed throughout the guide and apply them more effectively in their journey to become critical thinkers. The glossary should be comprehensive yet concise, providing clear definitions that enhance the reader's understanding and application of critical thinking skills.

References

- Abrami, P. C., Bernard, R. M., Borokhovski, E., Waddington, D. I., Wade, C. A., & Persson, T. (2008). Instructional interventions affecting critical thinking skills and dispositions: A stage 1 meta-analysis. *Review of Educational Research, 78*(4), 1102-1134.

- Allcott, H., & Gentzkow, M. (2017). Social Media and Fake News in the 2016 Election. *Journal of Economic Perspectives*, 31(2), 211-236.

- Allison, H. E. (2004). Kant's Transcendental Idealism: An Interpretation and Defense. *Yale University Press.*

- Anderson, L. W., & Krathwohl, D. R. (Eds.). (2001). A taxonomy for learning, teaching, and assessing: A revision of Bloom's Taxonomy of Educational Objectives. *Longman.*

- Anderson, T. (2008). *The Theory and Practice of Online Learning.* Athabasca University Press.

- Antonio, A. L., Chang, M. J., Hakuta, K., Kenny, D. A., Levin, S., & Milem, J. F. (2004). Effects of Racial Diversity on Complex Thinking in College Students. *Psychological Science*, 15(8), 507-510.

- Argyris, C. (1991). Teaching Smart People How to Learn. *Harvard Business Review*, 69(3), 99-109.

- Argyris, C., & Schön, D. A. (1978). *Organizational Learning: A Theory of Action Perspective.* Addison-Wesley.

- Aristotle. (1991). *On Rhetoric: A Theory of Civic Discourse.* (G. A. Kennedy, Trans.). Oxford University Press. (Original work published 350 B.C.E)

- Arum, R., & Roksa, J. (2011). *Academically Adrift: Limited Learning on College Campuses.* University of Chicago Press.

- Association of College & Research Libraries. (2016). *Framework for Information Literacy for Higher Education.*

- Bailin, S., Case, R., Coombs, J. R., & Daniels, L. B. (1999). Conceptualizing critical thinking. *Journal of Curriculum Studies, 31*(3), 285-302.

- Bain, K. (2004). *What the Best College Teachers Do*. Harvard University Press.

- Bakshy, E., Messing, S., & Adamic, L. A. (2015). Exposure to ideologically diverse news and opinion on Facebook. *Science*, 348(6239), 1130-1132.

- Banaji, M. R., & Greenwald, A. G. (2013). *Blindspot: Hidden Biases of Good People*. Delacorte Press.

- Barkley, E. F., & Major, C. H. (2014). *Learning Assessment Techniques: A Handbook for College Faculty*. Jossey-Bass.

- Barnes, J. (1995). Aristotle: A very short introduction. *Oxford University Press*.

- Baron, J. (1993). Why Teach Thinking? - An Essay. *Applied Psychology: An International Review, 42*(3), 191-237.

- Baron, J. (2000). *Thinking and Deciding* (3rd ed.). Cambridge University Press.

- Bar-On, R. (2006). *The Bar-On Model of Emotional-Social Intelligence (ESI)*. Psicothema, 18, supl., 13-25.

- Bawden, D., & Robinson, L. (2009). The dark side of information: overload, anxiety and other paradoxes and pathologies. *Journal of Information Science*, 35(2), 180-191.

- Bean, J. C. (2011). *Engaging Ideas: The Professor's Guide to Integrating Writing, Critical Thinking, and Active Learning in the Classroom*. Jossey-Bass.

- Bell, A. H., & Tang, N. K. H. (1998). The effectiveness of commercial Internet Web sites: a user's perspective. *Internet Research*, 8(3), 219-228.

- Bell, W. (2003). *Foundations of Futures Studies: Human Science for a New Era*. Transaction Publishers.

- Billett, S. (1996). Situated Learning: Bridging Sociocultural and Cognitive Theorizing. *Learning and Instruction*, 6(3), 263-280.

- Binkley, M., Erstad, O., Herman, J., Raizen, S., Ripley, M., Miller-Ricci, M., & Rumble, M. (2012). Defining twenty-first century skills. In P. Griffin, B. McGaw, & E. Care (Eds.), *Assessment and Teaching of 21st Century Skills* (pp. 17-66). Springer.

- Bitzer, L. F. (1968). The Rhetorical Situation. *Philosophy & Rhetoric, 1*(1), 1-14.

- Bloom, B. S. (1956). *Taxonomy of Educational Objectives, Handbook I: The Cognitive Domain*. David McKay Co Inc.

- Bloom, B. S., Engelhart, M. D., Furst, E. J., Hill, W. H., & Krathwohl, D. R. (1956). Taxonomy of educational objectives: The classification of educational goals. Handbook I: Cognitive domain. *David McKay Company Inc.*

- Bok, D. (2006). *Our Underachieving Colleges: A Candid Look at How Much Students Learn and Why They Should Be Learning More.* Princeton University Press.

- Bok, S. (1978). *Lying: Moral Choice in Public and Private Life.* Pantheon Books.

- Booth, W. C., Colomb, G. G., & Williams, J. M. (2008). *The Craft of Research* (3rd ed.). University of Chicago Press.

- Boud, D. (1995). *Assessment and Learning: Contradictory or Complementary?* In P. Knight (Ed.), *Assessment for Learning in Higher Education* (pp. 35-48). Kogan Page.

- Boud, D., Keogh, R., & Walker, D. (1985). *Reflection: Turning Experience into Learning.* Kogan Page.

- Bowell, T., & Kemp, G. (2015). *Critical Thinking: A Concise Guide.* Routledge.

- Boyd, D. (2014). *It's Complicated: The Social Lives of Networked Teens.* Yale University Press.

- Boyd, D. R., & Fales, A. W. (1983). Reflective Learning: Key to Learning from Experience. *Journal of Humanistic Psychology*, 23(2), 99-117.

- Brackett, M. A., & Salovey, P. (2006). Measuring Emotional Intelligence with the Mayer-Salovery-Caruso Emotional Intelligence Test (MSCEIT). *Psicothema*, 18, 34-41.

- Bråten, I., Strømsø, H. I., & Salmerón, L. (2011). Trust and mistrust when students read multiple information sources about climate change. *Computers in Human Behavior, 27*(3), 971-980.

- Brickhouse, T. C., & Smith, N. D. (1994). Plato's Socrates. *Oxford University Press.*

- Bridgstock, R. (2009). The Graduate Attributes We've Overlooked: Enhancing Graduate Employability through Career Management Skills. *Higher Education Research & Development*, 28(1), 31-44.

- Brookfield, S. D. (1987). *Developing Critical Thinkers: Challenging Adults to Explore Alternative Ways of Thinking and Acting*. Jossey-Bass.

- Brookfield, S. D. (1998). *Critically Reflective Practice*. The Journal of Continuing Education in the Health Professions, 18(4), 197-205.

- Brookfield, S. D. (2012). *Teaching for Critical Thinking: Tools and Techniques to Help Students Question Their Assumptions*. Jossey-Bass.

- Brookfield, S. D., & Preskill, S. (2016). *The Discussion Book: 50 Great Ways to Get People Talking*. Jossey-Bass.

- Broughton, J. (2002). Descartes's Method of Doubt. *Princeton University Press.*

- Brown, J. S., & Duguid, P. (2001). Knowledge and Organization: A Social-Practice Perspective. *Organization Science*, 12(2), 198-213.

- Browne, M. N., & Keeley, S. M. (2007). *Asking the Right Questions: A Guide to Critical Thinking*. Pearson Prentice Hall.

- Brundidge, J. (2010). Encountering "difference" in the contemporary public sphere: The contribution of the internet to the heterogeneity of political discussion networks. *Journal of Communication*, 60(4), 680-700.

- Bryman, A. (2016). *Social Research Methods* (5th ed.). Oxford University Press.

- Burt, R. S. (2004). Structural Holes and Good Ideas. *American Journal of Sociology*, 110(2), 349-399.

- Candy, P. C. (1991). *Self-Direction for Lifelong Learning*. Jossey-Bass.

- Chevalier, J. A., & Mayzlin, D. (2006). The Effect of Word of Mouth on Sales: Online Book Reviews. *Journal of Marketing Research*, 43(3), 345-354.

- Chi, M. T. H., De Leeuw, N., Chiu, M. H., & LaVancher, C. (1994). Eliciting self-explanations improves understanding. *Cognitive Science*, 18(3), 439-477.

- Cialdini, R. B. (2001). *Influence: Science and Practice*. Allyn & Bacon.

- Clarke, D. M. (2006). Descartes: A Biography. *Cambridge University Press.*

- Colby, A., & Sullivan, W. M. (2008). *Formation of Scholarship and the Advancement of the Purposes of Higher Education*. Wiley.

- Cooper, J. M. (Ed.). (1997). Plato: Complete works. *Hackett Publishing Company.*

- Copi, I. M., Cohen, C., & McMahon, K. (2016). Introduction to Logic. *Routledge.*

- Cottingham, J. (1992). The Cambridge Companion to Descartes. *Cambridge University Press.*

- Cotton, D. R. E. (1988). The Diverse Perspectives Problem. *Journal of Geography in Higher Education*, 12(2), 168-177.

- Cottrell, S. (2005). Critical thinking skills: Developing effective analysis and argument. *Palgrave Macmillan.*

- Covey, S. R. (1989). *The 7 Habits of Highly Effective People*. Free Press.

- Creswell, J. W. (2014). *Research Design: Qualitative, Quantitative, and Mixed Methods Approaches* (4th ed.). SAGE Publications.

- Cropley, A. J. (2006). In praise of convergent thinking. *Creativity Research Journal, 18*(3), 391-404.

- Cross, K. P. (1981). Adults as Learners: Increasing Participation and Facilitating Learning. Jossey-Bass.

- Daly, J. A. (2013). Advocacy: Championing Ideas and Influencing Others. Yale University Press.

- Damasio, A. R. (1994). *Descartes' Error: Emotion, Reason, and the Human Brain*. Putnam.

- Damer, T. E. (2009). *Attacking Faulty Reasoning: A Practical Guide to Fallacy-Free Arguments*. Wadsworth Cengage Learning.

- de Bono, E. (1970). *Lateral Thinking: Creativity Step by Step*. Harper & Row.

- de Bono, E. (1992). *Serious Creativity: Using the Power of Lateral Thinking to Create New Ideas*. HarperBusiness.

- De Janasz, S. C., Dowd, K. O., & Schneider, B. Z. (2002). *Interpersonal Skills in Organizations*. McGraw-Hill/Irwin.

- Deci, E. L., & Ryan, R. M. (1985). *Intrinsic Motivation and Self-determination in Human Behavior*. Plenum.

- Delli Carpini, M. X., & Keeter, S. (1996). What Americans Know about Politics and Why It Matters. Yale University Press.

- Derks, D., Fischer, A. H., & Bos, A. E. (2008). The role of emotion in computer-mediated communication: A review. *Computers in Human Behavior*, 24(3), 766-785.

- D'Esposito, M., Postle, B. R., & Rypma, B. (2000). Prefrontal cortical contributions to working memory: Evidence from event-related fMRI studies. *Experimental Brain Research, 133*(1), 3-11.

- Dewey, J. (1916). Democracy and education. *Macmillan.*

- Dewey, J. (1933). How we think: A restatement of the relation of reflective thinking to the educative process. *D. C. Heath and Company.*

- Dewey, J. (1938). Experience and Education. *Kappa Delta Pi.*

- Dillon, J. T. (1988). Questioning and Teaching: A Manual of Practice. Teachers College Press.

- Dillon, J. T. (1988). The remedial status of student questioning. *Journal of Curriculum Studies*, 20(3), 197-210.

- Doran, G. T. (1981). There's a S.M.A.R.T. way to write management's goals and objectives. *Management Review*, 70(11), 35-36.

- Draganski, B., Gaser, C., Busch, V., Schuierer, G., Bogdahn, U., & May, A. (2006). Neuroplasticity: Changes in grey matter induced by training. *Nature, 427*, 311-312.

- Drucker, P. F. (1954). *The Practice of Management*. Harper & Row.

- Drumwright, M. E., & Murphy, P. E. (2009). The Current State of Advertising Ethics: Industry and Academic Perspectives. *Journal of Advertising*, 38(1), 83-107.

- Durant, W. (1926). The story of philosophy. *Simon and Schuster.*

- Dweck, C. S. (2006). *Mindset: The New Psychology of Success*. Random House.

- Edmunds, A., & Morris, A. (2000). The problem of information overload in business organisations: a review of the literature. *International Journal of Information Management*, 20(1), 17-28.

- Eichenbaum, H. (2017). Memory: Organization and Control. *Annual Review of Psychology, 68*, 19-45.

- Ennis, R. H. (1987). A taxonomy of critical thinking dispositions and abilities. In J. B. Baron & R. J. Sternberg (Eds.), *Teaching thinking skills: Theory and practice* (pp. 9-26). Freeman.

- Ennis, R. H. (1996). Critical thinking. Prentice Hall.

- Ennis, R. H. (2011). The nature of critical thinking: An outline of critical thinking dispositions and abilities. *University of Illinois.*

- Eppler, M. J., & Mengis, J. (2004). The Concept of Information Overload: A Review of Literature from Organization Science, Accounting, Marketing, MIS, and Related Disciplines. *The Information Society*, 20(5), 325-344.

- Eraut, M. (2000). Non-formal Learning and Tacit Knowledge in Professional Work. *British Journal of Educational Psychology*, 70(1), 113-136.

- Facione, P. A. (1990). Critical thinking: A statement of expert consensus for purposes of educational assessment and instruction. *The Delphi Report*. ERIC Document Reproduction Service No. ED315423.

- Facione, P. A. (2000). The Disposition Toward Critical Thinking: Its Character, Measurement, and Relationship to Critical Thinking Skill. *Informal Logic, 20*(1), 61-84.

- Facione, P. A. (2015). *Critical Thinking: What It Is and Why It Counts*. Measured Reasons LLC.

- Festinger, L. (1957). *A Theory of Cognitive Dissonance*. Stanford University Press.

- Field, A. (2013). *Discovering Statistics Using IBM SPSS Statistics*. SAGE Publications.

- Field, J. (2000). *Lifelong Learning and the New Educational Order*. Trentham Books.

- Field, J. (2009). *Well-being and Happiness: A New Challenge for Adult Education*. The Adult Learner, 2009.

- Figley, C. R. (1995). Compassion fatigue as secondary traumatic stress disorder: An overview. In C. R. Figley (Ed.), *Compassion Fatigue: Coping With Secondary Traumatic Stress Disorder In Those Who Treat The Traumatized* (pp. 1-20). Brunner/Mazel.

- Fine, G. (1993). On Ideas: Aristotle's criticism of Plato's Theory of Forms. *Clarendon Press.*

- Fischer, G. (2005). Distances and Diversity: Sources for Social Creativity. *Creativity and Cognition*, 5(3), 128-136.

- Fisher, A. (2001). *Critical Thinking: An Introduction*. Cambridge University Press.

- Flanagan, J. C. (1954). The critical incident technique. *Psychological Bulletin*, 51(4), 327-358.

- Flavell, J. H. (1979). Metacognition and cognitive monitoring: A new area of cognitive-developmental inquiry. *American Psychologist, 34*(10), 906-911.

- Florida, R. (2002). *The Rise of the Creative Class*. Basic Books.

- Fook, J., & Gardner, F. (2007). *Practising Critical Reflection*. Open University Press.

- Freire, P. (1970). *Pedagogy of the Oppressed*. Continuum.

- Friedel, C. R. (2005). Lateral Thinking in Creativity: A Review of the Literature. *Triz Journal*.

- Galinsky, A. D., & Moskowitz, G. B. (2000). Perspective-taking: decreasing stereotype expression, stereotype accessibility, and in-group favoritism. *Journal of Personality and Social Psychology*, 78(4), 708.

- Gallo, C. (2014). *Talk Like TED: The 9 Public-Speaking Secrets of the World's Top Minds*. St. Martin's Press.

- Galston, W. A. (2001). Political Knowledge, Political Engagement, and Civic Education. *Annual Review of Political Science*, 4, 217-234.

- Gardner, H. (2007). *Five Minds for the Future*. Harvard Business Press.

- Garside, C. (1996). Look Who's Talking: A Comparison of Lecture and Group Discussion Teaching Strategies in Developing Critical Thinking Skills. *Communication Education*, 45(3), 212-227.

- Garver, E. (1994). *Aristotle's Rhetoric: An Art of Character*. University of Chicago Press.

- Gay, G. (2010). *Culturally Responsive Teaching: Theory, Research, and Practice*. Teachers College Press.

- Gibbs, G. (1988). *Learning by Doing: A Guide to Teaching and Learning Methods*. Further Education Unit.

- Gilovich, T., Griffin, D., & Kahneman, D. (Eds.). (2002). *Heuristics and Biases: The Psychology of Intuitive Judgment*. Cambridge University Press.

- Gilroy, M. (2008). *The Theory and Practice of Teaching*. Routledge.

- Gilster, P. (1997). *Digital Literacy*. Wiley Computer Publishing.

- Giroux, H. A. (1989). *Schooling for Democracy: Critical Pedagogy in the Modern Age*. Routledge.

- Glaser, E. M. (1941). *An Experiment in the Development of Critical Thinking*. Teachers College, Columbia University.

- Godet, M. (2000). *The Art of Scenarios and Strategic Planning: Tools and Pitfalls*. Technological Forecasting and Social Change, 65(1), 3-22.

- Goel, V. (2007). Anatomy of deductive reasoning. *Trends in Cognitive Sciences, 11*(10), 435-441.

- Goleman, D. (1995). *Emotional Intelligence: Why It Can Matter More Than IQ*. Bantam Books.

- Goleman, D. (1998). *Working with Emotional Intelligence*. Bantam Books.

- Goleman, D., Boyatzis, R., & McKee, A. (2002). *Primal Leadership: Realizing the Power of Emotional Intelligence*. Harvard Business School Press.

- Goleman, D., Boyatzis, R., & McKee, A. (2002). *Primal Leadership: Realizing the Power of Emotional Intelligence*. Harvard Business School Press.

- Goleman, D., Boyatzis, R., & McKee, A. (2002). *Primal Leadership: Realizing the Power of Emotional Intelligence*. Harvard Business School Press.

- Gorski, P. (2009). What We're Teaching Teachers: An Analysis of Multicultural Teacher Education Coursework Syllabi. *Teaching and Teacher Education*, 25(2), 309-318.

- Govier, T. (2010). *A Practical Study of Argument*. Wadsworth, Cengage Learning.

- Graff, G., & Birkenstein, C. (2010). *They Say / I Say: The Moves That Matter in Academic Writing*. W. W. Norton & Company.

- Granovetter, M. (1977). The Strength of Weak Ties. *American Journal of Sociology*, 78(6), 1360-1380.

- Gross, J. J. (2002). Emotion Regulation: Affective, Cognitive, and Social Consequences. *Psychophysiology*, 39(3), 281-291.

- Grube, G. M. A. (1993). Plato's Thought. *Hackett Publishing.*

- Guilford, J. P. (1956). The Structure of Intellect. *Psychological Bulletin*, 53(4), 267-293.

- Guilford, J. P. (1967). The Nature of Human Intelligence. *McGraw-Hill.*

- Gurin, P., Dey, E. L., Hurtado, S., & Gurin, G. (2002). Diversity and Higher Education: Theory and Impact on Educational Outcomes. *Harvard Educational Review*, 72(3), 330-366.

- Guyer, P. (Ed.). (2006). The Cambridge Companion to Kant and Modern Philosophy. *Cambridge University Press.*

- Halpern, D. F. (2003). *Thought and Knowledge: An Introduction to Critical Thinking* (4th ed.). Lawrence Erlbaum Associates.

- Halpern, D. F. (2014). Thought and knowledge: An introduction to critical thinking. *Psychology Press.*

- Hargittai, E., Fullerton, L., Menchen-Trevino, E., & Thomas, K. Y. (2010). Trust online: Young adults' evaluation of web content. *International Journal of Communication*, 4, 468-494.

- Hargittai, E., Fullerton, L., Menchen-Trevino, E., & Thomas, K. Y. (2010). Trust Online: Young Adults' Evaluation of Web Content. *International Journal of Communication*, 4, 468-494.

- Harris, J., & Mowen, J. C. (2004). *Consumer Behavior*. Prentice Hall.

- Harris, T. E., & Nelson, M. D. (2008). *Applied Organizational Communication: Theory and Practice in a Global Environment*. Lawrence Erlbaum Associates.

- Hart, C. (2018). *Doing a Literature Review: Releasing the Research Imagination*. SAGE Publications.

- Harvard Business Review. (2018). The Surprising Power of Questions. Retrieved from [website link].

- Hatfield, G. (2003). Routledge Philosophy Guidebook to Descartes and the Meditations. *Routledge.*

- Hess, D. E. (2009). Controversy in the Classroom: The Democratic Power of Discussion. Routledge.

- Hickman, L. A. (2009). John Dewey's Pragmatic Technology. *Indiana University Press.*

- Hirschberg, J. (2017). *Public Speaking and Influencing Men in Business.* ARC Manor.

- Hobbs, R. (2011). Digital and Media Literacy: Connecting Culture and Classroom. Corwin Press.

- Hodgin, E., & Kahne, J. (2018). Misinformation in the Information Age: What Teachers Can Do to Support Students. *Social Education,* 82(4), 208-211.

- Hoffman, M. L. (2000). Empathy and Moral Development: Implications for Caring and Justice. Cambridge University Press.

- Hofstein, A., & Lunetta, V. N. (2004). The laboratory in science education: Foundations for the twenty-first century. *Science Education,* 88(1), 28-54.

- Holland, J. H., Holyoak, K. J., Nisbett, R. E., & Thagard, P. R. (1986). *Induction: Processes of Inference, Learning, and Discovery.* MIT Press.

- Hughes, W. (2011). Critical thinking: An introduction to the basic skills. *Broadview Press.*

- Illeris, K. (2002). *The Three Dimensions of Learning.* Roskilde University Press.

- Jackson, P. W. (1992). *Handbook of Research on Curriculum: A Project of the American Educational Research Association.* Macmillan.

- Jacobs, H. H. (2010). *Curriculum 21: Essential Education for a Changing World.* ASCD.

- Janis, I. L. (1972). *Victims of Groupthink.* Houghton Mifflin.

- Jarvis, P. (2004). *Adult Education and Lifelong Learning: Theory and Practice*. Routledge.

- Jenkins, H., Clinton, K., Purushotma, R., Robison, A. J., & Weigel, M. (2006). *Confronting the Challenges of Participatory Culture: Media Education for the 21st Century*. The MIT Press.

- Johnson, D. W. (2001). The Value of Intellectual Conflict. *Peace and Conflict: Journal of Peace Psychology*, 7(1), 5-20.

- Johnson, D. W., & Johnson, F. P. (2005). *Joining Together: Group Theory and Group Skills*. Allyn & Bacon.

- Johnson, D. W., & Johnson, R. T. (1999). *Learning Together and Alone: Cooperative, Competitive, and Individualistic Learning* (5th ed.). Allyn and Bacon.

- Johnson, D. W., & Johnson, R. T. (2009). *An Educational Psychology Success Story: Social Interdependence Theory and Cooperative Learning*. Educational Researcher, 38(5), 365-379.

- Johnson, R. H., & Blair, J. A. (2006). *Logical Self-Defense*. IDEA.

- Johnson, R. T. (2009). *Making Cooperative Learning Work*. Theory Into Practice, 38(2), 67-73.

- Joinson, A. N. (2004). Understanding the Psychology of Internet Behaviour: Virtual Worlds, Real Lives. Palgrave Macmillan.

- Jonassen, D. H. (2000). Toward a Design Theory of Problem Solving. *Educational Technology Research and Development*, 48(4), 63-85.

- Kabat-Zinn, J. (1994). *Wherever You Go, There You Are: Mindfulness Meditation in Everyday Life*. Hyperion.

- Kahn, C. H. (1996). Plato and the Socratic dialogue: The philosophical use of a literary form. *Cambridge University Press*.

- Kahne, J., & Bowyer, B. (2017). Educating for democracy in a partisan age: Confronting the challenges of motivated reasoning and misinformation. *American Educational Research Journal*, 54(1), 3-34.

- Kahne, J., & Westheimer, J. (2006). The Limits of Political Efficacy: Educating Citizens for a Democratic Society. *PS: Political Science and Politics*, 39(2), 289-296.

- Kahneman, D. (2011). Thinking, Fast and Slow. *Farrar, Straus and Giroux*.

- Kahneman, D., & Tversky, A. (1979). Prospect Theory: An Analysis of Decision under Risk. *Econometrica*, 47(2), 263-292.

- Kant, I. (1781/1998). Critique of Pure Reason (P. Guyer & A. W. Wood, Trans.). *Cambridge University Press*. (Original work published 1781)

- Kashdan, T. B. (2009). *Curious? Discover the Missing Ingredient to a Fulfilling Life*. William Morrow.

- Kasser, T., & Kanner, A. D. (2004). *Psychology and Consumer Culture: The Struggle for a Good Life in a Materialistic World*. American Psychological Association.

- Kaufman, J. C., & Beghetto, R. A. (2009). Beyond Big and Little: The Four C Model of Creativity. *Review of General Psychology*, 13(1), 1-12.

- Kemerling, G. (2001). Descartes: The solitary self. In A. C. Grayling (Ed.), *Philosophy: A guide through the subject* (Vol. 2, pp. 160-194). Oxford University Press.

- Kennedy, R. (2007). In-Class Debates: Fertile Ground for Active Learning and the Cultivation of Critical Thinking and Oral Communication Skills. *International Journal of Teaching and Learning in Higher Education*, 19(2), 183-190.

- Kenny, A. (2008). A new history of Western philosophy. *Oxford University Press*.

- Kerlinger, F. N., & Lee, H. B. (2000). *Foundations of Behavioral Research*. Harcourt College Publishers.

- Khan, S. (2012). *The One World Schoolhouse: Education Reimagined*. Twelve.

- Kidder, R. M. (2009). *How Good People Make Tough Choices: Resolving the Dilemmas of Ethical Living*. Harper Perennial.

- Kidwell, B., Hardesty, D. M., Murtha, B. R., & Sheng, S. (2011). Emotional calibration effects on consumer choice. *Journal of Consumer Research*, 37(6), 1010-1022.

- King, P. M. (1995). Developing reflective judgment: Understanding and promoting intellectual growth and critical thinking in adolescents and adults. Jossey-Bass Publishers.

- King, P. M., & Kitchener, K. S. (1994). Developing Reflective Judgment. Jossey-Bass.

- Kirschner, P. A., & De Bruyckere, P. (2017). The myths of the digital native and the multitasker. *Teaching and Teacher Education*, 67, 135-142.

- Kitchener, K. S., & King, P. M. (1990). Reflective Judgment: Concepts of Justification and Their Relationship to Age and Education. *Journal of Applied Developmental Psychology, 11*(2), 179-208.

- Klapp, O. E. (1986). Overload and Boredom: Essays on the Quality of Life in the Information Society. Greenwood Press.

- Knowles, M. S., Holton III, E. F., & Swanson, R. A. (2005). *The Adult Learner: The Definitive Classic in Adult Education and Human Resource Development* (6th ed.). Elsevier.

- Koehler, M. J., & Mishra, P. (2009). What is technological pedagogical content knowledge (TPACK)? *Contemporary Issues in Technology and Teacher Education*, 9(1), 60-70.

- Kolb, D. A. (1984). *Experiential Learning: Experience as the Source of Learning and Development*. Prentice-Hall.

- Kouzes, J. M., & Posner, B. Z. (2012). *The Leadership Challenge: How to Make Extraordinary Things Happen in Organizations*. Jossey-Bass.

- Krumrei-Mancuso, E. J., & Rouse, S. V. (2016). The Development and Validation of the Comprehensive Intellectual Humility Scale. *Journal of Personality Assessment*, 98(2), 209-221.

- Ku, K. Y. L., & Ho, I. T. (2010). Dispositional factors predicting Chinese students' critical thinking performance. *Personality and Individual Differences, 48*(1), 54-58.

- Kuh, G. D. (2008). *High-Impact Educational Practices: What They Are, Who Has Access to Them, and Why They Matter*. Association of American Colleges and Universities.

- Kuhn, D. (1999). A developmental model of critical thinking. *Educational Researcher, 28*(2), 16-25.

- Lave, J., & Wenger, E. (1991). *Situated Learning: Legitimate Peripheral Participation*. Cambridge University Press.

- Lazarus, R. S. (1991). *Emotion and Adaptation*. Oxford University Press.

- Lazer, D. M. J., Baum, M. A., Benkler, Y., Berinsky, A. J., Greenhill, K. M., Menczer, F., ... & Zittrain, J. L. (2018). The science of fake news. *Science*, 359(6380), 1094-1096.

- Leary, M. R., Diebels, K. J., Davisson, E. K., Jongman-Sereno, K. P., Isherwood, J. C., Raimi, K. T., ... & Hoyle, R. H. (2017). Cognitive and interpersonal features of intellectual humility. *Personality and Social Psychology Bulletin*, 43(6), 793-813.

- Lewandowsky, S., Ecker, U. K., & Cook, J. (2017). Beyond Misinformation: Understanding and Coping with the "Post-Truth" Era. *Journal of Applied Research in Memory and Cognition*, 6(4), 353-369.

- Lilienfeld, S. O., Ammirati, R., & Landfield, K. (2009). Giving debiasing away: Can psychological research on correcting cognitive errors promote human welfare? *Perspectives on Psychological Science*, 4(4), 390-398.

- Lipman, M. (2003). Thinking in education. *Cambridge University Press.*

- Lloyd, G. E. R. (1996). Adversaries and Authorities: Investigations into Ancient Greek and Chinese Science. *Cambridge University Press.*

- Locke, E. A., & Latham, G. P. (2002). *Building a Practically Useful Theory of Goal Setting and Task Motivation*. American Psychologist, 57(9), 705-717.

- Loewenstein, G., & Lerner, J. S. (2003). The Role of Affect in Decision Making. In R. J. Davidson, H. Goldsmith, & K. R. Scherer (Eds.),

Handbook of Affective Sciences (pp. 619-642). Oxford University Press.

- London, M. (2002). *Leadership Development: Paths to Self-insight and Professional Growth*. Lawrence Erlbaum Associates.

- Longworth, N. (2003). *Lifelong Learning in Action: Transforming Education in the 21st Century*. Kogan Page.

- Lunsford, A. (2015). *Everyone's an Author*. W. W. Norton & Company.

- Lussier, R. N., & Achua, C. F. (2015). *Leadership: Theory, Application, & Skill Development*. Cengage Learning.

- Macan, T. H., Shahani, C., Dipboye, R. L., & Phillips, A. P. (1990). College Students' Time Management: Correlations with Academic Performance and Stress. *Journal of Educational Psychology*, 82(4), 760-768.

- Manktelow, K. I. (1999). *Reasoning and Thinking*. Psychology Press.

- Markie, P. (2004). Rationalism vs. empiricism. In E. N. Zalta (Ed.), *The Stanford Encyclopedia of Philosophy* (Fall 2004 Edition).

- Martin, A. (2008). Digital literacy and the "digital society". *Digital Literacies: Concepts, Policies and Practices*, 30, 151-176.

- Mayer, J. D., & Salovey, P. (1997). What is emotional intelligence? In P. Salovey & D. J. Sluyter (Eds.), *Emotional Development and Emotional Intelligence: Educational Implications* (pp. 3-31). Basic Books.

- Mayer, J. D., Caruso, D. R., & Salovey, P. (2016). *The Ability Model of Emotional Intelligence: Principles and Updates*. Emotion Review, 8(4), 290-300.

- Mayer, J. D., Roberts, R. D., & Barsade, S. G. (2008). Human Abilities: Emotional Intelligence. *Annual Review of Psychology*, 59, 507-536.

- Mayer, R. E. (1990). Problem solving. In B. F. Jones & L. Idol (Eds.), *Dimensions of Thinking and Cognitive Instruction*. Erlbaum.

- McComas, W. F., & Abraham, L. (2004). Asking more effective questions. *Rossier School of Education, USC*.

- McKeachie, W. J. (2013). McKeachie's teaching tips: Strategies, research, and theory for college and university teachers. *Cengage Learning.*

- McPeck, J. E. (1981). Critical thinking and education. *Martin Robertson.*

- Mehrabian, A. (1972). *Nonverbal Communication.* Aldine-Atherton.

- Merriam, S. B., & Bierema, L. L. (2014). *Adult Learning: Linking Theory and Practice.* Jossey-Bass.

- Metcalfe, J., & Shimamura, A. (Eds.). (1994). Metacognition: Knowing about knowing. *MIT Press.*

- Metzger, M. J. (2007). Making sense of credibility on the Web: Models for evaluating online information and recommendations for future research. *Journal of the American Society for Information Science and Technology,* 58(13), 2078-2091.

- Mezirow, J. (1997). Transformative learning: Theory to practice. *New Directions for Adult and Continuing Education,* 1997(74), 5-12.

- Miller, E. K., & Cohen, J. D. (2001). An integrative theory of prefrontal cortex function. *Annual Review of Neuroscience, 24,* 167-202.

- Mills, N. (1996). The Socratic Method: Teaching by asking instead of by telling. In G. J. Vlastos (Ed.), Socrates: Ironist and moral philosopher (pp. 179-192). *Cornell University Press.*

- Mittelstadt, B., Allo, P., Taddeo, M., Wachter, S., & Floridi, L. (2016). The ethics of algorithms: Mapping the debate. *Big Data & Society,* 3(2), 2053951716679679.

- Moon, J. A. (1999). *Reflection in Learning and Professional Development: Theory and Practice.* Kogan Page.

- Moor, J. H., & Bynum, T. W. (2002). Cyberphilosophy: The intersection of philosophy and computing. *Blackwell.*

- Moore, A. D., & Vitale, D. (2016). *The Online Library of Liberty.* Liberty Fund.

- Morreale, S. P., Osborn, M. M., & Pearson, J. C. (2000). *Why Communication is Important: A Rationale for the Centrality of the Study of Communication*. Journal of the Association for Communication Administration, 29, 1-25.

- Nemeth, C. (1986). Differential Contributions of Majority and Minority Influence. *Psychological Review*, 93(1), 23-32.

- Newell, W. H. (2001). A Theory of Interdisciplinary Studies. *Issues in Integrative Studies*, 19, 1-25.

- Nickerson, R. S. (1998). Confirmation Bias: A Ubiquitous Phenomenon in Many Guises. *Review of General Psychology*, 2(2), 175-220.

- Noddings, N. (2010). Moral education and critical thinking. *The Journal of Moral Education, 39*(3), 247-260.

- Nussbaum, M. C. (2010). Not for profit: Why democracy needs the humanities. *Princeton University Press*.

- Overholser, J. C. (1993). Elements of the Socratic method: III. Universal definitions. *Psychotherapy: Theory, Research, Practice, Training*, 30(1), 130-137.

- Pariser, E. (2011). The Filter Bubble: What the Internet Is Hiding from You. Penguin Books.

- Parker, W. C. (2003). *Teaching Democracy: Unity and Diversity in Public Life*. Teachers College Press.

- Parker, W. C., & Hess, D. (2001). Teaching with and for Discussion. *Teaching and Teacher Education*, 17(3), 273-289.

- Parker, W. C., & Ritson, M. (2005). Socratic seminars in high school: Texts and films that engage students in reflective thinking and close reading. *Seminar.net*, 1(1).

- Patchin, J. W., & Hinduja, S. (2012). Cyberbullying prevention and response: Expert perspectives. *Routledge*.

- Paul, R. (1990). Critical Thinking: What Every Person Needs to Survive in a Rapidly Changing World. *Center for Critical Thinking.*

- Paul, R. W. (1992). Critical thinking: What, why, and how. *New Directions for Community Colleges, 1992*(77), 3-24.

- Paul, R., & Elder, L. (1990). Critical Thinking: How to Prepare Students for a Rapidly Changing World. *Foundation for Critical Thinking.*

- Paul, R., & Elder, L. (2006). *Critical Thinking: The Nature of Critical and Creative Thought.* Journal of Developmental Education, 30(2), 34-35.

- Paul, R., & Elder, L. (2008). The Miniature Guide to Critical Thinking Concepts and Tools. *Foundation for Critical Thinking.*

- Peattie, K., & Charter, M. (2003). Green Marketing. In M. Baker (Ed.), *The Marketing Book* (5th ed., pp. 726-755). Butterworth-Heinemann.

- Perelman, C., & Olbrechts-Tyteca, L. (1969). *The New Rhetoric: A Treatise on Argumentation.* University of Notre Dame Press.

- Perelman, C., & Olbrechts-Tyteca, L. (1969). *The New Rhetoric: A Treatise on Argumentation.* University of Notre Dame Press.

- Perkins, D. N., Jay, E., & Tishman, S. (1993). Beyond abilities: A dispositional theory of thinking. *Merrill-Palmer Quarterly, 39*, 1-21.

- Pettigrew, T. F., & Tropp, L. R. (2006). A Meta-Analytic Test of Intergroup Contact Theory. *Journal of Personality and Social Psychology*, 90(5), 751-783.

- Phillips, K. W. (2014). How Diversity Makes Us Smarter. *Scientific American*, 311(4), 42-47.

- Porter, T., & Schumann, K. (2018). Intellectual Humility and Openness to the Opposing View. *Self and Identity*, 17(2), 139-162.

- Punch, K. F. (2016). *Developing Effective Research Proposals.* SAGE Publications.

- Ramage, J. D., Bean, J. C., & Johnson, J. (2016). *Writing Arguments: A Rhetoric with Readings* (10th ed.). Pearson.

- Resnik, D. B. (2015). *What is Ethics in Research & Why is It Important?* National Institute of Environmental Health Sciences.

- Ribble, M., & Bailey, G. (2007). Digital Citizenship in Schools. *International Society for Technology in Education.*

- Riggio, R. E. (2010). *Introduction to Industrial/Organizational Psychology.* Pearson.

- Robinson, K. (2011). *Out of Our Minds: Learning to be Creative.* Capstone.

- Rogers, C. R. (1957). *Active Listening.* The Free Press.

- Rogers, C. R. (1957). The necessary and sufficient conditions of therapeutic personality change. *Journal of Consulting Psychology,* 21(2), 95-103.

- Ross, L. (1977). The Intuitive Psychologist and His Shortcomings: Distortions in the Attribution Process. In L. Berkowitz (Ed.), *Advances in Experimental Social Psychology* (Vol. 10, pp. 173-220). Academic Press.

- Rothstein, D., & Santana, L. (2011). *Make Just One Change: Teach Students to Ask Their Own Questions.* Harvard Education Press.

- Rudinow, J., & Barry, V. E. (2004). *Invitation to Critical Thinking.* Thomson Wadsworth.

- Ruggiero, V. R. (2011). *Thinking Critically about Ethical Issues.* McGraw-Hill Education.

- Runco, M. A. (2004). Creativity. *Annual Review of Psychology, 55,* 657-687.

- Salmon, M. H. (1984). *Introduction to Logic and Critical Thinking.* Harcourt Brace Jovanovich.

- Salmon, W. C. (2013). Logic. *Prentice Hall.*

- Salovey, P., & Mayer, J. D. (1990). Emotional intelligence. *Imagination, Cognition and Personality, 9*(3), 185-211.

- Savery, J. R. (2006). Overview of Problem-based Learning: Definitions and Distinctions. *Interdisciplinary Journal of Problem-Based Learning,* 1(1), 9-20.

- Sawyer, R. K. (2007). Group Genius: The Creative Power of Collaboration. *Basic Books.*

- Schiffman, L. G., & Wisenblit, J. (2015). *Consumer Behavior* (11th ed.). Pearson Education.

- Schön, D. A. (1983). The Reflective Practitioner: How Professionals Think In Action. *Basic Books.*

- Schooler, C. (1984). Psychological Effects of Complex Environments During the Life Span: A Review and Theory. *Cognitive Development,* 4(4), 405-422.

- Schwartz, P. (1996). *The Art of the Long View: Paths to Strategic Insight for Yourself and Your Company.* Currency Doubleday.

- Sedley, D. (2007). Plato's Cratylus. *Cambridge University Press.*

- Senge, P. M. (1990). *The Fifth Discipline: The Art & Practice of The Learning Organization.* Doubleday/Currency.

- Shapin, S. (1996). The scientific revolution. *University of Chicago Press.*

- Siemens, G. (2005). Connectivism: A Learning Theory for the Digital Age. *International Journal of Instructional Technology and Distance Learning,* 2(1).

- Silverman, D. (2016). *Qualitative Research* (4th ed.). SAGE Publications.

- Slaughter, R. A. (1995). *The Foresight Principle: Cultural Recovery in the 21st Century.* Adamantine Press.

- Slovic, P., Finucane, M. L., Peters, E., & MacGregor, D. G. (2002). The Affect Heuristic. In T. Gilovich, D. Griffin, & D. Kahneman (Eds.), *Heuristics and Biases: The Psychology of Intuitive Judgment* (pp. 397-420). Cambridge University Press.

- Smith, R. (1989). Aristotle's logic. In E. N. Zalta (Ed.), *The Stanford Encyclopedia of Philosophy* (Spring 2021 Edition).

- Solomon, M. R. (2014). *Consumer Behavior: Buying, Having, and Being.* Pearson.

- Solomon, R. C., & Flores, F. (2001). *Building Trust: In Business, Politics, Relationships, and Life*. Oxford University Press.

- Sommers, N. (1980). Revision Strategies of Student Writers and Experienced Adult Writers. *College Composition and Communication*, 31(4), 378-388.

- Sparrow, B., Liu, J., & Wegner, D. M. (2011). Google effects on memory: cognitive consequences of having information at our fingertips. *Science*, 333(6043), 776-778.

- Spiegel, J. S. (2012). Open-mindedness and Intellectual Humility. *Theory and Research in Education*, 10(1), 27-38.

- Stanovich, K. E., & West, R. F. (2007). Natural myside bias is independent of cognitive ability. *Thinking & Reasoning, 13*(3), 225-247.

- Starko, A. J. (2013). Creativity in the Classroom: Schools of Curious Delight. *Routledge.*

- Stephan, W. G., & Stephan, C. W. (2013). Designing Intergroup Contact Programs. *International Journal of Intercultural Relations*, 37(2), 194-201.

- Sternberg, R. J. (1986). Critical thinking: Its nature, measurement, and improvement. *National Institute of Education*, U.S. Department of Education.

- Sternberg, R. J. (2003). *Wisdom, Intelligence, and Creativity Synthesized*. Cambridge University Press.

- Sternberg, R. J., & Lubart, T. I. (1999). The Concept of Creativity: Prospects and Paradigms. In R. J. Sternberg (Ed.), Handbook of Creativity (pp. 3-15). *Cambridge University Press.*

- Strunk, W., & White, E. B. (2000). *The Elements of Style*. Longman.

- Sue, D. W. (2001). Multidimensional Facets of Cultural Competence. *The Counseling Psychologist*, 29(6), 790-821.

- Sue, D. W. (2010). *Microaggressions in Everyday Life: Race, Gender, and Sexual Orientation*. Wiley.

- Suler, J. (2004). The online disinhibition effect. *Cyberpsychology & Behavior*, 7(3), 321-326.

- Sunstein, C. R. (2001). *Republic.com*. Princeton University Press.

- Sunstein, C. R. (2007). *Republic.com 2.0*. Princeton University Press.

- Tannen, D., & Trester, A. (2013). *Georgetown University Round Table on Languages and Linguistics 2011: Discourse 2.0: Language and New Media*. Georgetown University Press.

- Tarski, A. (2002). *Introduction to Logic and to the Methodology of Deductive Sciences*. Dover Publications.

- Thayer-Bacon, B. J. (2000). Transforming critical thinking: Thinking constructively. *Teachers College Press*.

- Thompson, L. (2009). *The Mind and Heart of the Negotiator*. Pearson Prentice Hall.

- Tindale, C. W. (2007). Fallacies and Argument Appraisal. *Cambridge University Press*.

- Ting-Toomey, S. (1999). *Communicating Across Cultures*. Guilford Press.

- Tough, A. (1971). *The Adult's Learning Projects*. Ontario Institute for Studies in Education.

- Toulmin, S. (1958). The uses of argument. *Cambridge University Press*.

- Toulmin, S. (2003). The Uses of Argument. *Cambridge University Press*.

- Toulmin, S., Rieke, R., & Janik, A. (1984). *An Introduction to Reasoning*. Macmillan Publishing Co., Inc.

- Turkle, S. (2015). *Reclaiming Conversation: The Power of Talk in a Digital Age*. Penguin Press.

- Tversky, A., & Kahneman, D. (1974). Judgment under Uncertainty: Heuristics and Biases. *Science*, 185(4157), 1124-1131.

- Tversky, A., & Kahneman, D. (1981). The Framing of Decisions and the Psychology of Choice. *Science*, 211(4481), 453-458.

- van Eemeren, F. H., & Groot endorst, R. (2004). A Systematic Theory of Argumentation: The Pragma-Dialectical Approach. *Cambridge University Press.*

- Vlastos, G. (1991). Socrates: Ironist and moral philosopher. *Cornell University Press.*

- Vygotsky, L. (1978). *Mind in Society: The Development of Higher Psychological Processes.* Harvard University Press.

- Walther, J. B. (2012). Theories of Computer-Mediated Communication and Interpersonal Relations. In M. L. Knapp & J. A. Daly (Eds.), *The Handbook of Interpersonal Communication* (4th ed., pp. 443-479). Sage Publications.

- Walton, D. (1996). Argumentation Schemes for Presumptive Reasoning. *Lawrence Erlbaum Associates.*

- Walton, D. (2004). Abductive Reasoning. *University of Alabama Press.*

- Walton, D. N. (1995). *A Pragmatic Theory of Fallacy.* University of Alabama Press.

- Walton, D., Reed, C., & Macagno, F. (2008). *Argumentation Schemes.* Cambridge University Press.

- Wardle, C., & Derakhshan, H. (2017). Information Disorder: Toward an Interdisciplinary Framework for Research and Policy Making. *Council of Europe Report DGI*, (2017)09.

- Wenger, E. (1998). *Communities of Practice: Learning, Meaning, and Identity.* Cambridge University Press.

- West, R. F., Toplak, M. E., & Stanovich, K. E. (2008). Heuristics and Biases as Measures of Critical Thinking: Associations with Cognitive Ability and Thinking Dispositions. *Journal of Educational Psychology*, 100(4), 930-941.

- Whitcomb, D., Battaly, H., Baehr, J., & Howard-Snyder, D. (2017). Intellectual Humility: Owning Our Limitations. *Philosophy and Phenomenological Research*, 94(3), 509-539.

- Wilberding, J. (2015). Socratic Method as a Way of Teaching Critical Thinking. In G. P. Lavery (Ed.), *Teaching Critical Thinking: A Pedagogical Treasure Waiting to Be Found* (pp. 85-105). Brill Sense.

- Wilen, W. W. (1991). Questioning Skills, for Teachers. *What Research Says to the Teacher*. National Education Association.

- Wilkinson, L. (2009). How to Build Scenarios. Wired Magazine

- Williams, B. (2005). Descartes: The project of pure enquiry. *Penguin Books*.

- Williams, J. M., & McEnerney, L. (2010). *Writing in College: A Short Guide to College Writing*. University of Chicago Writing Program.

- Williams, R., & Wessel, J. (2004). Reflective Journal Writing to Obtain Student Feedback about Their Learning during the Study of Chronic Musculoskeletal Conditions. *Journal of Allied Health*, 33(1), 17-23.

- Willingham, D. T. (2007). *Critical Thinking: Why Is It So Hard to Teach?* American Educator, Summer 2007, 8-19.

- Wilmot, W. W., & Hocker, J. L. (2011). *Interpersonal Conflict*. McGraw-Hill.

- Wineburg, S. (2018). *Why Learn History (When It's Already on Your Phone)*. University of Chicago Press.

- Wineburg, S., & McGrew, S. (2016). Why students can't Google their way to the truth. *Education Week, 36*(12), 22-23.

- Wineburg, S., & McGrew, S. (2017). Lateral Reading: Reading Less and Learning More When Evaluating Digital Information. *Stanford History Education Group Working Paper No. 2017-A1*.

- Wineburg, S., & McGrew, S. (2019). Lateral Reading: Reading Less and Learning More When Evaluating Digital Information. *Stanford History Education Group Working Paper No. 2017-A1*.

- Wood, A. W. (1999). Kant's Ethical Thought. *Cambridge University Press*.

- Wright, K. B., & Akgun, E. (2021). Emotional support and perceived stress among college students using computer-mediated communication and face-to-face communication. *Computers in Human Behavior*, 120, 106751.

- Zare, P., & Othman, M. (2015). Classroom Debate as a Systematic Teaching/Learning Approach. *World Journal of Education*, 5(5), 10-19.

- Zhao, Y. (2012). *World Class Learners: Educating Creative and Entrepreneurial Students*. Corwin Press.

- Zimmerman, B. J. (2002). Becoming a self-regulated learner: An overview. *Theory into Practice, 41*(2), 64-70.

- Zúñiga, X., Williams, E. A., & Berger, J. B. (2005). Action-Oriented Democratic Outcomes: The Impact of Student Involvement with Campus Diversity. *Journal of College Student Development*, 46(6), 660-678.